RACE, CLASS AND POLITICAL ACTIVISM

For my parents, Anne and Ian

Race, Class and Political Activism

A Study of West Indians in Britain

DAVID PEARSON

Victoria University of Wellington, New Zealand

Gower

© David Pearson, 1981

Published by
Gower Publishing Company Limited,
Westmead, Farnborough, Hants., England.

British Library Cataloguing in Publication Data

Pearson, David
    Race, class and political activism
    1   West Indians in the Midlands—Social conditions
    I   Title
    301.45'19'697290424   DA670.164

    ISBN 0-566-00353-8

Printed and bound in Great Britain by
Biddles Ltd, Guildford and King's Lynn

Contents

Tables

Preface

This book is a revised and updated presentation of the research submitted as a PhD thesis to the University of Leicester in 1975. Both the thesis and the present text would not have been completed without the advice and support of my family, teachers, colleagues and friends. In particular, I must express my thanks to Professor Ilya Neustadt for his consistent help and guidance; to Clive Ashworth for his perceptive and critical comments and, above all, to Eric Dunning for his conscientious supervision and continued support. Professor Asher Tropp also deserves mention for providing suggestions on the thesis and subsequent assistance with the book.

The Publications and Internal Research Committees of Victoria University, Wellington, assisted financially with the production of the text and I am grateful for their support. My thanks, also, to the editors of the *British Journal of Sociology* and *Sociology* for permission to reproduce those papers (Pearson 1978a, 1978b) that appear in revised form in Chapters 6 and 7.

A special debt of gratitude is owed to my wife, Suzette, who not only accepted the role of 'research widow' with great understanding but also made many editorial suggestions. Professor Jim Robb also read the final draft in its entirety and I am grateful for his comments. Of course I take full responsibility for any errors which remain. Once again Marjolane Ball deserves a medal for transforming my unenviable scrawl into an immaculate typescript.

Finally, my warmest thanks to the many people in 'Easton' who aided my research with patience, hospitality and friendship. In the book itself pseudonyms have been used in substitution for some place and personal names. I fully appreciate the difficulties associated with the use of pseudonyms but the wishes and security of those studied must take precedence. I hope all those who read this book will similarly protect their interests.

David Pearson,
Wellington, May 1980.

vii

1   Introduction

This book sets out to explore West Indian attempts at political mobilisation in Britain at the local community level. Drawing on extensive
field and survey research[1] in Easton, a medium sized Midlands city, a
detailed portrait of West Indian social organisation and voluntary association participation will be presented. Although the study of race and
ethnic relations in Britain has produced a considerable literature, the
political response of racial and ethnic minorities has received little
attention to date. Ward, for example, in a recent overview of British
research notes that 'politics and the state have only recently become a
significant focus of sociological research' (1978:477). He might well
have added, that even within this area of investigation much research
has been confined to the formal trappings of voting preferences and the
white response to the politics of race (Miles and Phizacklea, 1979).
Hopefully, this study will begin to fill the gap. It is fully appreciated,
of course, that the specific geographic and social situation of any ethnic
community must be related to a more expansive field of vision. As a
result, it will be useful to place this monograph within the general pattern of British ethnic and racial studies by providing a brief outline of
previous perspectives. This will serve the dual purpose of drawing
together existing findings whilst revealing one's own theoretical predilic-
tions.

The past three decades of race and ethnic relations research in
Britain have embraced the traditions of ethnography, social reformism
and political economy in roughly that order of historical succession. In
the late 1940s and early 1950s the pioneering ethnographic studies of
Little (1947) and Banton (1955) established a pattern of detailed por-
trayals of newly arrived African and West Indian immigrants. Additional
community studies soon followed in the sixties, for example, by Patterson (1965), Glass (1960) and Davison (1966). In the 1970s a growing
interest in ethnicity and the cultural nuances of minority existence was
observable (Khan, 1979; Wallman, 1979). However, unlike the early
community studies of 'coloured immigrants', that often tended to view
migrant settlements in particular cities as social isolates in space and
time, recent research on ethnic groupings shows a commendable sympathy for historical and cross-cultural comparison (Jeffery, 1976;
Watson, 1977; Foner, 1979). Nevertheless, as others have noted (Lawrence, 1977-8) this resurgence of interest in the cultural underpinning

1

of social organisation and group identity has been marred by a neglect of wider political and economic theoretical issues; most noticeably, with few exceptions (Foner, 1979), the complex links between class, race and ethnicity. If most ethnographic studies tended to be over-descriptive and often failed to bridge the relationship between culture and social structure, the majority of social policy orientated studies had even more limited theoretical pretensions. As soon as black and 'coloured' migrants were viewed as a 'social problem', a perception arguably dating from the Notting Hill and Nottingham 'race riots' in the late 1950s, racial scientists set about the task of surveying the prevalence of social prejudice and discrimination in Britain. Undoubtedly, the most publicised of these surveys have been the voluminous *Colour and Citizenship* study (Rose, 1969) and the two national PEP reports on racial discrimination and disadvantage (Daniel, 1969; Smith, 1977). These studies, together with other research initially funded by the Institute of Race Relations in the 1960s, indicated that the incidence of prejudice and discrimination against West Indian and South Asian immigrants was difficult to measure but was unquestionably substantial. Furthermore, the victims of such negative actions and attitudes were severely disadvantaged in the central institutions of the Metropolitan society. Levels of deprivation varied between diverse ethnic communities and different urban environments, but the chances of acquiring inferior housing, jobs and schooling were invariably higher for black workers and their children than for comparable whites.

The presence of ethnic and racial minorities in Britain predictably provoked statistical measures of inequality; but, somewhat curiously, an almost complete lack of theoretical attention to the structural placement of black workers in British cities. At least this was the case prior to the 1970s, with the outstanding exception of Rex and Moore's (1967) study of Sparkbrook, Birmingham. In this pathbreaking piece of research, the authors developed a Weberian model of market inequalities which placed the study of racial minorities firmly within a class analysis rooted in the historical continuities of colonialism.

In the 1970s with the onset of economic recession and an increasing interest in the expanding foreign labour force in the new European Community, many social commentators shifted the emphasis away from a model of immigrant adjustment towards one of worker exploitation (Moore, 1977). This recent interest in the political economy of migratory labour covers a variety of often opposing positions. Some writers, Marxist and Weberian, confront a broad scenario of historical and contemporary linkages which encompass the colonial histories of the Third World. Other, exclusively Marxist interpreters, debate the separate or incorporated status of European migrant workers as a sub-proletariat (Gorz, 1970) or part of a fragmented, but theoretically indivisible,

European working class (Castles and Kosack, 1973). Similar arguments surround the structural position of black workers in Britain as a separate underclass (Rex and Tomlinson, 1979) or a racially designated class fraction (Miles and Phizacklea, 1977).

Paradoxically, whereas those who stress the ethnic dimension of minority existence in Britain often neglect the structural questions raised by class analyses, proponents of political economy frequently de-emphasise the discontinuities raised by racial and ethnic divisions (Allen and Smith, 1974). Consequently, 'racial' distinctions are often over-simplistically perceived as conspiratorial justifications for white supremacy, whilst intra-class divisions centred on ethnic exclusivity are explained away as 'false consciousness'.

I accept the view that most West Indian and South Asian workers can be heuristically defined as an underclass; insofar as black workers invariably have inferior life chances to native workers in a variety of market situations (Rex and Tomlinson, 1979). But this Weberian inspired type of analysis does not preclude the possibility of some degree of economic and social differentiation within ethnic and racial minorities. Indeed, a small but significant sector of the black and brown labour force have attained equal or superior positions to some white workers (Nowikowski and Ward, 1978/9). I would argue, moreover, that group distinctions on the basis of believed or perceived physical differences or through an ethnic exclusivity maintained by beliefs of common ancestry and a 'sense of us' (Wallman, 1979:IX) are vital to a full understanding of British stratificatory patterns. Thus, the actions and perceptions that shape the day to day relationships between and within majority and minority groupings are viewed as an amalgam of structured inequalities, rigid or less rigid social conventions and inchoate images of individual and group placement. On one level the majority of black and brown workers share common social class backgrounds, but if we turn to the internal dynamics of minority group organisation and identification, particularly the bases for status distinctions, the essential task of separating out the social and cultural divisions within a common class position must be confronted. These internal distinctions not only apply to the major cultural and geographical divisions between, for example, West Indians, Indians and Pakistanis but also to the very important regional, linguistic, religious, political and other differences within these respective groupings. Such delineations are more readily apparent if there is an explicit recognition of the way in which these groups separate themselves into meaningful distinct communities.

Throughout this book, the total West Indian population in Easton will be referred to as a settlement, whilst the distinctive island divisions within the city will be called groupings or communities. This use of terminology corresponds to the way in which West Indians relate to one another and how they define the closeness or otherwise of the social bonds between themselves (Midgett, 1975). The term 'West Indian' is acceptable as a means of referring to individuals who originate from a common geographical area, namely the Caribbean or the West Indies, but it remains problematic at this point whether this common geographical background can be directly equated with social propinquity. This may appear over-pedantic, but it is essential to appreciate the implications behind the use of phrases such as 'West Indian community' which suggests a common, solidaristic social grouping at the settlement level rather than the more realistic picture of a collection of distinctive island communities.

The present study also seeks to apply an historical-developmental approach to the study of West Indian social organisation. A theoretical framework will be used which incorporates a number of different analytic levels which are nevertheless inter-penetrative. These levels range from personality formation to inter-societal relationships. Thus, we will be examining certain features of 'West Indian' personality formation and West Indian interpersonal and group relations both within and between island communities. We shall also be looking at the nature of the relationships between the West Indian settlement and the 'host community' and with other ethnic minorities in the locality.

Reaffirming the belief that black and brown workers in Britain can be placed objectively within an underclass, there will be a concern with the relationships between the 'immigrant settlement' in Easton (which is composed of all West Indian and South Asian groups in the city) and local whites. It can be seen that minority-majority relationships at the micro-level must be placed within the wider context of relations between native and settler populations at the national level. Indeed, the meanings with which members of both majority and minority groups impute colour and cultural differences may be dependent on micro- and macro-relations, face-to-face interaction or more indirect influences.

These individual and group relations within and between native and migrant groups must be placed within a theoretical framework which defines the social aspects of contemporary black settlement in Britain as a part of an on-going historical process which originated in the earliest colonial links between Britain and the Caribbean. There is a fundamental error in assuming a 'cut-off' point when a West Indian's migration to Britain has been accomplished. It is as if a Jamaican or Barbadian sheds the very substance of his previous existence when the gangplank rattles onto the dock at Southampton.

Those cultural traits of the home island which the West Indian brings with him are often perceived as merely a base for 'role-stripping'. It is assumed that the norms, indigenous to a particular West Indian society

4

are immediately constrained and a steady process of 'cultural erosion' is introduced as soon as the migrant enters the metropolitan society. This is a very static approach which fails to appreciate the dynamics of the continual inter-penetration which takes place of social factors from both the sending and the receiving society. Migration and settlement must be seen as an on-going process rather than a set of isolated actions. Therefore, the 'short-term dynamics' of the migrant's initial contacts with the metropolitan society must be seen against the background of the 'long-term dynamics' which blend past and present. The influence of a colonial past on West Indian family organisation, religious participation and island insularity in Britain, are only a few examples where these historical aspects (long-term dynamics) are introduced in the following chapters.

The links, both contemporary and historical, between Britain and the various West Indian societies which the former colonised need to be examined together with an analysis of the social structure of Caribbean societies. This point will be emphasised throughout the book, as the social organisation of West Indian island communities in Easton will be constantly compared with the social structure of those Caribbean societies from which these communities originated.

Most of the previous studies of West Indian settlements in Britain have remarked upon the paucity and ephemerality of West Indian communal associations, particularly those with political aims. This apparent dearth of formal political association is made all the more interesting by the noted presence of such associations within many South Asian settlements.[2] Thus, the mere fact of being lower class, black or coloured immigrants does not appear to explain the West Indian pattern. If the latter were the case, one would expect to find a similar lack of political organisation within South Asian groupings.

Michael Banton (1955) remarked on what he called a high level of West Indian 'disorganisation' in his early study of coloured immigrants in Stepney. He contrasted this with the more organised Asian communities in the area. Banton explained the lack of West Indian associations by referring to:

> The extent to which European influences have disrupted the culture of the country of origin, and it appears to relate closely to the attitudes adopted by immigrants after arrival. (1955:214)

Ruth Glass (1960) also found very few formal associations among the West Indians in her London study. She stated that:

> As integration with white British society is no longer expected as a matter of course, integration of the coloured peoples themselves appears to be the essential first step. (1960:211)

5

Glass argued that there was no reason to expect a high level of West Indian participation in voluntary associations because they were mostly newly settled migrants who were initially separated by island distinctions and so forth. Sydney Collins (1957), who also found a marked contrast between South Asians and West Indians in their levels of associational activity, attributed this disparity to religious differences between the two groups. He distinguished between 'traditional' associations which were similar to those found in the country of origin, and 'emergent' associations which were set up by immigrants to meet their needs in Britain. Collins noted that the Asian groupings he studied in Cardiff were united by their Moslem beliefs and the prevalence of traditional associations which were attached to these beliefs. The 'negroes' in Cardiff lacked these strong traditions and hence, Collins argued, they were fragmented.

Sheila Patterson (1965) attributed the lack of West Indian associations discovered in her Brixton study to 'culture shock' or cultural strangeness in the initial period of West Indian settlement. She stressed particularly the difficulties of maintaining solidaristic ties when the West Indian family and household structures are disrupted by migration.

Most of these early monographs were concerned with West Indian immigrants who were comparatively new arrivals in Britain. Thus, they could explain the lack of associational activity by pointing to the sometimes acute problems met in 'settling in' within their new surroundings. However, more recent studies of longer settled West Indian groupings found similar patterns of association. Thus, E. R. Braithwaite (1967) in a study which included an examination of West Indian attempts to establish housing societies in London, found that most West Indians 'were very reluctant to take any action themselves to improve their own circumstances'. Braithwaite mentioned island disunity again, but also argued that most West Indians whilst taking a very lively interest in politics in the Caribbean, are more content to be patient and wait and see what the host society has to offer before organising themselves in Britain.

Hylson-Smith (1968), in a comparative study of Cypriots and West Indians in North London, found that:

> With the West Indians there is a less well developed associational life, there is no pronounced geographical concentration of specifically West Indian associations ... and this stands in marked contrast to the Cypriot community. (1968:473)

Another brief discussion of the nature of West Indian associational activity was contained in the *Colour and Citizenship* report (Rose, 1969). Apart from reiterating the points made by Patterson, Rose argued that changes in the Caribbean could discourage West Indian organisation in Britain. He suggested that many West Indians came to Britain expecting to raise their status from lower class to middle class. However, they encountered unexpectedly high levels of prejudice and discrimination in the host society and this disillusioned them to such an extent that they were unable to organise themselves. Rose (1969: 423) also referred to evidence from the Rex and Moore study in Birmingham which confirmed the now familiar pattern. The Sparkbrook study yielded yet another 'explanation' for the lack of political organisation among West Indians:

> The lack of organised impact is due to ... the absence of institutions of their own which are significantly different from those of their hosts and the other is their affiliation to norms and organisations of the host society. (1969:155).

Finally, Rose alluded to some of the findings of Richmond in Bristol where a number of West Indians living on modern council estates were studied. Richmond, remarking on the reasons for West Indians not joining local associations, said:

> In this they preferred to behave as individuals, exhibiting the traits in their West Indian make-up which prompted emigration and which, given favourable circumstances, should equip the West Indian for individual adaptation to an English environment. (Rose, 1969:428)

Most recently published studies of West Indians or 'black Britons' confirm these earlier findings. For example, Banton (1972:146) reaffirms his much earlier study when he states in a recent work that 'West Indians have not so far been successful in building associations to represent their shared interests'. Lawrence (1974:153), in a recent appraisal of race relations in Nottingham notes a sharp disparity between the low involvement of West Indians in immigrant organisations and the greater participation of their South Asian neighbours. Philpott remarks on the dearth of 'formally-constituted voluntary associations such as clubs or mutual aid societies' (1977:111) among Montserratian migrants in London. A similar pattern is described in Foner's (1979) study of Jamaicans in Brixton. Also Pryce, drawing on a richly descriptive portrayal of West Indian life in Bristol, stresses that 'the vast majority of West Indians are indifferent to voluntary organisations' (1979: 220). Therefore, we can see that the existing material on West Indians in Britain shows a consistent pattern of low levels of participation in formal associations. Moreover, those few formal associations which have been established tend to be highly ephemeral and prone to fragmentation. This pattern can be discerned from the earliest period of West Indian settlement in Britain right through to the present day.

Whilst some attention has been paid to West Indian associational activity, most of the 'explanations' offered for the above pattern have been peripheral statements in studies which have been concerned with much wider issues. As yet, no detailed appraisal of levels of membership and participation in voluntary associations among West Indians exists. Similarly, no previous study has been primarily concerned with explaining the ephemerality and paucity of West Indian formal political associations. However, a recent study of Ben Heinemann (1972) provides a useful list of, as yet, untested propositions relating to West Indian politicisation that effectively summarise previous work.

The propositions, which Heinemann believes may serve to explain why 'West Indians have had difficulty in establishing united, cohesive organisations to help develop their communities in Britain and to fight discrimination' (1972:76) are as follows:

1 The heterogeneity of West Indians; which is demonstrated in terms of island, class, colour and political organisational difficulties.

2 The marked concern with individual economic activity, high residential mobility and a belief in the temporary nature of their migration may have impeded organisation.

3 The historical influences of slavery and colonialism have fermented self and group recrimination, possibly along class and/or colour lines.

4 The level of discrimination found in Britain may have incapacitated West Indians to such an extent that it has negated any attempts to organise themselves.

5 The difficulties of evolving a group identity from the strands of European and African historical links which emphasise fragmentation and marginality.

6 Political experiences in the West Indies may influence organisational problems in Britain. (1972:76—7)

Heinemann goes on to say that:

> The general phenomenon of the West Indians' failure to organise is extraordinarily complicated both to describe and to explain in depth, requiring tools from a multiplicity of disciplines—history, economics, sociology, anthropology, political science and literature. A cross-cultural framework embracing the West Indies, Africa and Britain is needed. (1972:76)

The exploratory nature of the present text, together with its deliberate focus on a specific urban location, negates any pretensions to present a complete explanation of the above phenomenon. The aim of the study is to look at a particular West Indian settlement with this problem as a central feature and to try and relate the nature of West Indian organisation, both in Britain and the Caribbean, to the observed pattern of formal and informal associational activity. Therefore, I am not only concerned with explaining *why* a particular low level of associational activity is apparent in this settlement, but also with an attempt to establish *how* some of the explanatory factors are produced and how they relate to one another.

I begin, of course, with the expectation that relatively low levels of participation in voluntary associations will be found amongst West Indians in Britain. This is due, not only to the evidence from previous studies, but also to the nature of present cross-cultural data on voluntary association membership and public participation in local politics. This information shows that, in most societies, high levels of voluntary association membership tend to be found mainly among the highly educated, powerful, urban based middle and upper classes.[3] The limited material on voluntary association membership and community activism in Britain confirms that this pattern is reproduced in the metropolitan society (Morris, 1965; Saunders, 1979). Consequently, one would not expect the majority of West Indians in Britain, who are predominantly black, working class, often not highly educated individuals, who come from societies which are not heavily urbanised and industrialised, to establish and participate in a great many voluntary associations. However, this overlooks the important differences between black, brown and white workers in Britain.

Black (and brown) workers, in common with many lower-class white workers in Britain, are in relatively powerless positions in the metropolitan society. That is to say, many of the urban poor in Britain are not able to exert much control over their life situations in a society that can be perceived as being composed of a number of competing groups who seek to maximise their opportunities in various markets for scarce resources. The ability to control one's life situation within these markets is governed by the nature of the power relationships between the respective groups and individuals who are competing for the above resources.

Within this 'conflict model' of society, black workers, together with other powerless groups, are faced with innumerable constraints in Britain when attempting to acquire, for example, jobs, houses and other resources. These constraints will be partly governed by how ethnic and racial differences influence the relationships of power and control between majority and minority members. Such differences must be seen within a system of group interdependencies which are governed by the nature of power relationships and the differing power

9

potentials of the respective groups and individuals in the market.

If relationships between West Indians and other groups in Britain are conflictual and competitive and if West Indians perceive their relative powerlessness in the host society, the formation of voluntary associations (by West Indians) could be most significant as agencies of political change; particularly, and this is the crucial difference between black and white workers, if the former feel that they are not even minimally represented by the traditional political representatives of the labour force—the Labour Party and trade union movement.

This argument is supported by a recent appraisal of black political activism by Miles and Phizacklea (1977). Drawing generally on current research on political action/inaction among West Indians, Indians and Pakistanis and more specifically on the earlier work of Lawrence (1974), the authors suggest three potential processes through which members of racial and ethnic strata could improve their present position in Britain.

> The first is for members of the racial and ethnic strata to become incorporated into the class structure of Britain, with the result that the problems that they face and experience will become defined as class issues. We will call this the *class unity process.* The second suggested strategy is organisation along ethnic lines and we will refer to this as the *ethnic organisation* process. The third strategy (also) identified by Lawrence is for members of the racial and ethnic strata to organise across ethnic lines. This we call the *black unity process*.(Miles and Phizacklea, 1977:492)

Miles and Phizacklea and Lawrence suggest that there are few signs of the class and black unity processes succeeding at present. The possibility that South Asian and West Indian groupings will combine in any cohesive and permanent sense is severely undermined by sharp cultural differences between the respective groups, cross-ethnic antipathies and the fact that both 'West Indian' and 'South Asian' labels gloss over considerable heterogeneity within these categories. Similarly, the immediate prospect of black, brown and white workers recognising their common class interests to the point where the traditional organisations and institutions of the native working class actively support ethnic minority members is viewed as equally implausible. Notwithstanding the acknowledged electoral support for the Labour Party and high levels of trade union membership found among black workers, Miles and Phizacklea (1977) suggest that much of this political allegiance is expedient. They argue that irrespective of isolated illustrations of class unity expressed during particular political or industrial disputes, the mainstream of the labour movement is usually apathetic, given to merely token gestures, or openly hostile to its black and brown fellow workers. Hence their conclusion that the current

failure of broadly based political movements centred on the commonalities of colour and/or class, strengthens the importance of the ethnic
organisation process. If specific ethnic groups cannot effectively voice
their demands through formal political channels or concerted action on
the basis of a shared non-white minority status, then it is vital that they
organise themselves on an ethnic basis. This brings us full circle back to
an analysis of West Indian formal and informal political associations and
the reasons for their organisational difficulties. Difficulties which are
highlighted by the apparent contrast with more cohesive South Asian
communities. Many South Asian (including East African) groupings *are*
considerably fragmented by factions that form along, for example,
regional, linguistic, religious, economic and political lines, but within
these boundaries a high degree of communal co-operation is often established (Watson, 1977; Khan, 1979; Wallman, 1979).

The differences between West Indian and South Asian family and
kinship patterns, community authority structures and politico-economic
formations will be briefly touched on in the text. At this juncture, it
will be useful to address ourselves to the underlying mechanisms that
promote or inhibit group solidarity within the various West Indian and
South Asian groupings in Britain. Michael Lyon (1972), for example,
has drawn a fundamental distinction between racial and ethnic minorities which rests on the crucial difference between race as an excluded
residual category, in contrast to ethnicity based upon an emergent cultural collectivity. This categorisation, contrasting West Indians and
South Asians respectively, has very important implications for group
identity, organisational cohesiveness and political mobilisation potential. Briefly, Lyon suggests that a history of colonial cultural depreda-
tion, particularly the experience of slavery, has left West Indians with a
racial stigma and a sense of cultural inferiority. Lyon argues that any
form of collective identity among West Indians arises from an externally
imposed racial ascription on the basis of colour and its symbolic reference to a colonial shame culture. In contrast, he points out, South
Asian communities being spared the form and degree of historical deprivation experienced by West Indians, have a far greater potential for
collective action arising from an internally generated ethnic solidarity.
This solidarity is reflected in communal kinship ties, systems of political
and economic reciprocity and a consequent greater incidence of viable
organisational forms.

Lyon's distinction between racial and ethnic minorities certainly has
some heuristic utility, particularly in stressing the importance of the
mechanics of boundary formation.[4] Nevertheless, I believe he dichoto-
mises the essentially interdependent nature of racial exclusion and
ethnic inclusion practices. For example, Lyon suggests that a racial
category cannot become an ethnic group because the basis for racial

11

collectivism is purely derivative. Conversely, he argues (Lyon, 1972:261), ethnic identity is relatively autonomous. I accept that exclusion on the basis of 'race' (i.e., outsider beliefs about immutable biological and/or phenotypical differences) and inclusion based on ethnic identification (a collective sense of cultural distinctiveness and common ancestry), are arguably the most significant alternative bases for 'West Indian' and 'South Asian' group closure;[5] but both 'minorities' embrace the dynamics of exclusion and inclusion.

As Wallman notes, 'Lyon draws only half the necessary inference. His usage implies that 'race' exists where one group is excluded by another, 'ethnicity' where the group considers itself or sets itself apart'. (1979:308). To be fair, Lyon fills in the other side of the equation for South Asian communities when he acknowledges in a later article (Lyon, 1973), that Indians and Pakistanis are also defined as racially separate by many majority members. But this still leaves the question of whether West Indians have any ethnic attributes which they can bring to bear against majority exclusion practices. We will return to this problem later in the text. Suffice to say at this point that I consider the possibilities of an emergent ethnicity amongst West Indians (Miles and Phizacklea, 1977:495) more complex than Lyon's somewhat dismissive premise would have us believe.

Irrespective of the above considerations, evidence to date indicates that South Asian groupings have been far more successful than West Indians in developing self-help associations. Even those recent studies that perceive a growing militancy among both black and brown workers document the greater organisational strength of South Asian communities (Moore, 1975; Rex and Tomlinson, 1979). Therefore, even within the limits of expected low levels of political organisation for lower class, powerless groups in Britain, West Indians still appear to have more difficulty in politically mobilising themselves than similarly situated migrant groups. The reasons for this will be fully explored in the following pages.

Before providing a brief outline of subsequent chapters, a few comments need to be addressed to the distinctions that will be made between informal and formal associations and how these relate to primary and secondary relationships.

The distinction between formal and informal associations is a subtle one and it is firmly emphasised that these categories are not mutually exclusive. A useful distinction has been made by John Rex between highly intimate and personalised primary relationships and more formalised associations within immigrant settlements. Rex (1973) distinguishes between what he calls 'primary communities' and 'associations'. Primary communities are those:

> Groups of individuals who are bound together by intimate
> personal ties ... they involve the whole life of an individual

... they are groups in which men reveal more of themselves, they turn to their fellow-members in times of emergency, they tell secrets about themselves, they share their excitements and joys. They feel able to relax and to let their hair down. (Rex, 1973:15)

Rex is referring here to the intimacy of the primary relationships to be found in family and kinship relationships, to friendship networks and highly informal, loosely-structured groups who meet in lodging houses, pubs and on street corners.

Associations, for Rex, are groups of individuals who are bound together 'through sharing a common set of cultural meanings, norms and beliefs, which structure the social forms within which they interact'. These groups have a clear purpose and their structure is related to this purpose. Rex (1973:20) suggests that a 'pure' form of association might be found in a trade union, a political party, or an immigrant association. Such associations may be functional to their members in a variety of ways. For example, Rex (1973:22) mentions four major forms of assistance—namely, overcoming social isolation, affirming cultural beliefs and values, goal attainment and, finally, pastoral work.

Particular associations may, manifestly or latently, perform all of these services or only relate to some of them. However, Rex confirms that ethnic and racial minorities, because of the powerlessness and social isolation of their position in the metropolitan society, need to develop 'community associations' which incorporate all the above functions. Thus, he states:

The community association so formed has four possible functions. It alters the social structure and creates new groupings of people through the group-work which it promotes. It does 'pastoral' work among those who present themselves as clients. It acts as a tension-management system serving to give expression to, but also to channel and manage, the conflicts of interest which do occur. And it is a body which may act as a political pressure group on behalf of the community as a whole. (Rex, 1973:30)

Rex's distinctions between primary communities and associations are particularly pertinent here because it appears more useful to use this type of generalised and flexible perspective rather than to make highly specific and somewhat mechanical distinctions between informal and formal associations. What can be suggested is that informal associations are more likely to be akin to 'primary communities' and thus incorporate highly personalised, primary relationships, whilst more formalised associations will be relatively distinct from the latter in terms of less personalised, secondary relationships.

13

Finally, a brief note about the organisation of the text. Chapter 2 sets the scene by outlining the structure of British West Indian societies, particularly patterns of political association and leadership. This is complemented by the description of the West Indian settlement in Easton, Britain, presented in Chapter 3. Chapter 4 will be concerned with an appraisal of recreational and political associations[6] that West Indians have established since their settlement in the city. Subsequent chapters, 5 and 6, explore the links between family structure and political organisation and the connections between West Indian religious participation and the formation of other types of voluntary association. In Chapter 7 the dynamics of West Indian activism will be discussed in some depth and I will re-examine some of the 'explanations' for the paucity and ephemerality of West Indian political associations which have been touched on in this Introduction. A brief Postscript will conclude the book by re-assessing the local scene in Easton in the late 1970s, dwelling on the growing political importance of second generation West Indians and addressing some final remarks to the possible future course of West Indian political mobilisation in Britain.

Notes

1   For a description of research methods, see Research Appendix.
2   Note that political associations tend to be formed within separate South Asian communities. There has only been limited success in forming associations that combine some or all of these diverse groupings. See, for example, Desai (1963); Aurora (1967); John (1969); Beetham (1970); Scott (1972); Lyon (1972/3); Ballard and Ballard (1977).
3   The ubiquity of higher rates of 'middle class, urban' voluntary association membership is well documented, see Smith and Freedman (1972). However, the question of 'black membership' is far more contentious, particularly if one appreciates the difficulties of cross-cultural comparison. See, for example, the ongoing debate over black membership in the United States *viz* Caplan (1970) and Olsen (1970).
4   For useful discussions of the boundary formation process, see Banton (1977) and Wallman (1978).
5   Even here we are using broad labels which disguise considerable heterogeneity. More precisely we should be speaking of Jamaicans, Sikhs, Mirpuris, etc.
6   A recreational and political association can be distinguished in the following manner. The former is seen (by the author) as primarily leisure orientated and has functions, aims and objectives which are concerned with the provision of supportive, leisure amenities. These are not expressly designed to alter the life situations of West Indians in Britain in any

14

fundamental way, but merely act as compensations or adjuncts to their present life situations. A political association, on the other hand, has aims and objectives which are mainly concerned with the utilisation of power for the purpose of promoting changes in the life situation of the members and other groups or individuals which the association purports to represent. However, there is no reason why an association cannot be both recreational and political in its functions and objectives. Nor is it suggested that a recreational association cannot be transformed or perceived by its members as a political association or *vice versa*.

2   Community organisation in West Indian societies

The briefest glance at the development of contemporary West Indian societies soon reveals that, 'there is a sense in which the Caribbean displays the essence of colonialism' (Mason, 1970). Certainly one cannot study any facet of the West Indian existence in Britain without taking a backward glance along the paths of colonial history. Thus, relationships between migrant and non-migrant in the metropolitan society must be seen as part of an on-going process of inter-relationships between the receiving society and the society of origin, coloniser and colonised. Within this perspective it is necessary for us to turn our attention back to the Caribbean in order to understand fully the factors which have contributed to the current position of West Indians in Britain. We need not concern outselves with a full appraisal of the historical links which bind certain island societies to the Metropolis, nor discuss extensively the social structure of particular West Indian societies. Both of these topics would require books in themselves and they have been closely documented elsewhere.[1] However, it will be useful to outline certain features of the social organisation of Caribbean societies, particularly the climate of formal and informal political participation, in order to under-pin the forthcoming examination of specific aspects of West Indian communities in Britain.

The history of the Caribbean is unique in many respects, for it provides a classic example of a purely colonially created social and cultural area. This area contains a variety of societies that originated in the fifteenth and sixteenth centuries when the arrival of European colonisers, through force of arms and disease, decimated the small indigenous populations of Arawaks and Caribs found in the Caribbean islands at that time. Today, very few West Indians are directly related to these indigenous groups. Almost all of them can trace their 'roots' back to the shores of the European and African continents. Over the last four centuries complex societies have been formed in the Caribbean out of these heterogeneous group formations.

The search for the 'New World' in the Americas made the West Indian islands useful stop-over points where, among others, the British, Spanish, French and Dutch settled or moved on. Initially, the precious metals of South America were the prizes sought by the Western powers, but soon the value of the Caribbean islands themselves was recognised and the lure of 'King Sugar' and other cultivated products proved irresistible.

Some islands were settled by one nation and remained under one rule throughout their history. The British settlement of Barbados is a notable example. However, most of the islands displayed the complexity of societies which were treated like trading stations, where different rulers passed and re-passed, sometimes with the tide. Most West Indian societies, therefore, can trace their lineage to a mixture of colonial influences. With the onset of slavery and later, indentured labour, an imported peasant/proletariat was placed within these societies to form a black mass dominated by their white or lighter skinned masters. Thus developed the plantation culture which is representative of much of the Caribbean and the surrounding areas of the Americas.

Plantation 'culture spheres' can be said to have certain basic features in common. Wagley (1960), for example, has attempted to provide a construct which he believes incorporates the most important facets of social organisation in the coastal regions of Brazil and Central America, the Caribbean and parts of the United States. This model embraces a peasant based plantation system and mono-crop culture, multi-racial societies with rigid class lines, matri-focal family organisation and finally, a weak community structure. This typology is useful in a very general sense, but it would be imprudent to view each of these features as present in every island in the British West Indies. It is important to distinguish between varying types of classificatory systems which cover the various societies in that area, without necessarily negating acceptance of the view, that the Caribbean 'comprises one cultural area in which common factors have forged a more-or-less common way of looking at life, the world, and their place in the scheme of things' (Knight, 1978: xi).

The most elaborate and sensitive typology of West Indian societies has been constructed by Sidney Mintz (1966), who argues that the Caribbean exhibits a wealth of cultural variation which defies easy classification. However, he agrees with Wagley that the 'Caribbean' can be seen as a social area (Mintz calls it a 'societal area') which has certain uniformities. These are expressed in a list of 'regional commonalities' which Mintz has outlined as follows:

1 Lowland, subtropical, insular ecology.

2 The swift extirpation of native populations.

3 The early definition of the islands as a sphere of European overseas agricultural capitalism, based primarily on the sugar-cane, African slaves, and the plantation system.

4 The concomitant development of insular social structures in which internally differentiated local community organisation was slight, and national class groupings usually took on a bipolar form, sustained by overseas domination, sharply differentiated access to land,

wealth and political power, and the use of physical differences as status markers.

5 The continuous interplay of plantations and small-scale yeoman agriculture, with accompanying social structural effects.

6 The successive introduction of massive new 'foreign' populations into the lower sectors of insular social structures, under conditions of extremely restricted opportunities for upward economic, social, or political mobility.

7 The prevailing absence of any ideology of national identity that could serve as a goal for mass acculturation.

8 The persistence of colonialism and of the colonial ambiance, longer than in any other area outside Western Europe.

9 A high degree of individualisation—particularly economic individualisation—as an aspect of Caribbean social organisation.

The above features provide a useful appraisal of the social structure of West Indian societies and will serve as a base-line for the examination of communal organisation in the British West Indies. Mintz's typology reminds us that even if we restrict ourselves to those islands largely or exclusively colonised by the British, any description of common features must also allow for variation within these commonalities.

For example, if one looks at the social stratification of West Indian societies, the complexity of cross-cutting class and colour gradations is readily apparent. David Lowenthal (1972:76) has distinguished between five types of West Indian society with different types of stratification systems:

1 Homogeneous societies without distinctions of colour or class.

2 Societies differentiated by colour but not stratified by class.

3 Societies stratified by colour and class.

4 Societies stratified by colour and class but with white Creole elites absent or insignificant.

5 Societies stratified by colour and class and containing sizeable ethnic groups in large measure outside the colour-class hierarchy.

Lowenthal (1972:78-79) argues that societies in the British West Indies, which are illustrative of these types are as follows:

1 Barbuda, the Grenadines, Turks and Caicos.

2 Anguilla, Cayman Islands.

3 Antigua, Jamaica, St Kitts, St Vincent, Barbados.

4 Dominica, Grenada, Nevis, St Lucia, Montserrat.

5 Trinidad, Guyana.

18

The above classification confirms the general proposition, that objective class differences tend to be reflected by colour divisions. Although the degree of variation between Barbuda with its relatively homogeneous black population and Trinidad and Guyana, with their highly differentiated societies cross-cut by significant ethnic divisions[2] is considerable. Historically, there is some utility in stressing that most British West Indian societies have moved from the classic three-tiered white/coloured/ black stratification system to the present two-tiered model of middle class coloured and black masses. But even the persistence of high correlations between wealth, income and phenotype (Cross, 1979:117) must be viewed against a rapidly changing social back-cloth. Some societies, notably Jamaica and Trinidad, have seen the introduction of newer industries—bauxite mining and oil extraction—which introduced new bases for social and economic differentiation. The past twenty years has also brought differing degrees of political independence to certain island societies, that promoted a redrawing of social distinctions.[3] Indeed, the relational aspects of class and concomitant status differentials have always been a delicate set of social balances, invariably, but by no means exclusively, centred on the pivot of colour distinction. Ambiguity and variation are of the essence in local systems of status evaluation (Kuper, 1976:61). However, as Cross points out:

> There remains (therefore), a racial element in deference within the Caribbean: to be black is still to be placed lower in a hierarchy of prestige than any other group. The force of these evaluations varies from society to society and is dependent upon ecological and demographic factors, moral and religious sentiments, the complex interplay of historical events and, perhaps more important than anything else, the degree to which racial ascription has correlated with access to economic and political power. But criteria of deference must be understood to have an important independent effect, albeit constrained by other factors. (1979:120)

Irrespective of political independence or constantly shifting self and group evaluations, there is a continuity of structured inequalities in the Caribbean enforced by economic dependence on the outside world (Best, 1968; Beckford, 1972; Cross, 1979). This level of external economic control, with its wider social and cultural ramifications, still dominates and largely explains the nature of contemporary West Indian societies. Gordon Lewis, for example, has concluded that:

> The Caribbean economy exhibits, in exaggerated form, all the major properties of the colonial regime—foreign ownership and control in the major sectors of oil, sugar, banking, insurance, mining and manufacturing; external decision making

with respect to investment and allocation of resources by the head offices of the big multinational corporations; structural unemployment and underemployment, combined with high salary-wage levels in privileged sectors; separation between local extraction of raw materials and overseas manufacture of the finished product; lack of indigenous technology; and concentration by overseas wealth in capital-oriented industries that do little to absorb the labour surplus inherited from the old plantation economy. (1971:34)

This form of external domination and control has led McDonald (1971:146) to call the Caribbean 'A beautiful house with an African personality', an outwardly attractive residence whose 'wealth and beauty have been the privilege and property of Europeans and North Americans for over three hundred years'.

The main point of this brief introduction has been to express some of the complexity and diffuseness of Caribbean societies. Mono-causal explanations of the nature of West Indian social organisation appear singularly inadequate when confronted with this plethora of historical contingencies. Therefore, those analyses which explain certain features of contemporary West Indian societies solely in historical materialist terms must be treated with some caution. Vera Rubin graphically illustrates the deficiences of such rigid models when he states:

The social structure of the colonial plantation extended beyond a simple dichotomy of land-owning aristocracy and a homogeneous mass of slaves. There was considerable differentiation within each segment of the free and slave social groups. The white population comprised estate holders and some smallholders, distinguished by the French as *grands* and *petit blancs.* There were also the various professional and managerial classes who performed essential services and stood in a ranked order in the hierarchy of colonial society. They were differentiated primarily by social position, also by creole or metropolitan origin, occupation, education, and other social criteria. For example, the Scots-Irish overseer or book-keeper did not rank as high socially as the absentee English landowner.

There was also considerable differentiation within the slave class on the basis of origin, occupation, skin colour and acculturation to European norms. Social strata among the slaves were defined by creole versus African origins by skilled versus unskilled, domestic versus field labour, and by the extent of the adoption of external symbols of European dress, speech and manners, which became significant status symbols in colonial society. The third major stratum of colonial society were the freemen of colour, who emerged even before emancipation. (1960:113)

This description shows that any simple statement about white elite and black masses is, at best, a pale imitation of what really transpired, and at worst, a serious distortion which de-emphasises intra-class nuances which are vital to a more than partial explanation of West Indian stratification patterns.

Similarly, any attempt to explain contemporary facets of West Indian social organisation solely by 'historical factors', may be mistaken if it adheres rigidly to those colonial or imperialistic influences so beloved by many social commentators. An interesting quote from Conrad Arensberg provides food for thought in this direction. Arensberg argues that:

A specialist in the culture of the Old World (Europe, Mediterranean, Middle East) is less likely to be sure that Caribbean marriage customs, or colour rankings or matrifocality and grand-mother families are simple responses to colonialism, plantations and slavery. Like susu, they may be traits, or re-working of traits, that must be pushed off the base-line which the classification 'Caribbean Culture' gives. Back before the English, the French, the Dutch, the Spanish and the Africans ever sailed the Spanish Main and settled the islands.

Till we know more of the culture of seventeenth and eighteenth century Europe, we are likely to forget that the islands were peopled and flowered in the Mercantilist Age, before the Puritan and Victorian victories and the Industrial Revolution re-worked England. As Herskovits traced susu to Dahomey; I would trace marriage as property validation and class legitimization of children to Hogarth's London. (1960: 97)

Here Arensberg is pointing out that care must be taken to be historically specific, that is to say the stage of development of the colonising society at the time of colonisation is significant. In addition, Arensberg is not denying the importance of colonialism and slavery in tracing the development of West Indian societies, which would be a patently false assumption, but pointing out that it is far too easy to hang a whole series of explanations on one hook. Western imperialism becomes in some works, a veritable cloak-room in which all the multi-coloured coats and cloaks of history can be hung.

What would seem to be required is a multi-dimensional approach which manages to embrace the power relations between and within contemporary West Indian societies, the relationships between such societies and those Western industrialised societies with which they are inextricably linked, all set against the back-cloth of history, which remains ever present in its influence. The latter point is borne out by Douglas Hall when he argues:

> Discussing our problems of today we too often tilt at the windmills of slavery and the post emancipation period, which lasted until the 1930s, when the style of today's social, political and economic predicaments was fashioned. The main features of the style are the complex human relationships and value judgements which, fashioned by our past, are of high relevance to any plans for the future. Social tensions, opportunism and irrationality in political behaviour and economic poverty constitute not three large problems, but one. (1962: 318)

The relationships between contemporary West Indian social organisation and the colonial history which shaped it are too expansive to analyse in depth in the present context. The richness of 'West Indian' culture, its complex history and the heterogeneous colour and class gradations which are developed within it should be an apologia for not attempting to 'explain' the social organisation of West Indian societies causally by working through the myriad strands of social development which preceded and thus helped to produce it. Nevertheless, it will be helpful to undertake a brief examination of present-day community organisation and political activism in the Caribbean in order to provide a basis for comparison with West Indian groupings in Britain.

Before concentrating on localised forms of association in West Indian societies, it is interesting to note that certain characteristics assigned to national political parties and trade unions are paralleled at the local level. The firm establishment of trade unions and political parties in West Indian societies dates back to the 1930s, although political association as such among West Indians (that is to say black and coloured West Indians), dates back to the slave rebellions in the earliest days of colonialism (Greene, 1974:9). In the late 1930s overpopulation, unemployment and the influx of emigrants from the United States and Latin America who were trying, unsuccessfully, to escape from the throes of the Depression, produced a spate of riots and strikes in the British West Indies which led to the establishment of trade unions and the labour parties. Discussing this period, Jesse Harris Proctor Jr. states that:

> This proved to be much more than merely a blind and ineffective outburst, for there quickly sprang up trade unions and labour parties throughout the area with leaders who articulated the grievances of the masses in such a way as to give the movement a positive content and direction. They pressed the workers' interests through political action as well as trade

22

union activity. The submerged majority was now at last politically activated and mobilised. (1962:283)

This period before the Second World War proved decisive in loosening, at least in a formal political sense, the bonds of colonial rule. Gordon Lewis (1971) divides the history of the British West Indies into three parts: first, the slavery period which ended with Nineteenth century emancipation; second, the period which corresponds with Proctors' analysis, namely the post-emancipation period which ended with the Second World War, and finally, the contemporary period of political independence at least for the larger islands. This broad spectrum of political and social change embraces far more than the formal acquisition of independent legislatures and enfranchisement. As Lewis stresses:

Whereas in other societies, culture and education, for example, can be left to other institutions, in the newly-found nations they come within the purview of politics. So, there is a mixture of politics, art, culture and education that defies the more conventional rules. (1971:12)

Bearing this historical legacy in mind, let us briefly examine the development of West Indian trade unionism.

The role of trade unions in the Caribbean has altered in conjunction with historical contingencies and the level of formal incorporation into the broader political system. As Greene (1974:22) notes: 'Historical conditions condition the role of trade unions which has shifted from 'mass movement' to 'pressure group' to 'party-union coalitions' '. In the 1930s the trade unions formed an important part of the spontaneous labour movements that produced certain reforms, if not radical changes, in the degree of political representation allotted to the masses. Subsequently, certain sectors of the labour force gained material benefits from unionisation and trade union leadership became a useful individual stepping-stone to wider political power. However, it is debatable whether the broad mass of workers (and certainly the unemployed) have made significant political gains through the movement. Indeed, the recent history of unionism in the British West Indies serves to confirm Clive Thomas's (1973:352) dictum that: 'Non participation is the characteristic condition of the West Indies'. Much of this condition can be explained by economic factors. The economic base of most islands incorporates wide fluctuations in prices and wages with a high pool of unemployed. As Knowles (1956:1396), for example, points out: 'The British West Indies economy is poor and its workers are poor'. With seasonal work, share-the-work schemes and low hourly earnings, many West Indian workers cannot afford to pay union dues even if they were so inclined. Only the genuine industrial unions and a few general unions can afford a strike fund or full-time salaried officials. Knowles (1956) also argues that many workers in the West Indies are used to estate and governmental paternalism. There is a tradition in many industries, particularly on the plantations, of fostering informal, paternal relationships between workers and owners rather than any encouragement by the latter of a move towards formal worker/management relationships.

This concentration of union representation in certain industries, which is invariably urban based (Cross, 1979:92), has led to a situation where:

> The trade union structure does not include two categories of the labour force which are, in terms of numbers, each as large as the working force itself. These are the twenty per cent of the labour force which are unemployed and the peasants.
> (Thomas, 1973:353)

This has led many commentators to confirm Thomas's point that the permanent working class is relatively privileged *vis-a-vis* the mass of unemployed and underemployed (Munroe, 1972: Stone, 1973). Knowles (1956), for one, sees this lack of union representation as indicative of a general trend of middle class paternalism in Caribbean politics. He points out that the working class do not generally produce their own leaders. There are low levels of literacy, little respect for members from their own ranks and a general preference for 'educated middle class leaders'.

Trade unions in West Indian societies are often closely aligned with political parties as labour organisations are seen as stepping stones towards political office. Union officials are commonly dependent on political offices for their incomes. Furthermore, there is a firm emphasis on trade union legislation introduced at the national level rather than collective bargaining at the local level. Paradoxically, those workers who have successfully organised themselves to improve local conditions, are often employed in newer industrial contexts—for example, the Trinidad oil industry—which already occupy a favourable niche in the West Indian employment market (Cross, 1979:92). Consequently, these organised attempts at self-improvement often exacerbate the fragmented nature of the labour movement alluded to above. Knowles (1956) found that West Indian governments tended to encourage training courses and trade unionism was supported by some employers, but this was mainly due to their preference for formalised union activities as opposed to spontaneous 'rioting' (as they defined it) among the workers. The increasing external influences of the multi-nationals moreover, has raised the level of unionisation, usually on a whole industry basis. But the general trend is towards incorporation of workers in specific vital industries into a reformist collective bargaining framework, whilst the majority of non-unionised or unemployed workers look on. There is certainly a long history of spontaneous collectivism within the labour force in the British West Indies, but a very limited involvement in the formal political arena on the part of the lower classes beyond the casting of their vote at election time.

A brief glance at the characteristics of West Indian political parties serves to confirm the above argument. Ayearst (1954: 1960), for example, reveals a number of parallels between trade union and political party participation. Both forms of organisation are marked by the importance of personalised, informal relationships and the prevalence of 'charismatic' type leaders. Most West Indian political parties are labour parties that are nationalistic and in Ayearst's terms, 'pseudo-socialistic'. This is not surprising as most parties have to rely on working class support through trade union connections, because the middle classes in West Indian societies are not large enough to act as an independent power base for electoral purposes. Hence, Ayearst points out:

> Enfranchisement of the black and coloured majority (in the West Indies) has proceeded rapidly under pressure exerted by local politicians, often identified with labour organisations and acquiesed to by British governments anxious to avoid political and economic dislocation. (1954:187)

This confirms Knowles' point that most trade unions and political parties are not separate in the West Indies. The labour unions are all-embracing in meeting both political and economic needs. There has been a constant fusion of economic and political interests and this has produced a combination of political parties and unions. Therefore, one cannot draw a clear line between the highly organised and formalised political activity of the middle and upper classes in the West Indies and the loosely organised formal associations of the lower class.

Nevertheless, as already mentioned, the leadership, particularly of political parties, tends to be concentrated within the middle classes. Furthermore, there have been wide restrictions on the degree of participation of the 'masses' in the political process. Ayearst (1954) argues that West Indian political organisations have a demagogic party structure with largely 'paper' constitutions. Local party groups are generally few in number and inactive except immediately before elections. Ayearst's general conclusion, as far as the West Indian worker is concerned, is that: 'His society is conspicuously lacking in community-wide organisations that he can identify with his needs and aspirations (1954:193). In part, this is due to the emergence of 'populist-type' parties which, as A. W. Singham (1973:279) has said, 'have been based on what can be characterized as a hero-crowd type of relationship, in which routinization, institutionalization and participation in the political system are minimal':

The hero emerges as a leader at a particular stage of colonial evolution, the terminal stage of colonial rule. This period is marked by the advent of universal adult suffrage. It is this sudden emergence of the mass into political life that enables a hero to arise and which at the same time encourages the caesarist tendencies in this type of leader. (1968:319)

Singham goes on to describe the main distinguishing features of contemporary West Indian political leadership, calling on this connection on the distinctions drawn by Lloyd Best between types of 'Doctor Politics'. Best, according to Singham:

Distinguishes between three types of 'Doctors': the 'Grammar School Doctor', produced mainly in Trinidad and Guyana, the new Plantation colonies where education rather than property holding has been the medium of advance, and whose prime examples are Williams and Burnham ... 'Sunday School Doctors', produced in the mature plantation colonies where there was no escape for potential leaders from organizing labour, where the education came chiefly from the Sunday School, and the rhetoric is Biblical, of which Bird of Antigua and Bradshaw of St Kitts are the best examples; and the 'Public School Doctors', a Jamaican phenomenon, where a local ruling class arose after the end of slavery, with many of the values of their English counterparts (for example, Norman Manley) ... (1973:279–90)

Irrespective of the type of 'doctor', Best argues, 'the distinguishing feature of Doctor politics is that the Leader is expected to achieve for and on behalf of the population. The community is not expected to contribute much more than crowd support and applause' (1973: 280). It has been argued that in many ways this 'populist' type of government also affects the middle class because they occupy a highly ambivalent position between the 'leader' on the one hand and the mass working and/or peasant class on the other. For example, C. L. R. James has stated that:

In the West Indies some of the politicians have or have had posts in the labour or union movement. But as a class they have no base anywhere. They are professional men, clerical assistants, here and there a small businessman, and of later years administrators, civil servants and professional politicians and, as usual, a few adventurers. (1962:131)

This 'populism' has been combined with an island nationalism which has further contributed to an island parochialism which the various Western powers have encouraged since the earliest days of colonialism.[4]

This parochialism contributed to the downfall of the Leeward Islands Federation in the 1920s and the attempt to establish a wider federation in the 1950s (Mordecai, 1968). In 1933, the Closer Union Commission reported that:

> Each (West Indian society) cherishes its own individuality, the product of its history and traditions ... To discover a common denominator is a baffling problem. With these differences in view it is small wonder that each community is interested solely in its own affairs and pays scant attention to those of its neighbour. (1933:19)

Recent attempts at economic co-operation on an inter-island basis, such as CARIFTA and CARICOM, have proved more successful. However these trading alignments have not been transformed into firm political alliances.

Island nationalism is also reflected in the weakness of local government in West Indian societies (Singh, 1972). This is particularly true of the smaller islands. However, this is due to disparities in power rather than any lack of political interest or acumen on the part of West Indians generally. Lowenthal reinforces this view when he says:

> In the smaller islands, where men of any influence are deeply involved in affairs at the territorial level, there is little impetus to allocate power to local authorities. But a more fundamental reason for the weakness of local government lies in the history of West Indian societies. West Indians have no tradition of self-rule; the drive for suffrage and for political autonomy came from the urban middle classes. It has only begun to percolate down from the territorial level to the localities, where conservatism, authoritarianism and paternalism are still entrenched. (1962:374)

This quotation highlights one of the problems of presenting material concerned with the social organisation of West Indian societies, namely the difficulty of knitting together different types of social organisation, in this case political organisation, in such a way as to allow for national and local differences and rural/urban distinctions. It has been argued that there are distinct differences between urban and rural environments which influence, for example, the level of political organisation and the likelihood of particular types of leadership (Braithwaite, 1968).

Thus, there appears to be a strict separation between the formal political institutions which exist at the national/urban level and the more informal associations which exist at the local/rural level. These distinctions could be important for the examination which follows of West Indian organisation in Britain. If there is a strict separation of the type suggested above it may indicate that leadership patterns in political

27

parties, governmental organisations and trade unions in the West Indies are not directly relevant to West Indian settlements in the metropolitan society. At the national/urban level in West Indian societies, power positions in political organisations are dominated by middle class and upper class activists. However, with the possible exception of the London area in Britain, with its greater concentration of West Indian intellectuals and professionals, the majority of West Indians in the host society have lower class origins in the Caribbean. Similarly, many of them have come from 'rural' areas in their respective islands. Therefore, one would not expect many of these West Indians to have had direct experience of participation in formal organisations of a political character in the Caribbean.

It will be shown, however, that many of the West Indians in Easton were skilled workers who occupied upwardly mobile, lower-class positions in their home islands (see Chapter 3). Furthermore, some of these individuals had prior experience of participation in formal organisations in the Caribbean, although not necessarily in positions of authority.

Much of the confusion in this debate may be due to the way in which some commentators have interpreted the supposed distinctions between national/local and urban/rural in the West Indies. Many sociologists in the Caribbean now question the validity of assuming these sharp distinctions. For example, Vera Rubin (1960) has argued that this strict separation between each island and between rural and urban intra-island situations is based on erroneous assumptions which assume that the contemporary situation in the Caribbean is comparable to past situations. Rubin suggests that:

> High population densities, inter-island communication
> increases, considerable migration between islands and else-
> where dispels the notion of insularity of cultural activities
> ... on the islands themselves the local markets and itinerant
> hawkers provide a human and cultural network between the
> rural peasants and the culture of the cities, i.e., between the
> urban and 'folk' subcultures. Schools, cinema, radio, roads
> and buses, improved public health and welfare services bring
> urban culture within the rural orbit and impinge on folk
> practices characteristic of isolated cultures. Thus, the urban-
> rural distinction is less sharp than elsewhere and we find in
> many areas of the Caribbean that the countryside appears
> more semi-urban than rural. (1960:119)

Note that Rubin is not saying that greater levels of inter-island communication have broken down nationalistic, separatist sentiments; nor that the traditional differences between rural and urban dwellers (among West Indians) have been eradicated, but that a form of cultural unification in terms of social activities is apparent. This would seem to indicate that, in examining levels and forms of participation in 'localised' organisation, the rural-urban distinction may be less important than has been previously thought. Certainly, when considering forms of lower class participation this would appear to be so. So, there may well be some justification for separating the informal cultural aspects of the social structure of West Indian societies from the formal political relations within and between them.

This point is confirmed by Cross (1979) in his excellent recent study of urbanisation in the Caribbean. Dwelling on the debate concerning 'traditional' and 'modern' sectors in underdeveloped societies, a duality which is usually taken to correspond with rural/urban differences, Cross argues: 'The fact is that there are no 'traditional' sectors to Caribbean societies. All are, or none are; a fact which throws into high relief the economic rather than the cultural causes and consequences of urban growth (1979:9—10)'. He concludes his text by suggesting that whereas urban migration within Caribbean societies promotes new life styles, 'small city size, as well as cultural affinity, adds to the impression that the two (rural/urban) areas are not worlds apart' (1979:152). The relative cultural and physical similarity between city and country has crucial implications for the role that voluntary associations play in assisting the transference of migrants from one social/geographical milieu to another. For, as Cross points out:

> At the middle class level urban based associations abound in
> the recreational and professional spheres and few identifiable
> ethnic groups are without an organization specifically formed
> to promote ethnic identity and act as a pressure group when
> collective interests are threatened. However, unlike West
> Africa,[5] there is little evidence to suggest that these associations
> have a direct or immediate relevance for socialising the rural
> migrant into the ways of the city. (1979:100)

If there appears to be little history of associational formation in easing the migrant experience within West Indian societies, this may have important implications for those lower class West Indians who venture to foreign urban shores.

The validity of assuming some degree of social uniformity among West Indian societies becomes an important issue when it is realised that there is a very little information on localised community organisation in the Caribbean, particularly among the lower classes (Greene, 1974). There has been a certain amount of work on religious associations (see Chapter 6) and considerable literature exists on family organisation (see Chapter 5) but little research has been done on voluntary associations and other forms of community organisation. This, in itself, may be an indication of the paucity of this type of organisation among lower class West Indians in the Caribbean. Nevertheless, the lack of material means that much of the literature cited in the remainder of this chapter is, perforce, taken from studies of particular islands (indeed, in most cases, particular communities within particular islands) so the degree of generalisation must remain problematic.

However, Michael G. Smith and G. J. Kruijer (1957:29) have constructed a list of types of organisations which, they believe, are commonly found in rural and urban communities in the Caribbean. They suggest that urban areas in West Indian societies contain the following forms of organisation:

1 Churches
2 Political and Trade Union groups
3 Friendly Societies
4 Ratepayers Associations
5 Social Welfare Associations
6 YMCA and YWCA
7 Women's Federations

It can be seen that such organisations correspond closely to forms of organisation that are familiar in Britain. In contrast, West Indian organisations in the Caribbean become more specialised at the rural level, as can be seen below:

1 Boards—Industrial—Coconut, coffee, etc.
2 Commodity Associations—Citrus Growers, Rice Growers, etc.
3 Authorities—Coconut Control Authority
4 Committees—Farm Improvement Committees, etc.
5 Co-operatives—Vegetable Growers, etc.
6 Manufacturer's Organisations—Sugar
7 Special Purpose Commodity Organisations—Citrus Loan
8 Credit Organisations

Smith and Kruijer (1957) argue that, to some extent, the latter type of organisations are found in both urban and rural areas. In addition, they point to the existence in local communities, both urban and rural, of a variety of informal, mainly recreational associations such as sports clubs and so forth. Smith and Kruijer (1957:30) also list the four types of leader which, they claim, may be found among these various organisations. These are:

(a) Professional leaders—officers of agricultural extension services, ministers of the major religious denominations, etc.
(b) Formal or Titular leaders—members of Parish Councils, members of Church Councils, Trade Union leaders, etc.
(c) Folk Culture leaders—the leaders of Revivalist sects

(d) Informal leaders—individuals who are influential in
     community life but who do not hold any formal office
     or position.

These types of organisations and leaders are found in both national
and local milieux and include all class positions. However, the present
study is particularly concerned with lower class associational activity
in the Caribbean so that a comparison with similar activities within
West Indian settlements in Britain can be made. In one of the few
studies of West Indian voluntary associations in Britain, D. R. Manley
(1959:296) distinguishes between West Indian associations which have
two types of lower class affiliates:

(a) Associations composed mainly of lower-class members with
     a proportion of members from higher status levels who
     hold most of the offices and run the organisations.
(b) Exclusively lower class associations.

Manley confirms that West Indian communities in the Caribbean have
not as yet been studied in great detail from the point of view of community organisation. But he suggests that there are many similarities between
lower class West Indian associations in the Caribbean and the West
Indian associations he studied in Britain. Manley quotes Smith and
Kruijer as saying that:

> In general the organisation (of lower class West Indians) into
> voluntary associations is so difficult, that at least one manual,
> for the use of agricultural officers and social workers, directs
> attention to it as a special problem. (1959:299)

In the rural areas, most group activities involving economic objectives
or mutual aid tend to be organised informally between relatives and
neighbours. As Manley puts it:

> Communities tend to be composed of isolated independent
> family groups and there are few formal mechanisms for main-
> taining inter-household discipline and control and for pooling
> of resources between households or other similar household
> groups. On the whole the pattern is one of individualism,
> competitiveness and aggressiveness in inter-personal relation-
> ships ... there is a strong accent on informality in community
> organisation and certain individuals have prestige and exert
> influence because of the facilities they control. (1959:299)

The community possesses an organisational pattern of its own, but
it depends upon spheres of influence and differences in status rather
than upon formal associations. Thus, Le Franc (1978), for example,
has argued that government attempts to introduce communal organisation among the Jamaican peasantry, particularly village based agricultural

31

co-operatives, have failed because of elitist bureaucratic practices that ignore informal modes of organisation already established among the lower classes. Associations which are formed by lower class West Indians include revivalist sects, friendly societies, sports clubs and informal or semi-formal economic co-operative groups. But nearly all of these groups are small and limited in scope. This informality of organisation means that very few West Indians in the lower classes have experience in voluntary associations. A study of Stycos (1957) estimated that only 10% of women and 20% of men are participants in such forms of association. These figures were obtained in a rural/urban study of lower class participation in Jamaica. It is interesting to note that, whilst Stycos believed that these were low percentages, the findings in the present study show that within a British urban situation the level of West Indian membership and participation in formal associations was even lower (see Chapter 3).

One form of association which is prevalent among the lower classes in the Caribbean is the friendly society. These societies were established in the Caribbean as early as the 1820s when visiting clergy and missionaries to the islands encouraged their formation. Friendly societies originated in Jamaica and Antigua but spread rapidly to the other islands. The societies, not surprisingly due to their origins, have strong religious affiliations which follow the major denominations. In St Lucia, for example, the majority of such societies are connected with the Catholic Church which predominates on that island.

In common with their counterparts in Britain, friendly societies in the West Indies are associations originally established for the promotion of thrift and self-help. They represent 'an attempt by working men to meet their social and convivial needs as well as to insure against the hazards of sickness and death' (Gosden, 1973:vii). However, these associations were often started by external agencies like the church. They were not, in most cases formed spontaneously within the lower class. Nevertheless, this type of association is certainly one of the commonest among the lower classes in the Caribbean. A. F. and D. Wells found that: 'In the West Indian colonies the Friendly Society idea has a great hold and these associations are prolific (1953:23). With respect to comparisons between the West Indies and Britain, the Wells' commented:

> In England the Friendly society tends to be, naturally enough, rather more an urban than a rural institution. Broadly speaking, the same holds in the West Indies in those colonies where there are large urban areas. (1953:27)

The Wells' study was carried out in the early 1950s, so it is likely that the rise, since then, of alternative financial institutions, such as banks, insurance companies and building societies may have made friendly societies less common. However, Le Franc (1979) confirms that credit unions and other forms of savings organisations are still widespread.

Whilst the friendly societies in the British West Indies owe their origins to the metropolitan society—in the sense that they are a continuation of their development among the British working class in the eighteenth and nineteenth centuries—other forms of economic co-operation among the West Indian lower classes are said to originate from Africa. Unlike the more formalised friendly societies and some American fraternal societies which have been introduced in the West Indies, the rotating credit associations (Philpott, 1968) are informal and almost exclusively working class in their membership. They have basically the same system of organisation but go under different names in the various islands. For example, in Jamaica they are called a 'pardner' or 'pardner-hand'. In Trinidad they are called 'susu', whilst in Antigua and Montserrat they are commonly known as 'boxes', in Barbados as 'meetings' and so on.

Basically the idea is for one individual to act as the 'banker'. A group of individuals contributes a set amount of money each week which is held by the banker. It may be as much as ten dollars or a smaller amount. The group may be just a few individuals or run to thirty or forty people. Each week, one individual is entitled to a 'partner-hand' and he collects the total investment of all members for that week. In a hand of thirty members contributing five dollars a hand, each individual will collect 150 dollars when his turn comes round. After each individual has gone through in rotation, the order is reversed. Therefore, once in every thirty hands each member will get the last hand in the last round plus the first hand of the next round. This doubles his share to 300 dollars. This system can give a sizeable sum of money to each member at fairly regular intervals. Often, of course, the 'hands' will be much smaller because the membership is lower or weekly payments less.

This system relies on a high level of mutual trust and, consequently, the banker is usually a person with a high degree of prestige within the household or kinship network. These associations are often restricted to family networks or close friends for this very reason. Rotating credit associations are usually confined to the lower classes in West Indian societies and may be compared with revivalist and sectarian religions as a predominantly lower class form of association. The middle and upper classes in the Caribbean utilise more institutionalised outlets for investment and credit facilitation.

The role of banker is an excellent example of 'informal leadership' within the Smith and Kruijer (1957) classification. Here, authority and prestige rest on highly personalised criteria, namely bonds of trust initiated through a family or friendship network. These credit associations are not marked by any level of formalisation in so far as they do not incorporate elected officials or formalised collective procedures. The collection, maintenance and distribution of money relies on personalised and informal social interaction. This latter characteristic introduces the question of leadership in voluntary associations in the West Indies, particularly with regard to working class activism.

Bearing in mind the four-fold classification of leadership presented by Smith and Kruijer (1957), it is apparent that 'professionals' and 'formal' or 'titular' leaders tend to be drawn almost exclusively from the middle class. This is in accordance with the prestige attached to middle class positions in West Indian societies which rests on status attributes like colour, occupation, income and education. Positions of authority are commonly equated with the dominance of European traditions in these societies, a dominance which is demonstrated by the high prestige accorded to a lighter skin colouring and other Caucasian-type phenotypical features (Nettleford, 1965). The latter are reinforced by the adoption of 'Euro-normative' standards, for example, in modes of speech, dress and general mannerisms. However, one cannot assume strict distinctions among colour gradations, particularly in recent years when some island societies have become independent. There is still a heavy emphasis on 'Euro-connections' but darker skin colouring may be overcome through education and/or wealth. Money 'whitens' in the Caribbean as it does, for example, in certain parts of Brazil (Ianni, 1972). Similarly, with the comparatively recent importation of Black Power ideologies, there have been some attempts, expedient or otherwise, officially to deny the predominant 'Euro-emphasis' in West Indian societies. These ideologies have split middle class leadership along the lines of 'conservatism' and 'radicalism' to use two rather imprecise terms.

An increase in graduates from the University of the West Indies in Jamaica and Trinidad has provided an intellectual base for the emergence of new leaders and ideas in the Caribbean which have been very influential in recent years. Parallel to this there have occurred spontaneous political movements in many parts of the British West Indies in the past two decades. Political activity which was labelled as 'black power' (by activists and West Indian governments alike) emerged in the early 1960s in Guyana with the formation of the 'New World Group' and the publication of the *New World Quarterly*. Other radical groups and publications followed in other West Indian societies, demonstrating the emergence of a new 'militancy' which owed much to the black movement in the United States, but which also combined those unique characteristics of the Caribbean that can be traced back through the centuries. Nettleford, for example, examining the history of 'black power' in Jamaica, argues:

The tradition of black assertion has never left Jamaican life.

There were the late Eighteenth and early Nineteenth century slave rebellions, 1865 and Paul Bogle, 1938, and the black working classes, 1960, and the Rastafarians, 1968, and the young sufferers. (1970:120)

In addition to the chain of 'unrest' in Jamaica, there have been a series of riots in Guyana, the so-called 'February Revolution' (Best, 1973) in Trinidad in 1970, and even more recent political movements in the Eastern Caribbean. For example, the late 1970s saw new radical governments established in Dominica, St Lucia and most recently in Grenada (Searle, 1979). This wave of political change, that in some ways resembles the militant years of the late 1930s, has been described in a variety of ideological tones. Commentaries run the gamut from reactionary cries of militant dissidence or anarchy to the liberationist hopes of 'the left'.

The former, representative of most West Indian governments of this period, couched their statements in terms of what they perceived as 'extreme' political behaviour that represented only those who were not prepared to work within the 'democratic' political process. Nevertheless, those who took this line considered such activities important enough to request foreign military aid and took steps to suppress freedom of political expression through censorship and the deportation of 'militants'.

An alternative viewpoint saw the upsurge of black power ideologies as a form of elitist 'pragmatism'. Moderate leaders were simply using the trappings of black militancy to keep themselves in power. Thus, the human dignity and majority rule aspects of such ideologies were extracted and brandished publicly but any signs of disaffection from the 'lower classes' were firmly denounced. Conversely, many so-called militants may have adopted black power slogans as a means to enrol the support of the dispossessed for their own ends rather than those of the majority they allegedly represented. This line of argument is forcibly demonstrated by Gordon Lewis when he writes:

The enemy in West Indian life is the perpetuation, by the new Middle Class elites of the successor states of empire, of the 'white bias' of society and in English life of a potent negrophobia so ingrained that it produces a 'Left-wing racialism' as easily as Neo-Facism. (1969:81)

This continuing reliance on things European still buttresses the authority of the middle classes in the Caribbean and thus they still continue to dominate leadership positions within more formalised organisations. But the phenomena of black power in its many forms may provide a basis for concerted effort incorporating black intellectualism and the strivings of the black proleteriat/peasantry. This form of mobilisation is fostered in a world climate where the mass media transmit a world-wide struggle of 'oppressed' against 'oppressor'.

Much of this political rhetoric is reminiscent of old forms of external control in new disguises. As Nettleford acknowledges:

> Black is seen by some non-American black intellectuals as
> merely another form of neo-colonial 'Imperialistic temper'.
> The importation of values and ideas which have been formed
> by the mass media rather than through a common bond of
> deprivation. Many West Indians and Africans wish to find
> solutions for themselves. (1970:120)

This viewpoint still reinforces the role of middle class leaders but undoubtedly in a new vein. Furthermore, it gives a role to the black proletariat, presumably in viewing the resurgence of spontaneous protest in West Indian societies in recent years as the start of a mass black 'revolution' in the Caribbean.

One can only speculate on future possibilities for a total transformation of British West Indian societies. Adam Kuper (1976), in a recent study of Jamaica, is dubious about any radical overthrow of the present political system. He argues that the middle class dominated, two party system is well entrenched in Jamaica. Support for these parties crosscuts racial and class divisions so a broad based platform for political revolt is not immediately evident. Kuper acknowledges that there has been a radical change in the local evaluation of status. Thus, the traditional impediments attached to colour distinctions have been largely replaced by new symbols of racial/cultural identity. These symbols have been successfully incorporated into the existing political structure so the possibilities for revolution (Kuper argues) are drastically reduced.

The radical shift in political allegiances recently observable in those smaller Eastern Caribbean societies mentioned previously, perhaps suggests greater potential for far reaching political reforms. The key to the political futures of the smaller islands, which often lack the party stability Kuper refers to above, rests with the possibilities for transforming largely rural, agrarian social structures that have traditionally encouraged the continued prestige of an Anglophile 'middle class', who have merely assumed the political mantle of their European predecessors and/or lower class folk leaders. These leaders are often tempted to re-introduce political systems based on authoritarianism and personal graft.

Such systems reproduce a form of autocratic leadership that is based on leader-follower relationships similar to those described previously in this chapter. A form of politics which John (1973) has characterised as a shifting alliance of populism, personalities and patronage. However, there are certainly signs that political activism in its many forms is volatile in West Indian societies at present, and that international and national issues are becoming more influential at the community level. Frank McDonald, for example, has noted that:

> In spite of the pressure from regional governments, the Commonwealth Caribbean radicals have continued to organize. And as in the past, when different conditions required changes in tactics, so now the Caribbean militants (ranging from Marxists to black nationalists) recognise that present circumstances dictate new strategy. So the shift from pure analysis to mass actions, to marches and demonstrations has become a foundation for the more serious work of organizing at community or village level, work that is certainly less dramatic and less obvious, but in the end far more likely to bring effective action. (1971:156)

This movement towards localised activism illustrates the fluidity of the situation and the diffuseness of leadership patterns. Manley (1959) has argued that the continual stress on informality in community organisations means that leadership may come from within proletarian or peasant communities, or from middle or upper-class elite groups. He argues that individual charisma is important within authority relationships and thus a lower status position in a community may be less disadvantageous if certain personal attributes are possessed and, more importantly, ranked prestigiously by others. Hence, recognised charismatic qualities can overcome the disadvantages of lack of education, income, and a black skin.

The continued centrality of informality and personalised relationships in associational activity among West Indians appears to indicate the existence of psychological characteristics that explain such behaviour. These traits may account for the emphasis upon individualism and the separation of personal qualities of leadership from those elements of prestige emanating from formal roles and group affiliations, a tendency which Manley calls 'an important trait in West Indian society' (1959:83).

The prevalence of 'individualism' in West Indian societies has been used by several writers to explain the low level of West Indian membership and participation in voluntary associations and formal organisations both in the Caribbean and in Britain (see Introduction). Michael Banton, for example, describes individualism as an 'evocative and rather dangerously vague' term but he suggests that 'factors of temperament may well be part of the answer' to the question of West Indian associational patterns in the host society (1972:146).

Certainly 'individualism' has a complicated ancestry as a concept. It is often dangerously close to psychological and/or physiological connotations with allusions to personality types and so forth. There would seem to be some evidence for suggesting that there are certain psychological characteristics which could be labelled as a lower class 'West Indian personality type' but one should hesitate to define such a term in any precise or concrete form. M. G. Smith has argued in relation to psychological types that:

> It would seem that outside the United States with its formal or informal caste systems, there is little unanimity about the nature and significance of differentiation within the societies examined ... however, it is interesting to note the agreement in definition of West Indian personality patterns among those students who lay such different stresses on different situations expressive of personality traits. (1965:48)

These 'traits' include aggressiveness, mistrust, jealousy, anxiety, insecurity and various forms of self-hate. The general tendency is to see an immensely complex personality which displays forms of insecurity and self-deprecation whilst at the same time possessing a spontaneity and outwardness which belies any form of introversion. Such tendencies are supposedly demonstrated through various social mechanisms observable in interpersonal relationships. There is a strong competitiveness among individuals, particularly with regard to money and material possessions. A person's wealth is surrounded by secrecy, mistrust, and considerable gossiping. Relationships are marked by anxiety and fear of being disliked but also intense jealousy. Mistrustfulness is paradoxically centred more on those one knows well than on outsiders. A description by Yehudi Cohen of a Jamaican village community illustrates some of these points. Cohen argues that economic competitiveness, particularly competition for land, undermines social co-operation to the point where deference to aspiring political leaders within the village is minimal. He describes how:

> Competition for land and its unequal distribution forces some members of the community to migrate to urban areas, thus reinforcing the brittleness and tenuousness of interpersonal ties within the community. This divisiveness is also seen clearly in the sphere of leadership. We noted that whatever leadership does exist in Rocky Roads is held by transient people. Important here is the fact that these persons do not own land in and around Rocky Roads. For the individual Rocky Roader this means that they are not competing for available land, food and wealth in the community. Hence, their leadership can be accepted. Where competition is absent in Rocky Roads, it seems possible to conclude, leadership can exist; where competition is present, it seems to militate against the acceptance

and functioning of social leadership. (Cohen, 1954:131)

A single, rather extreme, example from one village in Jamaica cannot be taken as indicative of interpersonal relations at different levels within that particular island society or indeed within the British West Indies as a whole. Furthermore, the relationships so described are not necessarily unique; elements of them may be found in all forms of social interaction to some degree. Aggression, materialism, and anxiety are surely just as applicable to Western industrialised, urban areas as to Jamaican rural villages. Nevertheless, work which has been done at this level of generality in the Caribbean, tends to substantiate Cohen's findings.[6]

The crucial problem in all these studies is how to define precisely the relationship between personality types and the social and cultural environments which may produce them. Thus, can it be said that a particular type of personality produces a given form of social action, or is the reverse true, or is the relationship between them problematic and inter-penetrative? These questions are similar to those raised by the controversy (Lane, 1971) over the nature of the personality types which developed among Negroes in the Deep South of the United States. This debate centres on the relationship between the social constraints of slavery and the relative degree of autonomy of slaves and how these two factors influenced personality formation over time. Thus, was the apparent docility of negro slaves a product of the harsh social constraints placed upon their life situation (and the degree of harshness is debated at length) or was it a demonstration of the social pragmatism of those in bondage; that is an exhibition of role distance in 'Goffmanesque' terms? This debate does not appear to have been resolved, nor perhaps is any conclusive, definitive statement likely to appear. The basis of the arguments of all protagonists, perhaps inevitably in terms of the 'delicacy' of the subject matter, rests on matters of personal belief as much as empirical fact. Bearing in mind the greater depth of knowledge in this area and the greater level of academic scrutiny to which it has been subjected in contrast to the Caribbean, one would be wise to tread somewhat warily along such paths.

Nevertheless, it can be suggested that despite the paucity and level of generality of the evidence collected for the Caribbean, 'West Indian individualism' should be considered as a social manifestation rather than a psychological one. This is not to deny that inter-disciplinary approaches which embrace psychological and social psychological forms of explanation are extremely important when attempting to explain inter-personal relationships within West Indian formal and informal associations.[7] However, for present purposes such concepts as 'individualism' will be discussed in relation to the social aspects of group relations. Hence, in what follows, 'individualism' will be loosely taken to describe the prevalence for independent thought and action among many West Indian individuals and groupings.

Viewing individualism as a social phenomenon, one could trace the development of various institutions in the Caribbean from the days of slavery to the present day and observe the degree of 'fragmentation' at the group level. This could be studied by examining, for example, family and household patterns, systems of land tenure, forms of social, economic and political control, etc. Therefore, it is suggested that if slavery was *the* crucial period for personality formation in the Caribbean, the particular level and form of constraint placed upon slaves at that time, produced a society in which individual rather than group actions were predominant. This could be illustrated by studying the constraints placed upon inter-marriage, the sub-division of land-holdings, the social distance encouraged between field and house slaves and so on. Above all, it may be demonstrated through the degree of differentiation along class and colour lines which emanated from wide ranging miscegenation and the gradual formation of complex forms of stratification based upon the perception of more phenotypical attributes than simply skin colour. Such a process has been called a form of 'creolisation' which describes what Edward Brathwaite (1971) terms 'an inter-meshing of Euro and Afro, both master and slave adapted to a new situation to produce a creole society'.

This originally produced a unique blend of European and African social and cultural mannerisms which left few 'pure' types (if one can talk in such terms) with the upper and middle classes owing more to their European ancestry whilst the black majority were predominantly African in origin. Thus, it can be seen that contemporary West Indian social organisation depicts a form of cultural and biological inter-mixing which, whilst not unique to the Caribbean, is perhaps best illustrated there. As Rex Nettleford remarks:

> What is remarkable about the West Indian is a sense of subtle links, the series of subtle and nebulous links which are latent within him, the latent ground of old and new personalities. (1970:155)

Therefore, it is suggested that there may be a characteristic form of West Indian social organisation within which West Indians demonstrate a type of individualism which is a product of their colonial history as the result of a consistent pattern of oppression and their reaction to oppression. This is demonstrated in the informality and competitiveness of West Indian interpersonal relationships and their concern with material stability. In group relations, it may produce fragmentation and ephemeral authority relationships which are easily altered by changes in individual loyalties. At the societal level, it is shown in an insularity and an island parochialism which was largely produced by an education system which gives many a West Indian child a knowledge of English Kings and Queens and the coalfields of Britain, but little about other Caribbean islands, in some cases, a few miles distant. It was also fostered by colonial policies of divide and rule which encouraged such insularity so that any thoughts of federation were considered impractical by the islands themselves.

Several points have emerged from the discussion of community organisation in the Caribbean presented in this chapter. It has been shown that formal associations predominate amongst the upper and middle classes in the West Indies but all levels of organisation are characterised by a high degree of informality and personalisation of authority relationships. This is particularly true of leadership patterns which are dominated by such characteristics. However, this emphasis on individual attributes renders the placement of leadership roles in class terms problematic. One cannot assume a sharp delineation between middle and lower class leadership potentialities, although it is recognised that the former group have a higher potential because of their greater economic stability, which provides a likely basis for prestige within a given community. Nevertheless, at a high level of generality one can discern certain class differences with respect to types of leadership.

Middle class leadership in the West Indies tends towards the formal and bureaucratic and is relatively stabilised, whilst lower class leadership tends to be charismatic and more ephemeral. However, all forms of organisation and association are prone to ephemerality and dissolution depending on their level of institutionalisation. The latter is influenced by the social structure of the given island society which, in turn, relates to stratification patterns, the level of economic 'viability', the political relationship with a coloniser or previous coloniser, and many other factors.

At the lower class level, which is our prime concern here, organisational patterns tend to be even more personalised and informal, based upon household or family networks rather than formalised economic or political institutions. Forms of association at this level tend to be more related to alternative forms of organisation to those incorporated within centralised, societal institutions; for example, cultist or sectarian as opposed to denominational religions and individualised economic associations (rotating credit associations) as opposed to centralised financial systems. Such types of organisation may provide the basis for initially spontaneous political action, as demonstrated by those kinds of 'militancy' which have been circumscribed by the label 'black power' and religio-politico groups like the Rastafarians in Jamaica. In general, there is a high degree of differentiation at all levels, which suggests that one can only talk about the 'West Indies' or the 'Caribbean' in very general terms. It still remains problematic whether one can speak in terms of a highly specific socio-cultural area. Therefore, particular attention should be paid to individual societal characteristics when comparing different islands and to possibly unique localised contingencies within a given West Indian society. This should be borne in mind when considering the nature of the different West Indian island communities in Easton, the possible differences in their social organisation and how these may affect the relationships within and between them.

Having injected a sufficient note of caution, we can now turn to the British setting; in particular, a description of the West Indian settlement in Easton, which will be presented in the following chapter.

Notes

1   For excellent overviews of the history and contemporary social structure of West Indian societies, which also contain extensive bibliographies, see Knight (1978) and Lowenthal (1972).
2   Both Trinidad and Guyana contain substantial East Indian populations.
3   Most notably Jamaica, Trinidad, Guyana, Barbados, Grenada, Dominica, St Lucia and St Vincent.
4   A number of studies have been concerned with populist leadership and island nationalism in the Caribbean; see, for example, Bell (1967); Oxaal (1968) and Wilgus (1967). Most of these studies are somewhat paternalistic towards the Caribbean. For a more radical interpretation of foreign influence, see De Kadt (1972) and Szulc (1971).
5   See Little (1965).
6   See, for example, the studies by Campbell (1943); Hadley (1949); Kerr (1952); Kruijer (1953) and Braithwaite (1954).
7   One important area is the relationship between colonialism and personality change; see, for example, Mannoni (1964); Memmi (1967) and Fanon (1970).

3 West Indians in Easton

The city of Easton has long enjoyed an affluence based on prosperous hosiery, engineering and other light industries. Industries that allowed the city to expand without the grime and vibrancy of the heavy forces of iron and steel. Therefore, the mill and furnace do not feature prominently in this Midlands landscape. In the nineteenth century Easton's wealth attracted Irish immigrants and, in the early part of the present century, they were soon followed by other migrant workers from Eastern and Western Europe. During the late 1940s and 1950s they were joined by increasing numbers of workers from the Caribbean; most of whom came from Jamaica, Barbados, and most notably, those small societies in the Leeward Islands that form part of the backbone that stretches from Florida to South America. These new arrivals met more hostility than their European counterparts but jobs were plentiful and small terraced homes could be purchased or rented cheaply.

In the 1960s and early 1970s Easton received another substantial boost to its labour force with the arrival of migrants from South Asia and East Africa. These workers, in common with their predecessors, represented a replacement labour force that swiftly filled those work slots vacated by indigenous workers who had already moved on to more salubrious housing and employment. A high proportion of West Indian and South Asian migrants moved into the central core of the city, particularly the decaying twilight area 'Lowdale', that offered a mixture of large and small, Victorian and Edwardian terraced housing. But, from the earliest years of settlement, some degree of geographical dispersal was a prominent feature of the residential patterns of black and coloured migrants. Consequently, many parts of the city display a mixture of cultures. Most noticeably, those central districts, akin to Lowdale, which have been redeveloped by South Asian entrepreneurship. These previously deteriorating areas now contribute some vitality to the city with new businesses and recreational outlets.

The West Indian population, in part, because of its smaller size[1] and greater dispersal, presents a less visible profile than its more numerous Asian neighbours. This presented some problems when a non-random sample of 108 respondents was selected for interview[2] but, eventually, a detailed profile of the various island communities in Easton was constructed. Unlike many recent studies of West Indians in Britain (Lawrence, 1974; Foner, 1979; Pryce, 1979) which have been concerned

43

mainly with Jamaican migrants, the Easton setting contains a variety of Caribbean communities. The island breakdown within the sample is a reasonably faithful replication of the respective sizes of different West Indian groupings in Easton. The largest groups are Antiguans (25 per cent), Jamaicans (19 per cent) and Barbadians (14 per cent). Also well represented are migrants from Nevis (10 per cent), St Kitts (7 per cent), Montserrat (7 per cent) and Barbuda (6 per cent) who comprise small but significant populations in terms of the total numbers of migrants from these Caribbean societies in Britain. Finally, a few respondents were also drawn from migrants from St Lucia, St Vincent, Dominica and Trinidad.

The presence of so many island communities in Easton is due to a mixture of fortuity and design. Settlement patterns have been influenced by employment demands and the early establishment of a network of relatives and friends that promoted a pattern of chain migration. This tends to reproduce a residential clustering of Caribbean groupings in many provincial cities and London boroughs. The Easton situation, therefore, represents a useful microcosm of different island clusters within a relatively small total West Indian settlement.

The sample was composed of 56 females and 52 males. This sex ratio relates to the construction of the sample on the basis of 68 household units, thus reflecting relationships of cohabitation and the balance between the sexes illustrated by the general pattern of West Indian migration to Britain (Peach, 1968). Most respondents were aged between 26 and 50 years, eighty eight per cent of the total sample (N = 108) falling within this range. Eleven respondents (10 per cent) were somewhat younger, in the 18—25 age group, whilst only two West Indians interviewed were over 50. The marked absence of older West Indians being typical of the general demographic characteristics of the Caribbean population in Britain (Lomas, 1973).

Migration patterns

With very few exceptions, most respondents had migrated directly from their island of birth to Britain. Only 10 West Indians (N = 108) differed from this general pattern, 6 having migrated from a different island in the Caribbean, whilst the remainder travelled from the United States. In all cases, this reflected a transitory migration in search of employment. None of these migrants had resided for more than two years in countries other than Britain or their birthplace.

Respondents were asked to mention whether they had lived in a town or village for most of their lives in the West Indies. Nearly half of the respondents (46 per cent) had spent all or most of their lives before arriving in Britain in the capital city of their respective West Indian societies. A further 17, (16 per cent) had rural backgrounds. There are, of course, innumerable problems in defining the meaning of 'rural' and 'urban', hence these figures only give a very rough guide to the residential background of respondents in the Caribbean. The differences between the sizes of West Indian societies and corresponding 'urban areas' is a case in point. Claiming residence in Kingston, Jamaica has vastly different connotations to past residence in Codrington, Barbuda. However, it is interesting to note that a majority of respondents did reside in what one can describe as 'less rural' settings within the context of their particular West Indian society. It will be useful to return to this question when describing the occupational background of respondents in the Caribbean.

The reasons for migration, unsurprisingly, centred around the quest for better opportunities, regardless of the manner in which these might be expressed. Table 3.1 indicates the reasons for migration from the Caribbean to Britain given by our respondents:

Table 3.1

Reasons for migration from Caribbean to Britain
given by West Indian respondents in Easton

Reasons for migration	No. of respondents mentioning it
Employment	36 (33.3%)
To join family and/or friends	38 (35.2%)
Travel and desire for change	16 (14.8%)
Better future	6 (5.6%)
Education	5 (4.6%)
War service	1 (0.9%)
Not given	6 (5.6%)

Apart from those who were unsure of their reasons or who arrived, rather fortuitously, by the fact of their war service, the two main reasons given for migration to Britain were the desire for better employment and the wish to join relatives or friends already settled in this country. A common pattern was for a husband to send for his wife after establishing himself in a job in Britain. Most West Indians (63 per cent) settled in Easton immediately on arrival in Britain, or settled there after short periods of residence in other cities, Birmingham and London being mentioned most often. This suggests some stability in the pattern of geographical mobility which the length of residence of respondents in Easton tends to support. The length of residence varied from 2 to 21 years, with the majority of respondents resident in Easton for more than 10 years. Over 75 per cent of respondents had lived in the area for at least 12 years. These figures, coupled with those pertaining to geographical mobility since arrival in Britain, suggest a settled community of some years standing.

The vast majority of West Indians in the sample were married or living within some form of settled union. This result was not unexpected in so far as the sample was constructed on the basis of residential units. Moreover, the age profile of respondents would tend to favour settled unions. Family sizes ranged from two to six children, with an average of 3.1 per family unit. A few families had children being looked after by relatives or friends elsewhere in Britain or the West Indies, but in the majority of cases all children were living in the household of their parents.

Education

All respondents had attended primary school in the West Indies, but only 32 (30 per cent) had gone on to some form of secondary schooling in the Caribbean. The latter group consisted of 21 men and 11 women. Although the figures for secondary education appear low, they reflect in fact a relatively high level of attendance when compared with overall patterns of school attendance in the West Indies. As Lowenthal notes: 'For the West Indian majority, formal education is brief and perfunctory. Primary schooling is mostly free and in theory compulsory, but there are far too few schools and teachers to enforce attendance. Many in the poorer islands have never been to school at all.' (1972:121)

Despite the possibility that some respondents, both in answering questionnaires and in interviews, might have consistently concealed non-attendance, the general picture still reflects the fact that a high proportion of West Indians in our sample had received a formal education in the West Indies. This has important implications for the measurement of status position and also geographical location within the home island. Secondary education is usually the prerogative of the elite and middle classes in the Caribbean who predominantly reside in urban areas. Rural dwellers are faced with problems of finance and transport which makes attendance at the largely urban based secondary schools difficult, if not impossible (Cross, 1979:125). Significantly, all of the 32 respondents who claimed to have received secondary schooling in the West Indies resided in the capital or other towns in their respective islands.

When one considers the pattern of secondary schooling in the West Indies, with all its related problems, it is hardly surprising to find that very few lower class West Indians go on to further or higher education. Although only 4 respondents had attended college after secondary schooling in the Caribbean this still reflects a high proportion compared with the total numbers of West Indians who reach that rung in the educational ladder. In the sample none of the respondents had attended universities in the West Indies. The 4 respondents with further education had been to technical colleges in their home island.

The educational backgrounds of the majority of West Indian respondents and their residence patterns in the Caribbean pointed to the fact that the sample in Easton was not drawn solely from West Indians with rural or lower class backgrounds in the Caribbean. This factor will have important implications when patterns of association and rates of membership in voluntary associations are discussed.

Very few West Indians in the sample had received any schooling in Britain. This was due to the fact that most respondents were above the age of schooling when they arrived in this country. Those who were young enough (7 respondents) had usually gone straight into the secondary level in Britain after completing the elementary level in the West Indies. Some respondents had attended or were still attending further education establishments in Britain. The latter group (16 respondents, 13 of them male) included a Barbadian who had acquired a degree in Social Studies, but the majority (11) were concerned with courses at Further Education Colleges. In all cases individuals were attempting to obtain qualifications related to their jobs. Finally, 4 respondents were attending Adult Education centres in Easton, all connected with recreational pursuits.

In all, 29 respondents out of 108 possessed some form of school, technical or professional qualification either acquired in the West Indies or since their arrival in Britain. This group was composed mainly of respondents who had completed their secondary (in some cases further) education in the West Indies; and a group of mainly younger men who were studying for qualifications at Technical or Further Education colleges in Easton. Some of the former group had acquired qualifications for particular occupations in the West Indies, for example, nursing, and 15 respondents had passed one or more General School Certificate examinations during their schooling in the Caribbean. The high proportion of women with qualifications is largely explained by the 11 nurses or nursing auxiliaries in the sample. The proportion of women in this occupation among West Indian females in Easton generally is not so high but nursing is well-known as an esteemed occupation for West Indian women both in the Caribbean and in Britain. It is one of the few occupations which allow women relatively free entry and is a common avenue by which women in the Caribbean can raise their status.

Employment

Table 3.2 shows the occupational composition of the total sample using the Registrar General's classification:

Table 3.2

Occupational background of West Indian sample employed in Easton

Category	Male		Female	
	No.	%	No.	%
Professional	1	(1.9)	—	—
Intermediate	5	(9.6)	11	(27.5)
Skilled (non-manual)	36	(69.2)	13	(32.5)
Skilled (manual)	—	—	2	(5.0)
Partly skilled	3	(5.8)	11	(27.5)
Unskilled	5	(9.6)	3	(7.5)
Other	2	(3.6)	—	—
Total	52		40	

The above figures in Table 3.2 show that very few West Indian men were employed in professional, intermediate or *skilled non-manual* work. This corresponds with previous studies which demonstrate that West Indians in Britain are proportionately heavily under-represented in white collar occupations, particularly in the professions (Smith, 1977). Within the sample, there was only one professional employee, a qualified researcher in a shoe factory. Intermediate jobs included social workers, a male nurse, a telephone engineer and a cabinet maker. There were no West Indian men in skilled non-manual work. Indeed, it was evident that very few West Indians, particularly men, had clerical or white-collar jobs.

Three men in the sample had semi-skilled occupations, all being employed as bus conductors. Unskilled employment was represented by railway porters, labourers, etc. A very high proportion of West Indian men were in skilled manual jobs, nearly 70 per cent of the total male sample. Most of them worked in local factories as drillers, moulders, welders and tool-makers. A variety of industries were mentioned as workplaces, including hosiery, boot and shoe, light engineering and rubber moulding. In addition to factory jobs, craft occupations were also common among male workers, for example, electricians, painters, printers and carpenters among others. Only two men were unemployed at the time of questioning.

In common with other studies (Smith, 1977; Foner, 1979), a high proportion of women in the sample, 71 per cent (N = 40), were working.

This was due to the demands of the household economy, the move towards greater economic independence among West Indian women and the overall high levels of female employment in the Easton labour market.[3] The local hosiery and light engineering factories provide a wide range of employment for female labour. However, most of these opportunities are in unskilled and partly skilled jobs. Consequently, many women were packers, examiners, and assemblers in local factories. None of the West Indian women in the sample had professional occupations. The relatively high figure for intermediate occupations is explained by the 9 nurses who fall into this category, the remaining 2 respondents being a laboratory technician and a qualified cook. The only West Indian women in skilled *non-manual* employment were a key punch operator and a secretary. Semi-skilled occupations also reflected a traditional interest in hospital work. Out of 11 respondents in this category, 8 were nursing auxiliaries. The remaining 3 women were in domestic work. A few West Indian women had unskilled jobs as cleaners, etc. Overall, the general pattern of female employment was in middle-range skilled and semi-skilled occupations. There were few unskilled workers and even fewer highly skilled or professional employees among the West Indian female labour force in Easton.

The general employment pattern illustrated in Table 3.2 is one of predominantly skilled and semi-skilled manual work. Over two-thirds (68 per cent) of men and women were in these categories. Only 15 per cent of the sample were unskilled, this figure being less than 10 per cent if only male workers are considered. However, there is a marked lack of West Indian workers employed in white collar jobs or occupations demanding high qualifications.

In addition to information about work patterns in Britain, all respondents were asked to give details of their previous employment in the West Indies. Thus some comparison could be made between work patterns in the society of origin and their present employment in Easton. Cross-cultural comparisons are extremely difficult when considering any aspects of the social structure of societies as diverse as Britain and the West Indies. In this respect, employment patterns are no exception. The structure of West Indian societies with large non-industrialised sectors, does not lend itself to a direct comparison with occupational categories constructed for use in Britain, the Registrar General's classification included. However, it was felt that some comparison, albeit a somewhat crude one, would be a useful exercise. Whilst accepting the additional difficulties of comparison with other West Indian societies, the occupational classification constructed by Cumper (1960) for Barbados, was used. Table 3.3 shows the jobs held by those West Indian respondents who were employed in the Caribbean prior to their move to Britain:

Table 3.3
Occupational background of total West Indian sample in previous employment in the Caribbean

Category	Male	%	Female	%
White collar	6	(12.2)	17	(51.5)
Skilled	16	(32.6)	2	(6.1)
Non-farm manual	7	(14.3)	2	(6.1)
Agricultural	18	(36.8)	4	(12.1)
Domestic	—	—	8	(24.2)
Unemployed	2	(4.1)	—	—
Total	49		33	

Occupations represented in the white collar category included nursing, teaching, clerical work and the civil service. The skilled category was centred on craft occupations, including West Indians who had been carpenters, printers, mechanics, a milliner and a mason. Other respondents in this category were, for example, shop workers and factory hands. The latter almost exclusively originated from Jamaica and Barbados where industrial jobs are more numerous. The non-farm manual workers were fishermen, stevedores, lorry drivers, etc.

Nearly 37 per cent of the men and 12 per cent of the women were employed in some form of agricultural occupation. All but 2 respondents with agricultural jobs in the West Indies came from islands other than Jamaica, Trinidad and Barbados. This reflects the predominantly agrarian based economies of the smaller West Indian societies. The relatively high percentage of women in domestic work (24 per cent) is also a feature of female employment in these societies. The low figures for unemployment are not necessarily significant for a variety of reasons. Many West Indians in the Caribbean are self-employed smallholders living on a small piece of land with some poultry and livestock. Similarly, a high rate of self-employment is combined with the seasonal nature of many types of work in the islands. This is particularly so with agricultural workers who are only employed when the crop is at a stage requiring quantities of labour. Very often, smallholding and reliance on seasonal work go together. The general picture of employment patterns in West Indian societies, particularly in those without some form of industry, is highly flexible and therefore difficult to compare with work patterns in industrialised societies.

Table 3.4 provides the figures for West Indian men claiming to have been unemployed for any period of time in the Caribbean and since their arrival in Britain:

Table 3.4

Periods of unemployment of male respondents in the Caribbean and Britain

Period of unemployment	Caribbean		Britain	
	No.	%	No.	%
Six months or less	27	(51.9)	17	(32.7)
One year	1	(1.9)	1	(1.9)
More than one year	1	(1.9)	1	(1.9)
Seasonal	9	(17.3)	–	–
Not given	1	(1.9)	1	(1.9)
Total	52		52	

Only 3 respondents claimed to have been unemployed in the West Indies for more than one period of time, in all 3 cases for less than six months, with the exception of those in seasonal, agricultural occupations. With regard to the figures for unemployment in Britain, only 4 men referred to unemployment in Easton. Most of the periods of unemployment mentioned were consistent with difficulties encountered acquiring jobs immediately on arrival in Britain.

Since arriving in Easton, only 16 West Indians in the sample had remained in the occupation which they had held in the home island. These respondents included nurses and men who had remained within certain skilled craft occupations, for example, printing and cabinet making. Very few West Indians had moved from a factory job in the Caribbean to factory employment in Britain. The employment pattern for women was relatively more consistent because many of them were still engaged in nursing and domestic work. However, it should be noted that many West Indian women were in regular employment for the first time in Easton, not having been in the same position before migration.

The pattern of employment for the male labour force reflected a move into skilled manual, often factory-based work in Britain. In many instances, there was a move from agricultural to industrial employment, but this was by no means a predominant feature of changes in employment from the Caribbean. West Indians who were teachers, clerks and policemen in their home island were now working as welders or lathe operators in local factories.

Over 60 per cent of the sample had held more than one job since their arrival in Britain. However, only 6 respondents (all men) reported more than three changes of job during this period. Thus, the West Indians work force in Easton, as demonstrated by the sample, was a relatively stable one not marked by frequent and long periods of unemployment or frequent changes of occupation. In addition, it was significant that the pattern of employment both in the West Indies and in

Easton did not demonstrate a preponderance of unskilled, agricultural workers. The labour force was fairly diverse, although it would be true to say that very few West Indians had been employed in industrial occupations in the Caribbean.

The pattern of employment in the city demonstrated that some West Indians had taken jobs which, even allowing for any differentials in skills between the West Indies and Britain, were not comparable to those they had held in their home island. For example, teachers in the West Indies were now employed as bus conductors, and a past civil servant now worked as a machinist. Many West Indians with white collar jobs in the Caribbean had blue collar jobs in Easton. This demonstrates the already well-documented difficulties of a black, migrant labour force constrained to enter occupations which are labelled suitable for them in Britain, irrespective of their work background or qualifications from their societies of origin (Foner, 1979:87).

Nevertheless, despite the fact that, in particular, many West Indian men had experienced a relative drop in work status and restricted job opportunities in Britain, the general picture in Easton was one of stability and limited, but not insignificant affluence, compared with fellow black migrants in other British cities.

All respondents were asked to compare their present position in Britain with their previous standard of living in the West Indies. Allowing for changes in life style, cost of living and their ages, 57 per cent of of the total sample (N = 108) claimed that they were better off in money terms in Easton than in the Caribbean. This figure includes a not insubstantial number, 12 per cent of the total, who stated that they were much better off in their present situation. Just over a quarter of the respondents, (26 per cent), thought that their present financial position in Britain was about the same as in the West Indies, whilst less than 6 per cent saw their present position as being worse or much worse than in the Caribbean. Overall, slightly fewer men than women saw their position in Easton as being the same or financially worse than in the home island.

The majority of West Indians claimed to have gained from their migration to Britain, in financial terms, but this must be seen in a relative context. Most of them were not claiming that they were as well off (however they defined this) as they could be, when relating their position to other groups in the city, including other migrants. Similarly, even being better off in financial terms did not necessarily compensate for the other forms of deprivation felt by many respondents. Nor did acceptable levels of wealth and income necessarily provide access to better resources, such as better housing and recreational facilities, which many West Indians expected they would or should do. Nevertheless, these assessments did indicate a relative level of economic stability which was partly confirmed by the occupational patterns previously described.

Turning to trade union membership, exactly half the male workers (N = 26) were found to be currently unionised. This is somewhat lower, but not remarkably so, than the generally high levels of trade union membership among West Indian men in Britain (Smith, 1977:191). In contrast, only one West Indian woman belonged to a trade union at the time of the survey. This is markedly below the average of one in three West Indian women unionised, reported by the PEP study (1977). However, the history of female employment in Easton has to be considered. Despite several recent strikes in the East Midlands that directly involved South Asian female workers, there is a long history of paternalism and weak unionism, particularly in the hosiery industry in Easton. Coupled with the additional factors of part-time or casual work and a past history of full employment, the low level of unionisation among West Indian women is more understandable. Specialised local work conditions also explain the relatively low levels of unionisation in the Caribbean, among those in the sample who were in employment prior to migration. Eighteen respondents (N = 49), all male, had belonged to a trade union at any time during their period of residence in the West Indies. Most of them were urban based, skilled workers. The structure of the island economies detracts from high levels of unionisation, particularly in the smaller islands where the plantation system is still prominent. Unionisation is either discouraged in the agricultural sectors or operates under highly paternalistic conditions. However, this situation is changing somewhat and one can point to a strong trade union tradition in many industries (Cross, 1979:89).

When questioned about their attitudes towards trade unionism in Britain and their participation in union affairs, very few respondents expressed any close interest or involvement in local union activities. Those few who did proffer firm opinions saw trade unions as protecting the workers' interests but very few West Indians appeared to believe that British trade unions were representative of West Indians' needs in Britain. The majority of respondents viewed themselves as outside of any bargaining frame of management and workers. West Indians were seen as forming a separate part of the labour force largely unrepresented by any official body or spokesmen. Thus, many West Indians perceived labour relations in local factories as a process involving relations between a white management and white workers. Black workers were, therefore, a special category tangential to the main bargaining framework (Castles and Kosack, 1973). A position neatly highlighted by a Jamaican welder:

> I think that in this society where there is still strong class differences, trade unions go a long way in reducing the differences between the rich and the working man, but we (i.e. West Indians) are outside of all this. The union should

be for black and white.

However, this is a somewhat atypical comment because most respondents answered non-commitally or expressed very little interest. Similarly, only one respondent was at all active in union affairs—an Antiguan employed in the building trade who was a shop steward and a regular attender of branch meetings. Only 3 other West Indians in the sample had ever attended a union branch meeting or taken any direct part in union affairs. A large majority of respondents, 76 per cent (N = 26), explained their membership of a union as an involuntary act, in so far as it was compulsory or the expected thing to do at their present place of employment. This corresponded closely to most West Indians' replies concerning their membership and participation in trade unions in the West Indies.

Housing

Residence patterns are another useful indicator of the economic position of West Indians in Easton. Table 3.5 shows the type of housing and accommodation occupied by the sample:

Table 3.5
Residential patterns of West Indian respondents
in Easton

Type of dwelling	No.	%
A house or flat which has been bought	11	(10.1)
A house or flat which is mortgaged	52	(48.2)
A house, flat or rooms rented privately	29	(26.9)
Council housing	9	(8.3)
Lodgings	2	(1.8)
Sharing with friends or relatives	5	(4.6)
Total	108	

It can be seen from the above figures that many West Indians had bought their own homes or were buying them through a mortgage; whilst a substantial minority (29 per cent) were living in some form of private rented accommodation. The latter included houses or flats but usually a number of rooms in the large three storied terraces, common to much of Lowdale. Most of the remainder (8 per cent) were living in council housing of some kind. The area of Lowdale and its environs is quite diverse as far as housing types are concerned. Victorian property is represented by artisan dwellings not only of the 'three up—three down' terraced type which face directly on the street with small yards at the rear, but also by much larger three-storied properties with imposing frontages and relatively large gardens at the back and front. These are usually in multi-occupation, broken into furnished or unfurnished private tenancies. The smaller terraces are mainly in single occupation, and account for the majority of West Indians who own or are buying their own houses. Adjacent to these types of property are more modern early Twentieth century semi-detached residences. More recent still is a newly opened council scheme, which replaced that part of Lowdale which has been re-developed. This consists of a variety of houses and blocks of flats, a shopping precinct and new primary and junior schools. These buildings face the older properties and stand in sharp contrast to them—in particular, the large, ugly red-brick secondary school which dominates a corner of Adelaide Street.

Many West Indians had been occupants of the older properties which were demolished to make way for the new council dwellings. This entitled them to one of the new council flats and therefore explains the number of West Indian respondents in the sample in council housing. However, the number of West Indians occupying similar council properties on estates in other parts of Easton is small. Some of these families are included in the sample or were interviewed through their connection with the West Indian formal associations described in the following chapter. They frequently commented on the dearth of fellow West Indians on the estates and some of the difficulties which this presented. It was noticeable that the council flats adjacent to Lowdale were included within the general stereotype of the area. Thus, occupants of the Lowdale council flats, both black and white, complained of being grouped together with residents of the older properties surrounding them, particularly those facing them across Adelaide Street.

The Lowdale area, often called the 'Khyber Pass' by local whites because of the predominance of more recently arrived South Asian migrants, is labelled as a district in Easton which contains all that is undesirable. Thus, many forms of deviant behaviour are attributed to its inhabitants, ranging from drunken parties, drug addiction and prostitution to the stereotypes commonly associated with overcrowded, insanitary housing conditions. Irrespective of the accuracy of these descriptions, it is significant that many West Indians within Lowdale subscribe to such beliefs and therefore sought to move to other, more desirable areas. This means that very few West Indians appear to desire council housing because there is a general belief that West Indians are restricted to those estates in or near Lowdale and therefore cannot escape from the area through this avenue.

Nevertheless, many West Indians have moved to better accommodation, often semi-detached properties near to their previous residence. In addition, some West Indians have moved to areas some distance away from Lowdale, often to districts which are beginning to decay and are becoming de-populated by local white residents who are moving to the newer, ever expanding suburbs.

Because of the wide availability of alternative, cheap housing for the indigenous (mostly white) residents of Lowdale in other parts of Easton, particularly during the 1950s and 1960s, migrants moving into Lowdale at this time encountered few difficulties in housing themselves. Only 27 respondents claimed any major difficulty in acquiring accommodation on arrival in Easton. The reasons given by the few West Indians who did have problems in housing themselves, included housing shortages, financial difficulties, and colour discrimination. The latter was mentioned by 15 respondents and was the main reason given for explaining any adversity met in finding accommodation.

It is difficult to estimate the degree of discrimination in the housing market in Easton. Certainly, the fact that most West Indian respondents did not mention such problems points toward the need for caution. However, there is ample evidence to support the notion that discrimination against black people in the housing sector exists in Britain (Smith, 1977) and there is no reason to think that Easton is a unique case where such difficulties are not encountered by the black and coloured groups within its boundaries. The availability of cheap properties for West Indians was mainly due to the existence of alternative areas of residence for the indigenous white population. Furthermore, despite the relative affluence of many West Indians, coupled with their desire to move out of Lowdale, the continued presence of West Indians in 'the twilight zone' has to be explained by the existence of barriers which restrict the entry of certain groups to more 'desirable' residential areas. Whilst many West Indians have succeeded in moving away from Lowdale, their transfer is often to other areas of the city which already contain 'mixed' populations, i.e., populations which cross ethnic and racial divisions. The appearance of black people in areas of Easton which are predominantly white, may indicate that such areas are entering a transitional period with significant population replacement. Alternatively, some black families may have sufficient economic and/or social status to enable them to separate themselves from the majority of black and coloured workers in the city and thus effect a degree of dispersal from the main zone of transition.

Certainly there was a low level of residential mobility within the sample. If there had been a change in residence since arrival in Easton, this was typically from rented to mortgaged property within or around Lowdale. Even the pattern of dispersal was centred on particular areas of the city which were marked for some or all of the characteristics previously attributed to zones of transition.

In spite of the high level of house purchase and single family occupation, many West Indians said that they would like to move to another area in Easton given the choice or leave Britain altogether. Just under half the sample, 49 per cent, expressed a desire to move from their present accommodation, 5 respondents were undecided, whilst the remainder indicated that they were satisfied with their present housing position. It was significant that out of those West Indians who did wish to move, only 4 respondents lived outside of the centre of Lowdale. Similarly, out of 50 respondents who had no desire to move, 38 did not live in this immediate area. This appears to suggest that negative evaluations of residence were congruent with the occupation of houses firmly located within the zone of transition. Whilst some dissatisfaction with the area of residence was indicated among those West Indians living outside of Lowdale, the level of discontent was significantly lower in their case.

When asked if they would like to move, given the choice, most West Indians expressed some dissatisfaction with their present location; but this response often took the form of a general feeling of discontent which had not crystallised into firm ideas of more desirable alternatives. Out of 53 respondents only 9 indicated a firm alternative preference when asked to name the residential area they would like to move to. Within the latter group, 4 West Indians mentioned some form of council housing, a further 4 had other cities in Britain in mind, whilst the remaining respondent wished to return to the Caribbean.

It is important to separate the desire to move to another area from the acknowledgement of the possibility of such a change. Thus many West Indians were disillusioned about housing and sought a move to areas with better 'names' or contemplated a move away from Easton, even to the point of returning to the West Indies. Despite these feelings, very few West Indians admitted that such changes were likely in the foreseeable future. Indeed, the acquisition of better housing and jobs was viewed as improbable in the light of current social and economic conditions. Many respondents argued that their present position was largely fortuitous and they had little control over what happened to them in the future. They argued, in effect, that there are particular types of housing and employment which are judged suitable for West Indians in Britain and that once the limited mobility within such areas had been exhausted, it was unrealistic to expect further mobility and the widening of opportunities. Those West Indians who did succeed were either lucky, or more able than their fellows. Similarly, when contemplating a return to the Caribbean very few West Indians thought this was likely in the near future. Indeed, it was often argued that to return was undesirable because so many West Indians would lose face by going back to their home island without the trappings of wealth which their friends and relatives in the Caribbean would expect from a 'successful' man who had been in Britain. To return with less than one set out with was shameful and demaning.

Furthermore, the recognition of greater material rewards in Britain did compensate to some extent for other forms of deprivation, but this is not to minimise the wide discontent and disillusionment felt among West Indians generally. An Antiguan nurse, for example, commented:

> Life in this country is quite different from the West Indies. In the West Indies it is warm and you can have quite a good time. Here in Britain life is different altogether for me, it is fight, fight, fight every day.

A Barbudan factory worker was somewhat happier, but remarked:

> I think mainly the changes from the West Indies are as follows: This country is a massive size to those at home, it is faster, plenty for the young people to enjoy. Plenty of food and meat, lots of sports, plenty of beer. I get more money than I got in the West Indies. For both black and white it should be a great place, but it is not right to feel you want to move on. It's the people, what really gets you—this prejudice to black people will never stop.

Associations and leisure

Leaving aside the important exception of religious participation (see Chapter 6), the level of West Indian membership and participation in voluntary associations in Easton was very limited. Only 14 (N = 108) respondents claimed membership of a local voluntary association. Of these only 2 respondents belonged to more than one association. The 'joiners' (Hausknecht, 1962) included 3 women who were members of the local Mothers' union and Women's Guild. Most of the male respondents belonged to recreational associations, usually connected with a sporting activity. Five men belonged to cricket clubs, 1 to a soccer club, and youth club membership was mentioned by 2 young men. Three West Indian men belonged to associations established along exclusively island lines, 2 in the Jamaican association, the other in a similar group established by Barbudans. Some associations mentioned were connected with employment. A couple of West Indian men were members of social clubs at the factories where they worked and another belonged to the Easton branch of the British Rail Staff Association. Not surprisingly, given such a low figure for membership of voluntary associations, very few West Indians occupied official positions in an association, or claimed to have done so in the past. Indeed, only 3 respondents, all men, came within this category. One was a past Treasurer of the Jamaican Association, while the other two were actively involved in cricket clubs, one as secretary, the other as team captain. Both clubs were exclusively West Indian.

Most West Indians, 87 per cent, of the sample, did not belong to any voluntary associations in the city. A very small number of women, only 3 respondents, belonged to such associations. These findings indicate that the level of membership of voluntary associations among West Indians in Easton is extremely low; thus confirming the well established pattern among Caribbean migrants in Britain described in the Introduction.

However, the low level of associational membership in Easton did not correspond with the level of 'joining' claimed by respondents in the Caribbean. When asked about the latter, 39 respondents (36 per cent of the total sample) indicated membership of one or more associations in the West Indies. Table 3.6 provides an illustration of the type of association mentioned and the number of respondents claiming membership of them:

Table 3.6
Voluntary association membership of respondents
in the West Indies

Category	Number of mentions		
	Male	Female	Total
Sports associations	12	2	14
Youth groups	8	5	13
Church groups	2	4	6
Friendly societies and credit unions	10	6	16
Work associations	4	—	4
Women's clubs	—	9	9
Social clubs	14	12	26
Political parties	2	1	3
Other	1	—	1

Table 3.6 shows that, whilst recreational pursuits were predominant, there is some evidence of membership of economic and political associations. No West Indians belonged to a political party or financial association in Britain akin to Friendly Societies but a significant minority did hold memberships of this nature in the Caribbean.[4] Similarly, membership figures for women respondents when resident in the West Indies were lower than for men, therefore following the pattern in Easton but the disparity between the sexes was less marked. Out of 39 respondents claiming membership of an association in the West Indies, 17 were women.

The range of memberships was also greater in the West Indies. Whereas most 'joiners' only mentioned one association in Easton, the tendency in the home island was to join two or three different associations. These findings still indicate that the majority of West Indians tend not to join voluntary associations either in Britain or the Caribbean. This is not surprising when one considers that the vast majority of West Indians would be placed in the lower classes both in the Caribbean and in Easton. They therefore follow the pattern of low voluntary association membership attributed to the working classes internationally (Smith and Freedman, 1972). Certainly the white working class in Britain appear to have similar patterns of membership (or more accurately non-membership) (Morris, 1965). Nevertheless, realising that voluntary association membership is likely to be a minority activity, we are primarily concerned with comparing the relative sizes of low levels of membership both in the West Indies and in Britain. On this basis it can be seen that the level of membership for West Indians in their home islands was significantly higher than their present levels of membership in Easton. Whereas, over a third of the sample belonged to some form of association in the West Indies, only 13 per cent of respondents claimed membership of any association in Britain.

This disparity becomes even more interesting when one considers that the age structure of the sample should favour a higher level of membership in Britain. Some respondents would have been excluded from many associations in the Caribbean because of their youthfulness. But the majority of respondents in the present sample, falling as they do within the middle age ranges, are at an age in Britain when their level of voluntary association membership ought to be at its peak. Bearing in mind that membership levels were higher in the Caribbean than in Easton, it is evident that factors other than age are of importance in explaining this disparity. These additional factors will be discussed in detail later (see Chapter 7). Suffice to say at this juncture that the comparison between membership figures for the West Indies and Britain would appear to detract from the argument that West Indians are 'non-joiners' as a matter of course. That is to say a pattern of non-joining might be seen as a cultural tendency among West Indians irrespective of their social or geographical location.

In addition to their actual membership of voluntary associations, respondents were asked about their attitudes towards joining local associations. When asked whether there were any associations in Easton which they would like to join, most West Indians (70 respondents) expressed little interest in seeking memberships of this kind. A further 10 respondents were undecided, but 28 West Indians (18 men and 10 women) did indicate a wish to join an association in the locality. When asked if they had ever attempted to obtain membership, 23 respondents claimed to have belonged to a local association in the past or to have made enquiries about joining one. Reasons given for not wishing to join an association, or why memberships had lapsed, included lack of time because of work and family commitments, the view that very few associations catered for West Indian tastes in recreation and the prevalence of colour prejudice in local white associations. Many respondents, particularly women, mentioned that bringing up a family and being employed in a part of full-time job did not leave them any free time for associational activity. Respondents complained that many associations, recreational or otherwise, were unlike comparable groups in the Caribbean. Predominantly white associations in Easton were too formal and had a different social atmosphere. Furthermore, many respondents feared rejection if they did apply for membership, for example, of a local sports or social club, because of their colour.

It is important to note that most respondents had not attempted to apply for membership and hence beliefs about colour prejudice were not necessarily based upon direct experience of rejection in this particular area. Thus, common beliefs surrounding colour prejudice and discrimination held by West Indian groups appear to have influenced individual actions. One case of rejection could lead to a widespread belief in general patterns of discrimination against West Indians locally.

Apart from asking about membership in existing white or mixed associations, respondents were also questioned about the likelihood of their joining exclusively West Indian associations. Over half the sample, 58 per cent, expressed considerable interest and stated that they would certainly join such associations if they were established. This revealed an ignorance of West Indian associations which had already been formed in Easton. The distinctiveness of island divisions amongst West Indians largely explains this. Many of the smaller West Indian associations which tended to be exclusive to one island group were often unknown to West Indians from other island societies. Thus Jamaicans may not have heard about Antiguan or Barbudan associations and so on. Complete lack of knowledge was uncommon but very few West Indians had acquired detailed information about associations other than those formed within their own island groupings.

It was interesting to note that many West Indians were active in a number of more informal recreational outlets. When asked about a range of activities which they might have taken part in during the period of four weeks previous to being questioned, the following results were obtained:

Table 3.7

Attendance of West Indian respondents in recreational activities in Easton

Activity	Number of mentions		
	Male	Female	Total
The theatre or cinema	11	8	19
A sports event	12	2	14
A night club or discoteque	6	4	10
A house party	29	15	44
A political meeting	2	1	3
A dance or social	28	21	49
A lecture of discussion group	3	1	4
Non-attendance at any of the above	7	16	23

Table 3.7 reveals that many West Indians took part in a variety of leisure outlets. The most popular activities were dances, 'socials' and house parties. The cinema and sports events were also fairly regularly attended. There was a marked lack of interest in political meetings, lectures or more formal discussion groups. It should be remembered in this respect that certain activities will be more frequent and more readily available to West Indians. Compared with most of the recreational activities listed, political meetings would be comparatively rare events unless respondents belonged to voluntary associations or political parties where this type of social interaction was a frequent occurrence.

Comparatively few West Indians, 21 per cent of the sample, had attended none of the activities given within the specified period of time. When questioned on the regularity of attendance of the activities mentioned 28 per cent of the sample claimed that they often attended such activities. A larger group, 42 per cent of all respondents, attended sometimes, whilst for 29 per cent of the sample attendance was rare. It was noticeable that West Indian men tended to be far more active than women when attendance figures were compared. This is partly explained by the limited amount of free time available to West Indian women, who often have to cope with work and family commitments. But the sexual division in recreation patterns also points towards the retention of Caribbean leisure habits (see Chapter 5) in the British context.

Summarising the pattern of membership and participation in secondary associations, West Indians in Easton revealed a low level of interest and activity in permanent and semi-permanent associations, with the exception of religious worship. A higher proportion of respondents were active in more ephemeral recreational pursuits, the majority of which were organised by and for West Indians themselves. This applied particularly to dances and house parties. This suggests that much of the recreational life of West Indians in Easton takes place within social networks which are ethnically specialised. These networks form a subcultural recreational system in the city and illustrate the existence of certain areas of social interaction outside of family and household relationships, which are exclusively West Indian. A further dimension of this exclusivity was examined by briefly studying patterns of friendship along inter- and intra-island lines.

Respondents were asked whether most of their West Indian friends (self defined) came from their home island, other islands or equally from both. A majority of West Indians, 52 per cent of the sample, indicated that most of their friends were from the same island as themselves. Just under a third of the sample (32 per cent) had a more mixed set of friends from a variety of islands, but only 9 per cent of the respondents claimed to have more friends from different islands than their own. Further questions were concerned with other aspects of West Indian friendship patterns, in particular with the variety of social situations in which West Indians interact and meet their friends and acquaintances.

The majority of West Indians met each other within their own homes or the homes of their friends, at dances and parties, and less often at work. Men often mentioned the pub whilst some women saw their friends at church. Friendship patterns and leisure interests confirmed that many West Indians, particularly women, are primarily home centred. Men may still pursue the traditional Caribbean pattern of mixing with their mates in the pub, barber shops or parties, but many males said they spent more time at home than they did in the West Indies.

The differences between recreational patterns in Britain and the Caribbean rest on different work patterns and social relationships. Furthermore, in Britain there is restricted access to many places of entertainment, and there are limitations placed upon social interaction by housing conditions. The urban setting in Britain is a far cry from the sun-lit yard life of the West Indies. The huddle round the television in a damp English setting stands in stark contrast to the freedom of movement in the Caribbean obviously relished by many respondents. In short, inclement weather, limited places for entertainment where one feels completely comfortable and welcomed, plus the restrictions of family and work commitments, tend to preclude a high level of social interaction among many West Indians. There is a marked tendency for West Indians to make their own entertainment within their own homes or in recreational settings organised amongst themselves. Family networks were generally viewed as important as friendship ones, although within many island communities friendship networks are highly intimate. Whereas the Jamaicans are divided along the lines of an urban or rural background in the home island, most of the smaller island groupings in

Easton are very close-knit. Nevisians, Montserratians and Barbudans, to name only three examples, commonly come from a small number of villages in the home island and this produces communities of some intimacy in Britain.

Island affiliation is extremely influential in maintaining communal ties among West Indians. Thus, 'close friends', those who are seen most frequently, whom one trusts with confidential information or relies upon for financial assistance are invariably fellow islanders. When situations become less intimate, kin and island affiliations become less important. A Barbadian may not bother about the island affiliations of his West Indian companions if he is involved in a casual conversation in a pub, but in other situations their origins in the Caribbean will be important. If a West Indian wishes to borrow money, or if he is asked to lend some, kin and island affiliations will certainly have some bearing on the transaction.

If there was considerable differentiation within and between island communities, this tendency was even more marked in relations between West Indians and other groups in Easton. Only 24 per cent of the sample claimed to have any white friends with whom they exchanged home visits. Within this group, very few West Indians had several white friends with whom they could claim close acquaintanceship. Many West Indians regretted that relationships with local whites were bounded by social barriers which prohibited all but superficial contact. Acquaintanceship ended at the factory gates or the pub door and did not cross the threshold of one's home. Those respondents who did claim a number of white friends were invariably living in higher status residential areas, had skilled occupations, or were active in associations which provided more opportunities for interaction across ethnic lines in more intimate social situations. The rare example of a West Indian with a professional job and a home in the suburbs, who had been completely accepted by his white neighbours is illustrative of the former group. Slightly more common were those West Indian activists who had developed friendships with whites through community relations work or similar activities. But both of these groups were exceptional; most West Indians restricted close friendships to other West Indians, whether by choice or otherwise.

Ethnic separation was even more entrenched between West Indians, Indians and Pakistanis. There were only three respondents claiming to have any regular acquaintanceship with Asians in Easton. The pattern which emerged was one of general suspicion and hostility. Many West Indians resented the fact that Asians were 'better organised', 'kept themselves to themselves', 'didn't try to mix with us because they look down on us', or 'were too intent on looking after their businesses to care about anyone'. A few respondents saw the Asians as fellow blacks or coloureds in a similar social category to themselves but this was untypical. Indeed, many of the comments from West Indians regarding neighbouring Asians were extremely similar to the views expressed by whites about West Indians!

This had more than a touch of irony about it. Certainly it firmly belies the notion, widely believed by many whites in the city, that the local black or coloured population is homogeneous or at least contains many common ties. It was clear that the lines of conflict between the various ethnically or racially separated groups in Easton were not clearly drawn. It would be erroneous to speak of black and white dichotomies, or black and brown ones for that matter. What emerged clearly from the data drawn from the sample, and confirming direct observation, was the complexity of intra- and inter-group relations both within and between West Indian groups, between West Indians and Asians and between black and white.

Caribbean ties

In order to attempt to measure some of the attachments West Indians had maintained with the Caribbean since their arrival in Britain, respondents were asked a number of questions about visits to the West Indies and the maintenance of financial links with kin or friends in their home island. They were also questioned about their reading habits with respect to newspapers produced in the Caribbean, or literature produced in Britain specifically designed for West Indians residing here. Almost three quarters of the sample (71 per cent), regularly read newspapers from the Caribbean, although only 17 per cent (N = 108) similarly perused such British publications as *West Indian World, West Indian Digest,* or locally circulated broadsheets. In most cases, West Indians relied upon family or friends from 'back home' to send them newspapers but they were also circulated in pubs, at parties and in the local 'barber shops'. Unlike the indigenous variety, these 'shops' were based in private houses where a room was set aside for use as a general meeting place for West Indian men. A place where they could get a haircut, sit and play cards and dominoes or just talk. These 'shops' provided a part-time job for the 'barber' who usually had a regular day-time occupation but used his house most evenings and weekends as a second business.

There would seem to be many parallels between the West Indian 'barber shops' in Easton and the rum shops in the West Indies (Wilson, 1973:166). Both play an important role in the everyday existence of West Indian males as centres for warmth and conviviality within a purely masculine preserve. This role was doubly important in Easton where the local pubs and clubs might lack the type of intimacy which pervaded the 'barber shops' and gave them a haven-like quality which was similar to 'home'.

A large number of respondents, 64 per cent of the sample, were sending money home to kin or friends in their home island. Most West Indians were reticent about disclosing the amounts of money involved or the regularity of payments. However, the general impression given pointed to relatively small sums being involved. Ten pounds a month was the highest figure mentioned but smaller amounts were more usual. The majority of respondents were sending money back to kin remaining in the home island, often parents, grandparents, a sister or sister-in-law who were caring or had cared for their children. No clear patterns of transaction along island lines could be discerned, for example whether respondents from small islands were sending more than those from larger islands. Nevertheless, it appeared that financial links were maintained between kin in the Caribbean and in Britain and that this was a common feature of West Indian migration and settlement (Frucht, 1967; Philpott, 1968).

Just over a third of the sample (36 per cent) had re-visited the Caribbean since settling in Britain. Usually, visits involved individuals rather than complete families. In a number of cases, husbands were unable to leave their employment for any length of time so re-visits by wives were more common.[5] This is reflected in the figures for re-visiting. Out of 39 respondents who had made a return visit to their home island, 24 were women. Very few respondents, hardly surprisingly, failed to express a wish to return to the Caribbean for a visit at some future date.

The frequency of newspaper reading, the levels of financial transaction between kin and the number of re-visits to the West Indies suggests that most West Indians maintained fairly close links with the Caribbean. Typically these links were concentrated on the home island, although newspaper readership demonstrated wider interests in Caribbean affairs. This was in spite of the fact that the majority of West Indians had lived in Britain for some years and ample time had elapsed for links with their Caribbean past to be somewhat 'stretched'. The maintenance of these connections with the Caribbean suggests that social changes in the West Indies directly influence the actions of West Indians in Britain. For example, events which reinforce island insularity in the Caribbean also tend to maintain the lines separating West Indian island groups in Britain.

This continuation of bonds with the Caribbean may point towards a persistent desire among West Indians eventually to return permanently to their home island but other factors would appear to deny this. Certainly it reflected the fact that, whilst most West Indians were now established in Easton and recognised that this settlement was likely to be prolonged if not permanent, they still desired to retain their interest

in and identity with the Caribbean and maintain close links with family
and friends who remained there.

Political participation

The final area of questioning for respondents was concerned with voting
patterns. Again we were concerned with material pertaining not only to
West Indians in Easton, but also to their voting patterns in the Caribbean.
However, there were innumerable difficulties presented in measuring the
figures for voting in the West Indies. With such a variety of islands en-
compassing a number of different electoral requirements for 'local' and
'national' elections, the figures for voting in the Caribbean, given in Table
3.8 following, should only be seen as a very rough measure of actual
voting patterns.

Table 3.8

Number of West Indian respondents voting in an
election during residence in the Caribbean

	Voters				Non-Voters				
	Male	%	Female	%	Male	%	Female	%	Total
Last local election	19	(22.1)	10	(11.6)	25	(29.1)	32	(37.2)	86
Last national election	31	(36.0)	21	(24.4)	13	(15.1)	21	(24.4)	86

In all, 86 respondents, 44 men and 42 women, claimed to have been
eligible to vote by virtue of registration in their home islands. Table 3.8
shows that 29 respondents (34 per cent) voted in the last local election
in their island of origin, whilst 52 (60 per cent) claimed to have voted in
elections at the national level. With all the difficulties surrounding these
figures one cannot draw any firm conclusions. Suffice to say that the
rate of voting in national elections was higher than in local elections
which corresponds to the pattern in Britain. As can be seen from Table
3.9 below:

Table 3.9

West Indian respondents voting in Local
and General Elections in Britain

	Voters				Non-Voters				
	Male	%	Female	%	Male	%	Female	%	Total
Last local election	18	(19.1)	14	(14.9)	30	(31.9)	32	(34.0)	94
Last General election	29	(30.8)	19	(20.2)	24	(25.5)	22	(23.4)	94

Out of a total voting sample of 94[6] just over a third (34 per cent) of respondents voted in the Easton local elections in 1969, whilst 51 per cent turned out for the 1970 General Election. In common with other studies (Rex and Tomlinson, 1979), the great majority of West Indians, 92 per cent (N = 48), voted for the Labour Party. This degree of commitment is not only attributable to a common (West Indian) perception that the Labour Party is 'The party of the working man', but also to the nature of Caribbean party politics. Most political parties in the West Indies are 'labour parties', because the middle classes are so small that any political organisation must gain wide support from the mass peasant/proletariat. Consequently, this is a West Indian voting legacy which the British Labour Party largely inherits. If the above voting figures belie a total commitment to the ballot box—a tendency well demonstrated elsewhere (Miles and Phizacklea, 1977)—even greater evidence of political disillusionment was displayed when future voting intentions were explored. Fully 73 per cent of the total sample (N = 108) expressed reservations about casting their vote if an election were to be held tomorrow.

The recent intensification of immigration controls, the failure of the 1968 Race Relations Act, and the growing threat of the National Front, were all commonly mooted as reasons for this degree of political cynicism. Most West Indians held firm views on these issues and frequently voiced their fears or anger about local re-housing policies, education, employment possibilities for their children, and alleged police harassment. However, the parliamentary process was rarely seen as a panacea for these social ills.

When asked whether any of the major political parties were particularly sensitive to West Indian needs, it soon became apparent that very few respondents thought any political party directly represented them. Political parties were seen in much the same light as trade unions. The former were a necessary and important part of one's life situation but they were exclusively white organisations which did not represent West Indians in any direct sense. Thus, the act of joining a trade union or a political party plus the exercise of one's voting rights was a matter of conforming to local mores or a token indication of one's views. There was hardly any support for the idea that West Indians could use voting procedures to influence local or national policies. Only 14 respondents (N = 108), 9 men and 5 women, held converse opinions and actively promoted the policy of direct West Indian participation in party politics both at local and national levels.

West Indian perceptions of party politics are extremely important when considering the nature of West Indian political association in the city. The revelation that the majority of respondents felt separated from the political process and unrepresented by any major party within it, distinguishes them to a considerable extent from the white working class.

Certainly it cannot be assumed that all native workers are content with their political representation (Hindess, 1966). However, large sections of the white working class do view the trade union movement and the political party system as suitable vehicles for expressing their interests (Rex and Tomlinson, 1979:8). If considerable numbers of West Indians in Britain consider themselves unrepresented in either of the above political arenas, the desirability of separate ethnic associations which could promote or force changes in their present life situations seems evident.

Such indeed were the views of many West Indians in Easton. But, as we shall see in the next chapter, there may be innumerable barriers placed in front of those who attempt to transform political awareness into political action. Bearing this in mind, we can now turn our attention to those voluntary associations which have been established by the various island communities in the city.

Notes

1   Exact population sizes for the various minorities in Easton were not available. However, estimates of 6—10,000 West Indians and 35—40,000 South Asians out of a total population of approximately 280,000 were current in 1974.
2   For a brief description of Research methods, including sample construction, see Research Appendix.
3   Female labour accounts for 40 per cent of the labour force in Easton. *Sunday Times Business News,* January 20, 1974.
4   The greater availability of State welfare and a wide range of alternative financial institutions in Britain are direct contributary factors here.
5   This may appear to contradict earlier evidence relating to high levels of female employment. However, much of this work was on a casual basis, so many West Indian women had jobs which were flexible enough to allow periods away on holiday.
6   This figure represents the total number of respondents eligible to vote at the elections mentioned. The sample was checked against the electoral registers and a high level of registration was confirmed.

4 West Indian voluntary associations

In the previous chapter, a detailed analysis of data drawn from a sample of West Indians covering the various island communities in Easton was presented. A general pattern emerged which indicated that comparatively few West Indians were members of local voluntary associations, particularly those with non-recreational functions. However, many West Indians claimed to have a number of recreational interests and took an active part in various forms of entertainment. The present chapter will be concerned with an appraisal of those voluntary associations, both recreational and otherwise, which West Indians have established since their earliest days of settlement in the city and, in particular, during the early to mid-1970s.

There were very few West Indians, or any other black immigrants for that matter, living in the city directly after the Second World War. The few exceptions were those West Indian ex-servicemen who settled in the locality after being demobbed from the RAF. They found suspicion but little antipathy in the locality, probably because they were in such small numbers and members of the host community did not see them as a 'threat'. 'L' related his first impressions of this period thus:

> When I came to Easton in '49 I must have been the only black face in the whole place. I had joined the RAF from Jamaica and decided to stay in Britain after I was demobbed. I had a mate in the forces who lived in Easton and he suggested I moved up ... I lived in London after leaving the forces, you see. He said the job situation was pretty good and I could stay with him and his wife until I found a place of my own. I married a local girl quite soon after that and we didn't really encounter any problems apart from curiosity. There were one or two other Jamaicans in the town by that time, most of them had been in the services. We used to get together for a few drinks and talk about back home. We formed a sort of small social club which met in the ... church hall back rooms ... mind you they stopped us using them fairly soon after because one or two of the locals had complained. But things were very quiet and most people were OK. It was really a case of adjusting to a new place and surroundings. We were sort of explorers in many ways because we had no friends or relations in the

place. You had to make your own way and find your own social life.

These sorts of experiences were shared by the small group of Jamaican artisans who first came to Easton. At the group level, they did not form a very significant part of the local community. As individuals, they encountered some difficulties but as we can see from their own words, it was debatable whether such problems were due to local prejudice and mistrust or their own isolation in the earliest years of settlement in the city.

'J', another Jamaican who had lived in the city for nearly twenty years also related his early experiences. He had established himself as a respected individual in the local Jamaican community and also in the eyes of many other local West Indians of his generation. Similarly, he had become accepted in the host community in his role as Headmaster of a local junior school. 'J' said:

> It's very disheartening in many ways to look back on one's arrival in the town and see how certain features of our life situation have deteriorated. I am fortunate in that my position and my roots in the community have allowed a fair degree of freedom in how I go about my daily business. I have many old friends from many nationalities and diverse ways of life who date back to our first arrival here.
>
> We had a restricted, but enjoyable, existence in those days. The social club was merely a group of friends with common interests. It gave us a common bond and the chance to develop certain interests like cricket, for example. We all used to play for local clubs and the only time we were a West Indian side was when a team was made up to play the local police force in a friendly. One of my earliest friends was in the force and he organised the whole thing. There was no sort of common purpose in trying to solve the difficulties we had because of our colour or the fact that we were Jamaican. In the early days after the war the Poles and other communities used to get all the stick.

By the middle of the 1950s more and more West Indians had come to settle in Easton and the forms of association among them changed accordingly. Attempts were made to provide social facilities not found in the locality, for example, parties and dances in the 'West Indian style'. One or two cricket clubs were formed, not always on island lines, and gradually the need for some form of local West Indian organisation became apparent. In 1957, a 'Sports and Social Club' was established by four ex-servicemen who were among the earliest West Indian settlers in Easton. All were Jamaicans. Initially, this club brought together members from different islands and different periods of settlement. The Club was purely recreational and was primarily concerned with providing facilities for cricket, boxing and weightlifting. Local halls and the back rooms in pubs were the venues for their meetings and training sessions.

The Club remained in existence until 1966 in a loose form of association which always remained centred on the original founders of the group. By this time, the West Indian settlement had reached its present proportions and formed a recognised minority in the city. The problems that the Club encountered in having to change their premises, and other difficulties, perhaps demonstrated that relationships between the West Indians and the host community at this time were somewhat conflictual even if the general atmosphere was not one of open hostility. Many of the changes in the Sports and Social Club in the late 1960s were a reflection of changes in the national situation, where the difficulties of coloured immigrants had prompted the establishment of a multi-racial organisation formed to represent the interests of coloured minorities in Britain. The Campaign Against Racial Discrimination was born in 1964 and by 1966 it was moving towards a policy of directly encouraging 'grass-roots' activity among coloured minorities, particularly those settled in the provinces (Banton, 1972; Heinemann, 1972).

This policy of CARD gradually filtered through to Easton and certain members of the Sports and Social Club were prompted by it to seek changes in the aims of their association. A serious split developed between those members of the Club who wanted it to take a more political stance in the community in accordance with the aims of CARD and those (a large majority) who wished to retain it as a purely recreational association. These general policy disagreements and the serious rifts which they produced between members led to the eventual demise of the Club and finally to its complete disbandment.

By the end of 1966, the Sports and Social Club had become a small cricket club for those few members who still remained. The acrimony displayed in its break-up prevented the formation of new associations for some considerable time. But by the early 1970s, a number of West Indian associations were established in the city, some involving participants from earlier voluntary groupings.

The Jamaican Welfare Association

The Jamaican Welfare Association (JWA) was established in 1969 by a nucleus of members who had been active in the Sports and Social Club. In the Autumn of that year, the Jamaican High Commissioner visited the local West Indian settlement, in particular the Jamaican community, to view local conditions and to suggest possible ways of forming a local association. The High Commission agreed to fund the group, which originated from this meeting, provided it came under the auspices of a national Jamaican organisation. Such an alignment proved to be a mixed blessing when attempts were made to draw support from the other island communities.

The main focus of the JWA was to act as a support organisation for West Indians in the city and, in particular, to raise funds for the establishment of a community centre. The main method of fund raising was the promotion of dances and 'socials'. Initially these were fairly modest ventures but some special occasions, for example, Jamaican Independence Day, warranted more ambitious arrangements. These events were the only forms of large-scale entertainment specifically provided for West Indians in Easton and therefore they drew support from fellow migrants in neighbouring towns. The regular 'house' parties and 'shebeens'[1] to be found in Lowdale every weekend were shunned by many 'respectable' West Indians, whilst indigenous community leisure outlets lacked the congeniality and distinctive blend of Caribbean music and cuisine found at West Indian organised dances.

Very few of the West Indian associations in Easton combined to arrange dances or other activities and the JWA was no exception. However, there were a few occasions when the JWA and another local West Indian association, the British-West Indian Club, did co-operate with one another. One such occasion was when the local Community Relations Commission asked both associations to arrange a 'Caribbean evening' as part of a 'Community Relations Week' in the city. This event consisted of an exhibition of Caribbean crafts, a buffet of Caribbean foods from a number of islands and a concert of music and dance. Many members of the JWA expressed delight that on this occasion more than the customary handful of regular activists were able to come forward and participate. However, other projects met with very different reactions from the West Indian settlement.

Some of the JWA committee members complained that many West Indians in Easton availed themselves of the facilities provided by the association but most of them refused to take an active part in the running of these projects. Hence a member of the JWA Executive grumbled:

> It's pretty hard trying to put on anything round here, you put in your time for them and when it's all set up they turn out, but you try getting anybody to help you before they've tasted the goods.

The emphasis on recreational events was a constant source of irritation to many of the younger members of the JWA who wanted the association to have a more overtly political role. However, there were very few 'militants' in the group. The majority of committee members were first generation, upwardly mobile Jamaicans. The main activists had skilled manual or white collar jobs. The Executive Committee, for example, comprised a toolmaker, printer, design engineer, trainee youth worker, and an accountant; whilst other activists included a section leader in a local tyre factory, a bus driver, the headmaster of a local Junior School, a clerk/typist and one or two nurses. There were three women active in the group, but none of them held office on the main committee.

In the main the committee was composed of individuals who had lived in the area for a considerable number of years and had thus bene-fited from the early pattern of settlement in Easton when West Indians were able to acquire houses and jobs more easily than more recent arrivals. Length of residence was also influential in shaping the attitudes of the JWA activists towards the receiving society and their fellow West Indians. The majority of members could remember a time, when, with a much smaller number of West Indians in the city, black/white relation-ships had been more harmonious; not necessarily because the level of hostility towards them was low, but mainly because West Indians were far less visible as a group at that time and they lived away from the main centres of the white population. Factors such as these went hand in hand with a high degree of deference towards the host community in the sense that most JWA members recognised that they were 'immigrants' and therefore expected an unequal slice of the cake in terms of access to local resources. As one member, a Jamaican woman, who had lived in Easton for sixteen years, put it:

> I can understand many white people not accepting us on equal terms. You keep reading about West Indians arriving in this country and expecting the streets to be paved with gold and it's true I did myself up to a point. But we were being unreal-istic. A man or woman likes to hang on to what he sees as his own and that's right I suppose, but my sons who were educa-ted here in Easton won't see it that way because they're really British and expect to get what every other kid in school wants. So they don't overlook a lot of things. Maybe we are wrong in being quiet and just wanting a few necessities out of life, but to be anything else is to invite trouble and frustration.

This view was common to many members of the JWA and it explain-ed their reputation as a 'moderate' organisation. The label 'moderate' is equated with the advocacy of non-militant forms of protest against any observed forms of discrimination against West Indians and also with a non-separatist outlook with regard to co-operating with local white activists. Only two members of the Executive, the Secretary and Social Secretary, objected to the use of white participants in the association and wanted little to do with them. The vast majority of JWA members tended to adopt the view that all ethnic or racial groups should be subsumed under one group, even if West Indian needs come first.

The 'militants', on the other hand, took an opposing view and tended to see the association as having a specialised role within the West Indian settlement. They complained that white liberals were not to be trusted and should be treated with suspicion because they tended to dominate or 'take-over' black organisations. However, it was noticeable that both 'militants' and 'moderates' were highly ambivalent about the numerous local Asian communities which were generally seen as being more than capable of looking after themselves.

The following comments give an impression of the way in which different JWA activists saw their role in Easton. The Chairman, for example, expressed the viewpoint of a considerable number of members when he said:

> I don't really see the role of the JWA as a political one, at least in any open sense. West Indians get very suspicious of the word 'politics'. They also fear anything to do with it in many ways. They often see politics as a means for someone to make a little money or for a personal gain of some description and in some respects thinking of what used to happen back home particularly in the past (in Jamaica) maybe this isn't too far from the truth, but it's very demoralising for us because when you ask someone to join they often say what's in it for me or what are you getting out of it? We want to do things on our own so we haven't any English members on the committee but we do have white members. I see the role of the JWA as representing all the local community. If we want help we should go for it whoever that person might be, but mainly we need to help the West Indians because they're getting left out in Easton and we're the least well-equipped to help ourselves.

A slightly more 'militant' line was put forward by the Secretary:

> West Indians have got to learn to look after their own interests. I don't mind getting assistance from any man, whatever his colour, but it's got to be on our terms. You ask someone to help you out and sooner or later they are dictating the show. We used to get this with white radicals like students and that. Some of them were really good, but others only wanted to help if they could run the whole show. Anyway, a lot of West Indians, particularly the kids, don't want a mixed set-up any more; they want to do their own thing. So if we get lots of whites on the committee we destroy our

chances with them for any support.

Finally, the following quote, from the Social Secretary demonstrates that attitudes towards local Asian groups, although guarded, were less than amicable:

> I know one or two Asians and they are OK, but most of them look after their own and look down on West Indians. Maybe it's our colour or our background in the old days, but they just don't want to know. They stick together and organise themselves much better than we do. It's their religion you know, it binds them. West Indians want to go their own way and they mistrust one another too much. It's like we are two different sorts of people; they keep to themselves as a group and want to keep separate from anyone else. The West Indians want to mix in, but there have been too many disappointments and for some strange reason, which I can't explain, most of them are not prepared to come together as a community and do the sort of things we have in our minds.

One of the general policies of the JWA was actively to encourage the establishment of certain facilities to assist West Indian children and adolescents in Easton. This involved the setting up of a youth club in a local school and assisting with the running of an adventure playground, which had recently been established in Lowdale by a number of local action groups. The JWA also tried to organise films, talks and discussion groups with an emphasis on extra education for local West Indian school children. The desire to provide a community centre for the West Indian settlement was prompted by the realisation among JWA members that all other major ethnic groups in the city had provided themselves with this facility. This was particularly noticeable among the local South Asian population which had over 80 voluntary associations, many with their own buildings, which acted as a focal point for the various regional, religious and linguistic communities.

This profusion of Asian organisations and facilities was a subject of some embarrassment for many JWA activists. The JWA had approached the local Council for assistance with premises or finance, but these overtures had met with little success. The secretary explained the situation thus:

> We approached the Council and asked them for assistance, either in the form of some financial help or a building of some kind. They told us that we shouldn't try and build a community centre as two local council estates had them already. We said that they didn't provide the sort of entertainment that we wanted and anyway they didn't make us welcome in these places. Then we suggested we build a specialised building just

as a club. They said this might be alright, but they couldn't provide funds for a building which was to be set up by just one group of West Indians; it had to be a combined project. They also said it would be rather awkward giving us some money for such a building when no other group in the city had had some money for the same thing. We have given up trying in that direction, and will try and do things on our own, but we think it will cost about £50,000 for a building and that's an awful lot of money to raise by dances and socials.

These negotiations with the City Council demonstrate some of the difficulties of the JWA and other West Indian associations in the city. It appeared quite plausible for the Council to deny the JWA funds on the grounds that no other ethnic group in the city had required such assistance, but it also demonstrated that the Council was either unaware of the island distinctions and other lines of conflict which prevented West Indians from forming 'representative' communal groups, or that they chose to ignore these difficulties. The latter appeared more likely to the JWA, because an additional reason given by the Council for refusing funds was the argument that the JWA was not representative of all West Indians in the city (a correct assumption) and hence could not claim to be a 'community' group. The Council stipulated that funds could only be advanced if the proposed club was a 'West Indian' rather than a Jamaican one and, furthermore, if the club was run jointly by all island communities in the city.

The final irony was that the JWA was the only West Indian association in the city which was represented on the local Community Relations Council. Whereas the City Council recognised the unrepresentativeness of the JWA in the West Indian settlement, the local CRC had included them as representative delegates for the West Indian 'community' as a whole. The CRC was aware that the JWA was primarily a Jamaican group but it considered that the policies advocated by the JWA were designed for all West Indians. The City Council were not prepared to accept this, thus forestalling one of the major aims of the JWA.

A further activity of the JWA was the establishment of a local 'West Indian' newspaper which could be used as a form of communication among West Indians throughout the city. One of the members of the Executive had worked on the local city newspaper and was able to use certain contacts and his relevant experience in setting up a project of this nature. A previous colleague on the same paper was also available to advise on the technical details of layout and so forth. An editorial staff was formed, comprising several West Indians and white assistants.

The publication aimed to provide a vehicle for publicising many events and issues which concerned West Indians both within the city and elsewhere. A typical edition might include a detailed list of forthcoming 'social' events plus a feature on an individual's legal rights if stopped and questioned by the police. Scanning through the pages one came across a variety of local news, for example, articles about a local Antiguan woman who was having difficulty getting the relevant documents to bring her son across to Britain. A local Barbadian woman who had won a cookery competition was also featured, together with a review of a recent book on race relations. The headmaster of a secondary school in Lowdale recounted how a Dominican boy had won a place at Cambridge University. The sports news was particularly extensive; cricket, football, boxing and the local dominoes team were all covered.

The advertisements were all written with West Indian needs in mind. Cheap holiday flights to the Caribbean, and West Indian dances in Easton and neighbouring cities were typical examples. Apart from those pertaining to a local finance broker, a furniture warehouse and a local builder, all the adverts were concerned with West Indian entertainment, food and records, etc. The newspaper was a mixture of the type of material which would be associated with any local broadsheet, but the contents were illustrative of many facets of the daily lives of local West Indians. Consequently, it had some potential for the establishment of closer links within the local Caribbean population.

Nevertheless, after only five monthly editions, the paper was officially suspended by the JWA for what were said to be 'staffing problems'. Many members suggested other, more unofficial reasons for its demise. There was the suggestion that the editorial staff had not consulted the Executive Committee and that there had been certain anomalies in the financing of the paper. There were other members who argued that the financial committee had disagreed with some of the content of certain editions. One article in particular, which criticised the local police force, met with considerable hostility from some members of the Executive. An interesting feature of the closure was the apparent lack of publicity given to the newspaper. Respondents were asked if they had ever read the publication and very few had even seen it. It was noticeable that most of the respondents who had read the paper were Jamaicans. Hence, the distribution of the newspaper may have been so limited that this became an additional reason for its failure. Certainly, other activists in associations which were formed by different island communities attributed the demise of the JWA newspaper to its island exclusivity, at least as far as circulation was concerned.

The JWA was established by a few individuals who can be seen as representative of the small number of activists who appear recurrently in most voluntary associations formed within the West Indian settlement in Easton. However, the suggestion that this pattern of 'joining' denotes a recognised leadership structure is highly problematic. One member of the JWA Executive, for example, admitted that:

> If you join a group you set yourself up as a target for all
> manner of abuse and suspicions. There is so much mistrust,
> particularly about money, that it gets really demoralising.
> You spend nights on committee meetings and running around
> after people who often don't want to know, and you get
> little thanks. They just turn around and say, 'what you gettin'
> out of it man?'

The group's Treasurer expressed similar sentiments:

> Back home you hear about so and so walking off with the funds,
> or this chap has set up a group just to make money out of it.
> It happens over here all the time. There was this Antiguan who
> started a group and said it was a charity for some association
> back home, and he ran dances every Saturday night for a few
> weeks. Then he just drifted away and the next we heard of
> him he had just bought a posh house in ... No-one even sniffed
> that money in Antigua. You get these things going on and
> every group is under suspicion. I'm in a particularly awkward
> position as Treasurer. You should hear some of the things I'm
> accused of!

Finally, the Chairman explained his commitment to the association in
the following terms:

> I'm never really sure why I do it. It's taking plenty of my
> time and we can see what we want, but getting it is another
> matter. You get so down seeing support dwindling but I
> have some conviction that what we are doing is worthwhile.
> That's all that keeps me doing things. Maybe I just like to
> be seen trying, even if we get little thanks or recognition.

Irrespective of these activists' self-evaluation of their motives, many
West Indians who were non-participants, equated community activism
with social climbing. The mere existence of these beliefs within Caribbean groups in the city was sufficient to form and maintain gossip
channels which dissuaded many individuals from allying themselves
with the JWA, or any other association for that matter. Island divisions
were also very important in this regard and the JWA suffered accordingly.

Many West Indians in Easton believed that the JWA was solely a
Jamaican group and, therefore, they had no intention of joining if they
came from another island. This had the effect that the dances and socials
organised by the JWA were seen as an amenity provided for personal
profit in the same way as any other commercial undertaking. Such activities were still supported by West Indians in this light, but many refused

to buy the JWA publication because they believed it to be a propaganda vehicle for local Jamaicans. The content of the newspaper did not sub-stantiate this belief, but these suspicions of island exclusivity were not completely unfounded, as many members of the JWA seemed to accept that, because Jamaica was a larger and more 'developed' island in their terms, they were better qualified to organise themselves than other 'smaller' islands.

The following example is illustrative of the importance of these island status evaluations: On one occasion a meeting was organised where representatives from all West Indian associations in Easton met to discuss a programme for the eventual building of the community centre. Nothing was decided because agreement could not be reached on any concrete proposals. Each association wished to retain its own identity and its own policies, with the result that the meeting fragmen-ted and finally broke down when arguments between individuals became heated and personal differences became uppermost. The dynamics of group interaction within the meeting centred on a small nucleus of activists who were well-known to most of the audience. It was apparent that policies put forward by an association were perceived by the audi-ence as representative of a particular individual, rather than of the association which that individual purported to represent. Thus the occu-pation of an official position within a West Indian voluntary association was again seen as a platform for the promotion of individual status. Con-sequently, it was very easy for any debate to be transformed into a clash of personalities rather than a group discussion of general policies.

This is not to suggest deep hostilities between particular activists or island associations—although they existed in a limited number of cases—for the conflictual relations between groups and individuals in respective island communities in the city were subtle and usually covert.

Suffice to say that, after the meeting, several members of the JWA were disillusioned by what they saw as pedantry and an over-concern with inessentials. Their criticisms were couched in terms of 'small island' narrow mindedness as most of the other associations present at the meeting were representative of island communities from Antigua, Nevis, Barbuda and so forth. After the meeting, the JWA adopted a policy of attempting to build a community centre on their own. Its members could not see any possibility of maintaining agreement between the various island communities for such a project to be achieved as a joint effort. This policy decision was interpreted by the non-Jamaican associations, or at least many of their officials, as the final confirmation of the supposed arrogance of 'those Jamaicans' who wanted to do every-thing themselves.

One further problem encountered by the JWA centred on the role of key activists within the association and the relative importance which was attached to them within the group. One such figure, the Secretary, entered a course of full-time education and it became critical as to whether the association could maintain itself without this individual. The Vice-Chairman was also planning to emigrate to the United States in the near future, thus leaving a further gap in the 'leadership' of the group.

Those West Indian associations which are mainly organised by upwardly mobile individuals face the recurrent problem of leadership replacement. West Indians who have 'made good' in Britain are often in a position to move to other areas in the host society, to emigrate elsewhere or return to the Caribbean. The latter group consistently form the majority of active participants in West Indian associations and this 'leadership loss' is a continual problem of voluntary association formation and maintenance within West Indian settlements in Britain.

Many West Indian associations rely on the projection of certain activists within their leadership who are able to construct a following based on their reputation in respective island communities. This reputation tends to be based upon a number of criteria, subtle and less subtle, depending upon factors only known to the particular social network from which a certain association may be formed. In the smaller island communities, village friendship and kinship ties are particularly important. In the JWA, organisational skills and expertise were highly rated in prestige terms. Hence, prestige is relative to the contingencies surrounding group formation among West Indians.

A reliance on personalities to project group images and amass support, renders group solidarity dependent upon the continued presence of such prestigious individuals. The loss of this group image through the withdrawal of key personalities, even temporarily, can produce a crisis of identification and possible group fragmentation. The latter is also probable if certain personalities indulge in activities aimed at forwarding their own power positions in the community rather than those of the associations which they 'represent'. The dissolution of several West Indian associations was claimed (by West Indian respondents) to be due to a chain of gossip built around certain key figures within associations which tended to discredit them and the associations with which they were connected.

The JWA was the most highly organised and most patronised West Indian association in Easton (approximately 60 members). It had a fairly elaborate administrative structure and was actively involved in a wider range of activities than any other West Indian group in the city. Furthermore, despite many of its members' firm denials that the association was in any way political, the JWA was concerned with a number of projects which were designed to change the life situation of the local West Indian settlement. Unlike most of the other West Indian groups described in this chapter, the JWA was not a purely recreational association.

One was left with the impression (in 1974) that if JWA members were able to establish a community centre by themselves and then open these facilities to other West Indians, general support could be forthcoming. However, it seemed doubtful whether a single West Indian association could achieve anything as ambitious as this without financial support from for example, other associations or the City Council in Easton.

The British-West Indian Club

The British-West Indian Club (BWIC) was formed in 1970 and differed from the JWA in many respects, not least in the fact of originating as solely a women's organisation, although this pattern changed marginally after its formation. The BWIC was started by a small group of West Indian women who decided that a club should be started in Easton in order to encourage harmonious relationships between various groups and nationalities in the city. The group had approximately thirty members (all but two were female), comprising several English women, a West African, and West Indians from a variety of island backgrounds. Not surprisingly, given the composition of its membership, the BWIC focussed on the daily problems encountered by West Indian women in the locality. Discussion groups organised by the Club, occasionally in conjunction with the JWA, examined, for example, the problems of finding child-minders for mothers at work, the educational problems of West Indian children, and the difficulties faced by families in inadequate housing.

The BWIC made several attempts to encourage local West Indian mothers to discuss their problems with the teachers of their children. One of the meetings arranged by the Club was a discussion of the educational needs of West Indian children and it brought together many West Indian parents and some local teachers. A West Indian schoolteacher from a neighbouring city was the guest speaker and he spoke of some of the problems which West Indian children meet in the British educational system. He particularly objected to some of the value premises, the stereotypes of black and white, and the neglect of the role of black people in history, found in many school textbooks.

This parents' meeting provided an opportunity for an exchange of ideas between parents and teachers which was often impossible in the normal school situation. Many West Indian parents expressed fears of the type of reaction which they might receive if they went to their child's school on their own. One anecdote which can be related from this meeting demonstrates, once again, how inter-island distinctions can influence group perceptions. During the course of the meeting, the Jamaican headmaster who was a member of the JWA recounted how he had been a member of a recent educational delegation sent out from Britain to study teaching methods in the Caribbean. He mentioned that the delegation had only visited Jamaica on this trip. This brought an immediate rejoinder from some of the women present who pointed out that here was another example where the smaller islands had been ignored in preference to Jamaica. In this case, the tone of the accusation was light-hearted but it was illustrative, nevertheless, of the underlying island distinctions which represent an ever-present frame of reference for first generation West Indians in Easton.

It was noticeable, however, that the BWIC was one of the very few first generation West Indian voluntary associations which had a variety of island backgrounds represented by its leadership. The Club President, and Secretary, were both Jamaican; the former being a nurse who had lived in Easton for many years, whilst the latter owned a hairdressing salon which acted as a focal point for West Indian women in the city. The Social Secretary, a typist who came from Antigua, the Treasurer, a housewife from St. Kitts, and two other members, one from Nevis and an English schoolteacher, made up the remainder of those most active in the group. The success of the BWIC in combining disparate island backgrounds can be attributed to its mainly recreational and non-competitive organisation. The BWIC, being relatively isolated from most other groups in the locality, tended to avoid many inter-island squabbles. All other West Indian associations in the city were predominantly male preserves and they tended to ignore or deride the women's club as being unimportant. Similarly, the type of leisure pursuits which the BWIC were concerned with were entirely separate from the competitiveness of, for example, the island based cricket clubs. Therefore, the group was able to maintain a membership which was not island exclusive.

However, there were signs that even the BWIC was facing internal conflicts within its membership. This came about through the attempt to organise joint activities with the JWA and the suggestion by some members that an amalgamation between the two associations might be possible. Notwithstanding efforts from both sides, all attempts to promote any kind of union between the groups met with little success. Members of both groups tended to blame the other for the relative lack of rapport between the two associations. Most of the BWIC members did not want to become connected with an association which they perceived as openly political in its objectives. They also believed it to be insular, island based and not prepared to include other groups within its framework. On the other hand, many JWA members did not want to join with an association which they saw as small, ill-organised and unable to make a strong contribution to 'important issues' like founding a community centre. In addition, many of the men in the JWA were afraid of losing face among their peers if they amalgamated with a women's group. These sex differences were not voiced openly, but many informants alluded to them and believed them to be a major cause of friction between the two associations.

In all other respects the BWIC closely resembled the JWA in its membership and aims. Both groups were politically moderate and basically believed in effecting some degree of rapprochement between black and white in Easton. This was in sharp contrast to the following association.

The Black Power Group

Although the Black Power Group was formed in 1969, at the same time as the establishment of the JWA, there were few links between the two associations. Most of the original members of the BPG were drawn from what has been called the 'misplaced generation' (Pryce, 1979) of West Indians in Britain. These are West Indians who were born in the Caribbean but were partly educated in Britain. Therefore, most members of the BPG had completed a few years in secondary schools in Easton. They had left school at fifteen to enter mainly unskilled or semi-skilled jobs. In many cases, they soon drifted into unemployment or underemployment and the BPG became the central feature of their day to day life situation. There were about a dozen members when the association was first formed and this had grown to approximately twenty at the time of fieldwork. However, it was difficult to obtain accurate membership figures because records were not kept by the association. Island representation does not seem to have been particularly important either in the general recruitment of members or in 'leadership' patterns. This can be largely attributed to the youthfulness of its membership. Many younger West Indians, born or largely educated in Britain, find their parents continued attachment to Caribbean conceptions of 'home' somewhat meaningless (Midgett, 1975). It can also be explained by the 'black power' ethos which disavows any form of distinctions within a common 'black' identification. Thus, apart from a few white students, this association was exclusively West Indian. Asian members were noticeable only by their absence.

Initially, the general organisation of the BPG was based on the Black Panther movement in the United States (Bracey, 1970; Carmichael and Hamilton, 1967). The leading members of the association lived in a small terraced house which they called the 'Black House'. This was used as a base for some young West Indians, local students and hustlers. The

Black House was also used for regular commercial parties. These she-beens, which involved the illegal sale of drinks and drugs, were the main source of income for many BPG members. Such activities attracted the attention of the police on innumerable occasions.

Although the BPG disavowed any notion of a formal leadership, certain members held specific 'ministries' within the association. The main aims and objectives of the group included:

1 To re-educate black people on politics so that they can see clearly just what politics is doing to them.

2 The Organisation will, whenever possible, give practical and ideological aid to other black people in other parts of the world, fighting for the freedom of black people.

3 To fight for the rights of black people in England for economic and social justice, and to defend these rights by the most effective means at its disposal.

4 To raise funds by all legitimate means; to advance the aims and objectives of the Party.

5 To demand that African history and culture be added to the education programmes, for all black children so they too can be proud of their ancestry, and also see the reasons for migration.

These aims were pursued through regular discussion meetings, liaison with other militant groups in neighbouring cities and political demonstration. Typical discussion topics ranged through Black People and the Police, Garveyism, and Pan-Africanism, to Black Children and the ESN system.[2] Some members of the BPG assisted with local educational programmes for West Indian youth, including the youth club mentioned earlier. The principal organisers frequently travelled to political meetings and demonstrations from Birmingham to London.

Regular activists within the BPG were drawn from three loosely linked groups: local black students, usually West Indians, who tended to take an active but ephemeral role within the group; young West Indians who were in regular employment but who maintained some connections with the BPG; and finally, a nucleus of unemployed and underemployed youths and young men who depended on BPG activities, crime, and casual work for their subsistence. All members who occupied official positions were in the third category, apart from the Secretary and the Minister of Information who were local West Indian students.

It is important to stress that the level of influence and importance of any action group can far outweigh the level of active adherence within its boundaries. The BPG was classic proof of this maxim. Its political militancy and real or imagined connection with a variety of deviant activities, attracted newspaper coverage, police surveillance, and provoked considerable comment among the local population, black, brown and white. The group was seen as decidedly disreputable by many older West Indians, but it provided a communal atmosphere for the young and unemployed who were attracted by the idealisation of a form of 'black power' with its ramifications of negritude; separatist inclinations and an active avowal of a positive identification with an alternative life style. The political commitment of many black youths attached to the group was problematic, but the militancy of its leadership was unquestionable.

The ideological commitment of the BPG was reflected in the content of its journal which differed significantly from the subject matter presented in the JWA's publication. Whereas the latter was eventually dissolved because of its alleged 'political content', the BPG journal was openly concerned with circulating the political views of 'black power' as it was perceived by BPG members. Copies of the journal included articles on alleged police brutality towards local black people, racial discrimination, black political activities in Africa, the United States and the Caribbean, and a number of articles concerned with 'black ideology'.

The following excerpts from an interview printed in the journal give some indication of the views expounded by the BPG. The Chairman is being quoted in the following extracts:

> The blacks have always felt the urge to fight, but they haven't realised the advantage of collectiveness until the last few years. I don't think that we are influenced by the Panthers to any extent. The movement here arose simply because the blacks were being pressurised by society. We take certain lessons off the Panthers, of course. They have been at it longer than we have and are highly organised. But it must be remembered that Black Power is just part of a world revolution, a feeling of brotherhood between oppressed peoples.

In answer to a question about the BPG's attitude to white radicals:

> Of course, they can help the struggle. In the final analysis we're both fighting against the system and we'll co-operate with the white radicals if we feel that it will benefit us. But on our terms never theirs.

As regards the police:

> We believe that the image of the police has got to change before we want to see blacks joining the force. We're quite aware that blacks can be bad too, and then it's even more pathetic. No, the police must change. At the moment they act like Hitler's storm-troopers.

Finally, when questioned about his attitudes towards the local Asian communities, the Chairman replied:

> They have their own thing, of course. They are organising
> themselves and we can get together when its needed, because
> we are all fighting the same fight against the same enemy. Of
> course, there has been the language difficulty for one thing,
> but we all consider ourselves part of the Third World.

These excerpts represent a reasonable cross-section of the views formally expressed by the BPG, but the opinions given in interviews and
the contents of other journal articles were more 'militant'. Most of the
latter were strongly anti-white and anti-police. Both 'whitey' and the
'Pigs' were portrayed as the enemy in highly inflammatory tones.

The relationships between the BPG and other West Indian voluntary
associations in the locality were heavily influenced by the nature of the
adverse publicity which surrounded the group. Many of the West Indians
in other associations were highly critical of the BPG and saw it as a
major disruptive influence within the West Indian settlement. The views
of a former member of the group being a case in point:

> I belonged to the BPG from its formation in '69 when a group
> of us got together to form the group. We wanted to get some
> sort of radical association going instead of all the tea parties
> and such like which was going on. At the beginning, most of
> us were in jobs and I was studying at night school in my employ-
> ment. When I thought about getting married and settling down,
> I moved out of Lowdale and came here on the outskirsts of
> Wigton. I don't know whether I was resented for getting on and
> getting above myself. I didn't want to get involved in the pimp-
> ing and drugs scene. We were always getting busted because of
> these sorts of things and some of the ideas got mixed up and
> became a bit wild. I still believe in the basic philosophies of the
> group, but I joined the JWA because it seemed to be moving
> towards some sort of political voice but without the stupidness.
> The group (BPG) is now just seen as a bunch of layabouts who
> don't want to work and who live off their women and ganja
> (marijuana) peddling. I still know one or two guys in it, and its
> not true of them, but these things go on and it makes us unpopu-
> lar in the area.

These views were typical of two or three former members of the
BPG who, after becoming established in their jobs, had moved into the
suburbs and subsequently became marginal participants in the life of
Lowdale. Furthermore, they were representative of the moderates in
most other West Indian associations in the city, and, indeed of many
West Indian parents who expressed considerable concern lest any of
their children became connected with the group.

Other West Indians, however, were more ambivalent about the BPG. On the one hand they firmly disapproved of all of the 'deviant' activities assigned to BPG members, but they did have some sympathy with the ideology or ethos which the BPG represented. For example, some members of the JWA and other associations stressed that an identification with their colour or common heritage was a useful focus for West Indian solidarity. But these members tended to differentiate between an identification with a distinctive 'West Indian' life style or background and what they considered to be the somewhat ethereal ethos of negritude or Afro-culture. The latter was seen as too abstract for most West Indians to identify themselves with. Furthermore, such idealisation was criticised because many West Indians did not accept that the British situation was similar in all respects to that in the United States. They also disagreed with the notion that West Indians should destroy all affinities with European culture. Whilst it was accepted that West Indians should organise themselves effectively, independently and without reliance on whites, nevertheless it was felt that the historical links with Britain could not be erased by simply turning toward Africa. As one Antiguan said, 'If we try to replace our European heritage with an African one, we are merely replacing one borrowed culture with another'.

This ideological gulf between the BPG and other West Indian associations tended to isolate the former. Such isolation was reinforced by the fact that the BPG officials who took part in the few meetings arranged between all West Indian groups in the city, consistently used a rhetoric and a form of ideological argument which most other associations found impractical or irrelevant. As one JWA committee member commented:

> Who the hell wants to hear about African heritage when you're talking about a building fund or the weekend dance?

BPG activists answered in turn that the JWA were middle-class aspirant 'Uncle Toms', who, with the aid of 'whitey', avoided what to them were the bitter realities of black exploitation.

The eventual demise of the BPG was due to the lack of direct political commitment among West Indian youth in Easton in the early 1970s, the apprehension of many of their officials by the police, and finally, by the possibility that alternative West Indian associations, for example, the JWA, were becoming more overtly political in their objectives. However, the remnants of the BPG partially aligned themselves with a similar group in a neighbouring city. As events were to prove, the rise of new ideological foundations more relevant to younger West Indians provided a continuity between a militancy modelled on the United States, and a new radicalism more specifically based on the Caribbean and Britain.

Island development societies

These associations were recent innovations in Easton and were organised strictly along island lines. The three associations of this kind established in the city represented the local Nevisian, Barbudan and Antiguan communities respectively. Their main purpose was to promote fund raising activities to support development programmes which were intended to contribute to the economies of the respective islands. The islands represented were all small in size and relatively impoverished, so funds from their island communities in Britain could make a substantial contribution to their economies (Philpott, 1973). The Antiguan and Nevisian groups were local branch associations of national organisations, but they differed considerably from each other in their memberships and activities.

The Antiguan group was primarily based in London and the majority of activities organised by this association took place in the Metropolis. Consequently, the local association in Easton consisted solely of one representative of the national organisation. Thus, its membership was only meaningful in a national context because the local branch did not have a committee or elected officials except for the branch secretary. This lack of formal structure at the local level meant that the Antiguans, despite being the largest West Indian group in Easton, were underrepresented in inter-island associational activities within the West Indian settlement in the city.

Nevertheless, the branch secretary was very well-known among West Indians in the neighbourhood. This was mainly due to the fact that he had many interests outside of his duties in the Antiguan Association. He was involved, for example, in running a local youth club for West Indians and he also acted as an agent for a West Indian firm in London which specialised in charter flights to the Caribbean.

The activities of the Antiguan Association and the other island development societies were largely hidden from West Indians in other island communities in Easton. Apart from the usual dances which these associations held on infrequent occasions, the nature of their organisation was exclusive to their own island communities. The West Indian associations which were formed by 'small island' communities were organised on an informal basis centred on kinship and friendship relationships which originated in the home island. Most of the West Indians from Antigua, Barbuda, Nevis and the other small islands represented in Easton came from a small number of villages in their home societies. Thus, most Nevisians or Barbudans knew one another before their arrival in Britain. An elaborate kinship and friendship network tended to replace or at least to complement any formal associational network which might have existed within these communities. Although this pattern held for all West Indian communities in Easton, it was particularly the case for those smaller island groupings which lacked a formal associational structure.

One exception to this was the Nevisian Development Society which had a local committee and formally elected officials. This association had approximately twenty members at the time of the research, and these included an elected Chairman, a Secretary and a Treasurer, who were the most active participants in the group. The occupations of these officials were a schoolteacher, a foreman in a shoe factory and a telephonist, respectively. In common with the JWA and the BWIC, all the 'leaders' of the development associations were upwardly mobile working or middle class West Indians who had been resident in Easton for some years. The main aims and objectives of the Nevisian Association were to raise funds for development programmes in Nevis and, in particular, to provide equipment for the improvement of medical and educational facilities in the home island. These funds were raised by personal subscriptions or the organisation of dances and other recreational events. The Nevisian Association in Easton maintained links with similar associations in Leeds, Manchester and Birmingham, cities which all had sizeable Nevisian communities.

There was little contact with other West Indian associations at the local level. The JWA was avoided as a 'Jamaican' group and, therefore, likely to be 'uninterested in smaller islands'. Unlike the Antiguan Association which was based outside of Easton, the local Nevisian Association held regular meetings in the city and combined these with visits to Nevisian communities elsewhere in Britain. All members of the committee planned to return to Nevis within a few years after, as they put it, the home island had been 'redeveloped'. They considered that Nevisians in Britain had a duty to transfer funds to the home island not only to provide for their fellows in the Caribbean, but also in order to stimulate the island's economy so that Nevisians could leave the 'hardships of Britain' and return home.

The Barbudan Association was very small and run by very few individuals. Membership figures were unavailable and the only active participants who could be traced were the 'Chairman' and the 'Secretary', whose sole duties appeared to be organising regular dances. The aims of this 'association' appeared to be similar to those of other island development societies. That is to say, the Barbudan Association was basically a fund raising organisation for the home island. The Barbudan community in Easton, although comparatively small in numbers, was in fact, one of the largest groupings of Barbudans in Britain. The links between these islanders were once again based on kinship and village networks which, in part because of the smallness of the island society, were highly intimate. Most Barbudans knew one another and many were directly related through family and kinship ties. Both formal and informal associational activities were, therefore, highly exclusive and completely separate from those of the other West Indian communities in Easton.

These very close-knit social networks are possibly not so important among larger island groupings where a greater number of individuals tend to be strangers. Moreover, in the case of islands such as Jamaica, where industrialisation and urbanisation are sufficiently advanced to have produced more pronounced rural/urban distinctions, formal associations tend to be more common (Kuper, 1976:21). However, it can be seen that the degree of informal interaction between West Indians is a crucial factor in influencing the level of formal associational participation in all West Indian communities in the city. The lack of formal associations within certain island groupings may not be indicative of a lack of associational activity *per se,* but possibly that informal kinship and village networks which were predominant in the home island are similarly present in Britain. However, the significance of this informal type of activity is important in relation to the links between and within particular West Indian communities and also in connection with relationships between the West Indian settlement and the 'host community'. The relative enclosure of highly informal networks which are based on intimate normative prescriptions at least partially excludes neighbouring island groupings. Thus, group solidarity based on this type of affiliation may be irrelevant or detrimental to the establishment of West Indian communal associations, that is to say those associations which transcend intimate island distinctions.

The latter point is illustrated by the attitudes which many members of the JWA had towards the formation of island development associations in Easton. Many JWA activists were disquieted or openly annoyed about the formation of these groups, because they perceived them to be a danger to the establishment of some sort of corporate association representative of all West Indian communities in the city. The JWA considered that development associations would not only increase the competition in arranging dances and socials and thus disperse funds throughout the settlement, but that they would also reinforce island insularity and endanger the possibility of establishing a community centre. Some JWA members, somewhat ironically given their own 'reputations', also insinuated that some of these development associations might be merely a cover for certain individuals striving to build a power base for themselves or, even more likely, that they were a means of making personal financial gains.

These views were understandable in many ways for there had been several occasions in the past when local West Indians had established 'associations', some with supposedly charitable aims, and gone off with the funds accumulated from putting on dances in the 'association's' name. The running of dances was the most common abuse because most local halls would only book their rooms to associations rather than individuals to prevent private profiteering. However, these stipulations led to the formation of bogus organisations or groups with false objectives, which were purely private profit-making enterprises. There was no evidence that any of the development associations were bogus organisations, but the important factor is that they were believed by activists in other associations and many West Indians from other island communities, to be spurious.

The main significance of the formation of island development associations in Easton was the confirmation of a definite move away from the so-called generally representative associations like the JWA and the BWIC. Their formation pointed towards a resurgence of island exclusivity within the West Indian settlement in Easton. This was recognised by the JWA and BWIC, who saw this new development as detrimental to West Indian solidarity in the city, as it tended to factionalise the local settlement.

The reasons for the fragmentation of West Indian associations will be examined in Chapter 7. At this point it can be noted that the move away from communal to island associations was partly due to the recurrent quarrels between the various associations in Easton, some of which have been described in this chapter. These conflicts led to a further erosion of inter-island relationships, that had always been mistrustful, and contributed to a situation where internal island solidarity was perhaps perceived by many West Indians at the time as the only viable basis for group cohesion. However, since at the time of fieldwork most of the island development associations were only recently established, it remained a matter of conjecture whether their formation indicated a concrete trend towards a hardening of island distinctions, or whether such associations were simply ephemeral formations.

West Indian sports associations

The importance of recreational voluntary associations within the West Indian settlement in Easton has already been mentioned. Certainly the number of exclusively West Indian sports associations in the city confirmed this emphasis. There were five cricket clubs, a football club, local facilities for boxing and weightlifting and finally a domino club in the locality. The provision of these separate sporting facilities stemmed from the previous attempts to maintain a Sports Association which would encompass all such activities within one West Indian recreational association.

The organisational pattern of local cricket clubs followed the trend of the island development associations and further confirmed the degree of group separatism among West Indians in Easton. One cricket club, mainly composed of Antiguans, was the last remnant of the old Sports and Social Club. Another was associated with a local youth club which had a predominantly West Indian membership and this included players from a number of different islands. The other three clubs were predominantly or exclusively Barbudan, Jamaican and Barbadian teams respectively. The Barbadian club can be seen as illustrative of the ways in which island insularity influences the composition of local West Indian cricket teams and the nature of the power struggles within these associations. Initially, this particular club was a mixture of Antiguans and Barbadians, but there were many quarrels about the island composition of the elected committees within the club. The Barbadians argued that the Antiguans were trying to 'take-over' the club, whilst the latter expressed similar sentiments about the 'Bajans'. One particular point of contention between them was focussed on whether the team should play in a Saturday or Sunday league. The religious affiliations of many of the Antiguan members were significant in this decision for many of the latter were Seventh Day Adventists, which meant that they could not play on Saturdays. The Barbadian members of the committee, one of whom was Match Secretary, were accused of organising the club fixtures so that matches fell on a Saturday. The Antiguans argued that this was a political ruse to force them out of the club. The result of this quarrel was that the majority of Antiguans did leave the club and organised a cricket club of their own, leaving behind them a predominantly Barbadian cricket club which continued to recruit members on an island basis.

Although one or two members of non-recreational voluntary associations in Easton were members of sports clubs in the locality, no links were apparent between these various groups. The majority of participants in sports clubs did not appear to be involved in any other types of association. Similarly, island affiliations were important in the formation and maintenance of certain cricket clubs which were either exclusively or predominantly composed of players from a single island. But there was no observable connection between cricket clubs and other West Indian associations primarily based on island affiliations. The only exceptions were two members of the JWA committee who belonged to cricket clubs, and the captain of the football team who was active in the cultural association which will be described later in the chapter. However, these activities were perceived as entirely separate from one another which confirms previous studies which have suggested that West

Indians, in common with many members of the host society, tend to compartmentalise their social activities (Banton, 1972:132).

The role of sporting activities in the West Indian settlement did not appear to go beyond the function of providing an outlet for recreational and athletic endeavour. Those members of cricket clubs who joined other groups of a political nature in the past, or who attended meetings and discussions connected with, for example, the Community Centre project, appeared to do so as individuals not as representatives of the sports clubs which they might be associated with. This is not to say, of course, that politics are unimportant in the composition of teams or in West Indian cricket generally. The power struggles within West Indian cricket teams in Easton have already been mentioned. Moreover, one has only to look at the inter-island rivalries which influence the selection of West Indian Test teams in the Caribbean to see that political considerations permeate the sporting world to a significant degree (Patterson, 1969).

The local Domino club was illustrative of a popular form of West Indian recreation. In the Caribbean it is played by men in bars and rum shops, as well as in their own homes. West Indians play dominoes competitively and have organised regional league and cup competitions in Britain. It is part of the local West Indian scene in Easton to see a group of men or youths playing dominoes in the part-time barber shops or in the youth club. Participants are often surrounded by a huddle of spectators who loudly acclaim or denigrate each move.

The club had approximately twenty-five members, most of whom were young men, although a few older members had been introduced into the club in order, to quote a phrase used by the Club President, 'to act as figure-heads'. These officials, a President, Chairman and Secretary, complained that most of the younger members could not be bothered with the club's administration. They were only interested in the actual playing, so the older men had offered to join the club in an administrative capacity. Following the pattern of other West Indian sports associations, the Domino Club could not be said to exist for any purpose other than for the specific recreational pursuit for which it was formed. Similarly, its mixed island composition, predominantly Jamaican but with several other islands represented, corresponded with the pattern observed in other purely recreational associations.

This brief appraisal of West Indian sports associations in Easton suggests that these forms of association have limited recreational goals and do not constitute groupings which are likely to provide a basis for formal political activity. Such degrees of formalisation as do exist, in the sense of elected committees and officials, are merely administrative provisions which are seen as necessary within the specific limits of sporting activities. In this way, West Indian sports clubs share many common characteristics with similar associations in the host society. They perform certain functions in providing recreational and sporting outlets for their West Indian members and, in the case of cricket and soccer clubs, they promote a limited kind of interaction with similar local white and Asian clubs.

The Caribbean Cultural Group

The Caribbean Cultural Group was a drama and music association established by the JWA to promote forms of Caribbean artistic expression among West Indian youth in Easton. It grew out of the 'People to People Week' organised by the local CRC in 1972. During a 'Caribbean Evening' which was jointly staged by the JWA and BWIC, a group of local West Indian teenagers performed a number of dance routines and recited their own poems. The success of this venture prompted the youngsters taking part to form a cultural group which would meet regularly to develop their interests in Caribbean literature and drama. An active member of the JWA was largely instrumental in establishing the association and arranging for premises where they could meet. The Group had about twenty members at its inception, all of whom were in their teens or early twenties.

During the first few months of its existence, the group was very enthusiastic and established a regular programme of concerts which they performed at West Indian dances and 'functions', both locally and in neighbouring towns. A dance teacher from a local college was introduced by the JWA and facilities were provided for the group in a room attached to a local adventure playground. Soon after its formation, however, the group started to disband due to internal conflicts and disagreements between its members and the JWA. The latter had intended to form a general co-ordinating committee which would meet infrequently and serve as an advisory body for the group. This proposed committee was never formed, however, and no clear objectives were established among the membership. The latter resented the 'assistance' from the JWA who were seen as attempting to control the activities of the group. JWA members denied this and argued that the youngsters were intransigent and would not accept any advice, even though they were unsure of their objectives or how to organise themselves. These disputes decreased the membership until finally only a very small number of youths still attended weekly meetings.

The interesting feature of the Caribbean Cultural Group was the attempt to re-impose West Indian culture, in particular literature, through its activities. The latter is a cultural area in which the Caribbean is richly endowed. Much of the material used by the group was written by members and displayed a strong concern with their search for identity. Poems depicted the problems of living in a society which offered no clear symbols of acceptance or rejection, but a confusion of actions and attitudes which created ambivalence and insecurity among West Indians in Britain. Half-forgotten remembrances of a Jamaican or Antiguan childhood were contrasted with their more recent experiences in Easton. The rhetoric of black consciousness was also present. Some members reinforced their island backgrounds and sought to draw the parameters of their life experience around a specific West Indian society. Others categorised their life situation as part of a world-wide phenomenon which embraced the Caribbean, Africa and North America.

The JWA was hopeful that the Cultural Group would be able to establish a viable association which could provide some form of clear identification for its members, whilst at the same time, serve as a cultural reference group which might unify disparate interests and possibly promote a form of solidarity similar to that which the BPG had sought. The Cultural Group was seen as a form of association which could encompass the 'radicalism' of the BPG, but within a group context which disavowed the violence (of the BPG) and the 'deviant activities' which were connected with it. It remained problematic whether the group's search for a new identity would lead to a reinforcement of the island exclusivity common to their parents, or, more probably, whether new forms of expression would develop out of a shared awareness of being black and British.

Entertainment groups

One of the focal points of most West Indian parties and recreational gatherings is provided by distinctive forms of music played by West Indian musicians or provided by tapes and records. The presence of a large radiogram or hi-fi set is a common sight in many West Indian homes. Similarly, at dances and house parties, particular forms of West Indian music are the main attraction. The recreational function of most West Indian associations has constantly been stressed and this creates a demand for specialised forms of musical entertainment. This demand has led to the formation of several 'Entertainment Groups' within the West Indian settlement in Easton. There were at least four regular bands in the area, one of which had been mildly successful beyond the locality and had issued recordings nationally. Many of these West Indian groups play in neighbouring towns and are not confined to exclusively West Indian dances.

However, most groups play at social gatherings which are organised within those areas of heaviest West Indian occupation. In many 'twilight areas', the basement rooms of large Victorian houses are given over to dances, 'shebeens' and blues parties where every weekend the walls throb to the heavy bass beat of a high wattage 'sound system' (McGlashan, 1973). Some of these parties are gatherings of friends and relatives, but others are run on a commercial basis with the (usually illegal) sale of drinks supplementing the money taken at the door. The particular forms of music are an important part of the cultural expression of a subculture where music and dance express the 'style' of folk entertainment. Dances are noisy and crowded, characterised by uninhibited participation in 'reggae', 'rocksteady', 'blue beat', 'ska' or 'saga ting' or whatever is the latest 'scene stealer' (Pryce, 1979:100). Most of the time, the music is Jamaican reggae with its distinctive bass line setting the dance rhythm. Local whites are rarely in evidence apart from some white girls who have black boyfriends or who are attracted by the unique excitement of forms of recreational expression which are far removed from the local 'Palais'.

Whilst individual members of dance groups may have or have had links with other West Indian associations, their main interests were centred on the provision of entertainment through participation in the local music scene. Two West Indian bands in Easton could be classed as semi-professional with regular paid 'gigs' in local dance halls and clubs throughout the city and elsewhere. Most of the musicians treated their participation as a means of supplementing their earnings though, in some cases, it was their sole source of income. Entertainment groups are an important part of the day-to-day life of West Indians in Easton. But this role is strictly confined to a specific form of commercial enterprise or recreational association. There was no indication that these groups constituted any form of political expression. Moreover, their economic functions are individualistic as they provide private incomes rather than funds for island communities or the West Indian settlement as a whole. The relationship between these entertainment 'entrepreneurs' and other West Indian associations who use their services is a strictly commercial one, although the negotiation of playing fees and booking dates may be influenced by informal contacts between musicians and the members of the associations hiring them.

Conclusion

It can be seen that the majority of West Indian voluntary associations are recreational and non-political in their functions and objectives. Similarly, in common with most of the previous studies of working class participation in voluntary associations, memberships in most of the West Indian associations described are low and the number of West

Indians who can be described as 'activists' is extremely small. A limited number of 'leaders' tend to operate and control the organisation of those formal and semi-formal associations which have been established within the West Indian settlement. The vast majority of these activists, irrespective of their political allegiances, remain unknown to the majority of West Indians beyond their own circle of acquaintances or island networks.

In most West Indian associations there appears to be a blend of formalised procedures, for example, a concern with 'procedural etiquette', and a high degree of personalised debate. This is not to suggest that these associations are completely informal in their decision making. Indeed, there is a marked concern with formal agendas and so forth, but these procedures are often seen (by members) as outward manifestations of respectability. They are the 'right thing to do', as one West Indian described them. Therefore, there is a kind of formal ritualism observable at most West Indian meetings which partly conceals the informal nature of the group interaction within this context.

Within this framework, group situations are often dominated by 'personalities' and highly individualised debate. These key figures in West Indian associations produce conflicting results. In many ways their presence initiates a form of organisation in which an individual, provided he has the necessary support from other members, can dominate an association and thus overcome the factionalism which is common in such organisations. Conversely, and more commonly, the rigidity of this situation provokes further internal conflicts. Criticism is often used in a negative manner so that individual proposals are often discarded without any substantive alternative policies being offered in their place. The demise of the Sports and Social Club and the failure of the JWA to organise communal support for their Community Centre project can be seen as illustrative of the repercussions of these organisational difficulties.

Island distinctions within the West Indian settlement are extremely important in explaining the 'forces' which make for variations in the balance between centripetal and centrifugal tendencies in communal or island-exclusive associations established by West Indians in the locality. These island distinctions appear to be more important in affecting those West Indian associations which have overtly economic and/or political objectives rather than purely recreational aims. The mistrust which surrounds financial matters is also quite marked and corresponds to similar social patterns in the West Indies (see Chapter 2).

Most of the voluntary associations in Easton which have some political aims or functions, for example, the JWA, the BWIC, the Cultural Group and the Island Development Associations are 'moderate' organisations which seek changes within their own communities in Britain and/

or the Caribbean, without resort to violence or any methods which might disrupt relationships between themselves and the host community. Most West Indian activists within these associations are middle or upwardly mobile working class West Indians who have acquired a living standard which is somewhat better than the majority of West Indians in Easton. In many cases these activists are first generation West Indians who have resided in the city for many years.

The exceptions to the above were provided by the BPG, and a minority of activists within the Cultural Group and the JWA. These were younger, second generation West Indians, mainly from working class backgrounds who lived in Lowdale. They advocated more 'militant' forms of political expression which were likely to be socially unacceptable both to the host community and the majority of West Indians in Easton.

The pattern of West Indian activism in Easton shows many similarities to the patterns of leadership in the Caribbean which have been previously described. We have shown, for example, that 'leadership' in Easton is commonly, but not exclusively, the prerogative of the middle and upwardly mobile working class West Indians in the city. However, irrespective of class position, very few West Indians are prepared to adopt 'leadership' positions in local West Indian voluntary associations because of a recurrent pattern of what might be termed 'leadership deprecation'. This pattern can be partly attributed to the existence of an egalitarian value system within the West Indian settlement which deprecates any group or individual who is perceived by other West Indians as 'getting above themselves'. Similarly, there is a general ethos of mistrust and jealousy among West Indians in the city which surrounds the occupancy of leadership positions or 'influential roles' within West Indian voluntary associations, particularly those connected with financial matters. These factors, together with others which will be discussed in greater detail in Chapter 7, contribute to the scarcity and ephemerality of West Indian non-recreational, political associations in the city. This pattern of associational 'fragmentation' corresponds not only with previous studies of West Indians in other urban settings in Britain, but also with those general features of lower-class West Indian political organisation in the Caribbean which I described earlier in the book. Thus, we have established a consistent pattern of political association—or more accurately, political disassociation—which appears to be typical of West Indian social organisation in a variety of social and geographical milieux.

This being the case, we can turn our attentions to some possible explanations for this phenomenon. In particular, the problem can be approached by an attempt to relate certain features of West Indian social organisation to forms of political association. Hence, the following chapter's concern is with West Indian family and household patterns and their possible influence on political mobilisation.

Notes

1   A 'shebeen' is a commercial party where food and drink are sold, invariably illegally.
2   This title refers to the categorisation of West Indian children as educationally sub-normal (Coard, 1971).

5   Family and social organisation

There are few aspects of Caribbean social structure which lend themselves to explicit statements and nicely rounded definitions. The passage of history has contrived to weave a tapestry of social relationships which are as varied as the colour gradations found among the individuals who exist within them. Nevertheless, even with this rich profusion, the area of family and kinship has produced a greater variety of debate (and confusion) than most other aspects of the social structure of West Indian societies.

It will not be necessary for us to delve too deeply into the more contentious areas of this debate. Nevertheless, an outline of the main characteristics of family and household structures in the Caribbean[1] will be useful for purposes of comparison with the family and kinship patterns observed among West Indians in Easton. It is important to realise at the outset that variations in Caribbean family and kinship patterns have to be viewed against the systems of social stratification of the different West Indian societies. 'Caribbean sociology has always stressed the different institutional forms characterising lower and higher classes, and in particular the differences in family form and religious expression' (Kuper, 1976).

The higher strata usually adhere to the legal marriage unit common in most Western industrialised societies, although there are certain subtle distinctions which are of importance. However, our main concern is with those family household units which typify the lower classes, and they, it must be remembered, represent the majority of individuals in each of the West Indian societies in the Caribbean. At this class level, there is considerable variation both between islands and regionally within them. These variations must be kept in mind throughout the discussion which follows. It should be emphasised, moreover, that the characteristics singled out in this discussion are not intended as a definitive typology of 'lower class' family structures in the Caribbean.

Katrin Fitzherbert (1967) has stressed the importance of regarding the West Indian family unit as a highly flexible and variable type of social organisation. She believes that it is more important to consider differences in locality rather than those between island societies. There are rural/urban distinctions within islands, but rural and urban patterns may be similar in different islands. Patterns of family organisation depend upon a number of local contingencies, political, economic and social. These contingencies depend very largely on how individuals and groups view their own life situations and those of their neighbours. Thus, 'family' as a local phenomenon may be more dependent on how the term is meaningful to the individuals within this social group than on more concrete features such as blood ties, marriage forms and patterns of land tenure.

Legal marriage among the West Indian lower classes usually coincides with 'economic maturation'; that is to say, at a time when common-law partners are approaching middle-age, and when the male has sufficient wealth or income to marry, with all the necessary ceremonies. Typically, sexual relations follow a 'developmental cycle' (Cross, 1979:80) where early unions are marked by 'visiting' which defines the presence of sexual relationships without cohabitation; followed by 'common-law' and/or legal marriage. A study, carried out by Cumper (1958) in Jamaica, illustrates the complexities which exist within a particular society. What he shows is the way in which different forms of economic organisation influence the pattern of 'economic maturation' in the sense of determining whether this comes in middle, old age or earlier.

According to Cumper, two economic subsystems can be distinguished in Jamaica. He calls them the 'estate' and the 'peasant' subsystems and they contain, respectively, landless wage-earners and landed, self-employed peasants. He shows how economic relationships, particularly as they affect the male role, help to shape family forms. Therefore, among the landed, self-employed or 'peasant' group, economic relationships act to strengthen family ties and, in particular, to reinforce the central position of the father. Among the landless wage-earners in the 'estate' subsystem, however, the degree of coincidence between economic and family relationships is considerably lower. The estates display sharp status differences in terms of economic and monetary rewards, differences which do not arise to the same extent in the more homogeneous peasant communities. In the estate society, the fact that status is vested in male workers coincides with the fact that the male-centred family has high prestige. This produces a family form which, while normatively similar to the peasant one, is functionally different. Thus, in the peasant community, common-law marriage is a transitional state, a stage on the road to legal marriage. As with advancing age, the male head of the family grows economically more secure, for example, being able to increase the amount of land under his control, so he tends to establish a legal relationship with his common-law spouse. On the estate, by contrast, legal marriage is not, to anything like the same extent, a normal 'end-state'. Moreover, the permanence of common-law marriages tends to vary, not in relation to age, but in relation to the performance of the worker in his economic role.

In a study of family and household units in Jamaica, Grenada and

Carriacou, Michael G. Smith lists certain common features of lower class family organisation in these islands:

> Their household heads are of either sex, their members are differentiated by birth status, they practice alternative forms of mating, they differentiate parental roles in correspondence with these alternative mating forms. Their domestic units vary widely in size and constitution. Consensual cohabitation is ambiguous in so far as it may dissolve or develop into marriage, which is therefore structurally indeterminate (1962:244).

He goes on to state that:

> All the societies we have been studying have a formal commitment to monogamy, a ban on polygamy, a plurality of mating forms and of elementary and domestic family organisation alike (1962:255).

The general features of family organisation must be related to the historical context out of which they have evolved over the past few centuries. Smith shows how the persistence of high illegitimacy rates and distinctive forms of domestic grouping in the West Indies, are all due to the same historical conditions. Such conditions had their origin in slavery[2] in particular the mating organisation of slaves within a system of permanent domination. West Indian slaves were not allowed to marry, but they were free—indeed they were encouraged—to 'cohabit consensually' or to mate extra-residentially without any limitations other than the provision that they could not establish a common home:

> In both the hill and plains populations of Jamaica, and in other West Indian societies, emancipation merely permitted the adoption of a new mating form; it could not abolish the old mating system; nor could the new form introduced into this traditional dual system displace either of its original forms (1962:261).

Smith's emphasis on a dual system of values, the one modelled on European prescriptions of legal marriage and legitimacy of offspring, the other an alternative set of values developed over time by the lower classes, has been questioned by Hyman Rodman. Rodman (1971), drawing on material from his Trinidadian study, suggests there is but one single value system which has become 'stretched' over time:

> By value stretch I mean that the lower class person, without abandoning the general values of the society, develops an alternative set of values. Without abandoning the values of marriage and legitimate childbirth he stretches these values so that non-legal union and illegitimate children within that union are desirable (1971:195).

103

However, as Wilson (1973) points out in his study of Providencia, the emphasis on alternative values still indicates a plurality of institutional forms. Wilson's plausible solution to the dynamics of differing systems of relationships is to stress the dialectical nature of historically changing social patterns. 'These historically separable value systems are, in the Caribbean constituents of a single, sociologically dynamic system whose crux is the relations between the constituents' (1973:220). The basis of the dialectic, for Wilson, is a set of social and cultural oppositions that reflect 'the *respectability* of European white stratification and the *reputation* of indigenous black differentiation' (1973:222). Respectable institutions, in this case legal marriage, derive from those externally imposed by the metropolitan society over time, whereas:

> The origin of reputation is *within*, and in a sense it is a reaction to respectability. It provides the majority of the population with the basis for self-recognition, since otherwise they would exist only as an 'inferior' and anonymous 'mass' in the class-structured society (Wilson, 1973:223).

Hence, the European and 'indigenous' family forms co-exist in a dynamic relationship which incorporates a flexibility and ability for adaptation far removed from any thoughts of 'marginality' and family 'disorganisation'. As Rodman (1971:197) points out, West Indian lower class family units are solutions not problems for their members; such units only become 'deviant' by the labelling of the middle class or outside observers. In this case, Rodman is referring to labelling by the middle classes in the Caribbean, but I would wish to extend this to incorporate those members of the white population in Britain who may also 'perceive' the social organisation of immigrant West Indian families in this way.

There is ample evidence from Caribbean studies of the pervasiveness of a striving for 'respect' among the lower classes. Wilson (1973:220) argues that marriage and legitimacy are prerequisites for respectability, though not guarantees of it. Henry and Wilson (1975) and Cross (1979) also refer to a number of studies which view the pursuit of 'respect' as a major reason for eventual marriage. The woman in the partnership is often the main seeker after status, for contrary to popular myth, whilst West Indian men may only have a restricted role within the household they are very far from powerless. The flexibility of sexual relations, the prevalence of male unemployment or underemployment, and high levels of migration, have all led to a position where the woman is the constant factor within the household. Men commonly seek social gratification among their male peers so leisure and friendship patterns reveal a strict separation between the sexes (Henry and Wilson, 1975:168). This segregation has led many writers to describe Caribbean households as matrifocal, i.e., 'mother focused'. But past usage suggests the concept is less than precise. Morris (1979), for example, has recently argued that 'matrifocality' is ill-defined and frequently ill-used. She stresses that the Caribbean male is dominant in both structural and cultural terms; suggesting that: 'The mother is the centre of domestic activity, holds the central affective position, (and) has considerable power over offspring and influence through the female members of the kin network. This does not preclude the man from making significant contributions to the running of the home, or from holding ultimate authority' (Morris, 1979:332). Indeed, Henry and Wilson (1975:165) conclude, after a wide survey of the literature, that: 'by and large (Caribbean women) play a subservient role to men particularly in economic and social areas'. This apparent contradiction between the idea of the 'absent male' and the relative powerlessness of women is partly resolved if the household is placed within a wider community and societal framework. Wilson (1973), for example, accepts that lower class Caribbean men are often peripheral to household and domestic organisation. But (he suggests) they retain ultimate authority through land ownership and inheritance, economic remittance (even when removed from the household), and the informal system of social contacts maintained outside the household. This prevalence of male extra-familial relations has considerable significance, for, as Wilson notes:

> Since males are peripheral to household and domestic organisation, the household is not a political unit; its integration into sections (of the community) is a function of legal relations between brothers and the rules of inheritance, but the sociability and solidarity of these sections depends upon the age and affinal 'structure' of relations between women. And this is complemented by the kinship ties that bind women (and certain men) closely to each other, but across community boundaries. Women living in the same community are not as closely related to each other as they are to women living in different communities (1973:40).

This distinctive pattern, which Wilson believes can be observed throughout the Caribbean, has important consequences for community cohesion. If men play little part in the social life of the immediate community organised on the basis of households and women, who are active participants, look beyond the residential community to kin residing elsewhere, then kinship *per se* does not bind them to their locality. 'From this point of view, then, we can understand why the residential community is rarely an active structured entity or even a sentimental one' (Wilson, 1973:145). The latter point is merely suggestive but worthy of further attention. At this point we can only reiterate that controversies abound in the family literature of the Caribbean, and thus the above outline has to be seen as a tentative basis for the purposes of comparison with the British situation.

Despite these debates, one can discern certain generally accepted features of West Indian family organisation. These include the flexibility of role relationships within the family unit; the general acceptance of legal marriage as a status prerequisite, the attainment of which is equated with a degree of personal and economic maturity; the relative importance of 'matrifocality'; the highly personalised and individualistic role expectations embedded in the overall framework of the family structure; the class and status divisions which are believed to characterise various family types; the existence of stereotypes both within and between classes which generate group images which may extend beyond the parameters of family and household organisation; and finally, the important point that these general features can be extended to the metropolitan society and the effects which this may have in the new urban industrial *milieu*.

Comparatively few indepth studies of West Indian groupings in Britain have been carried out so far. Most of the information currently available has been gleaned from 'community' studies which examine various groups within a given geographical location (see Introduction). This is a useful approach, but it often, by necessity, lacks depth by attempting an overall appraisal which often has to neglect some constituent parts of specific group structures.

Katrin Fitzherbert represents an exception. In her study of West Indian families in London (1967), a study connected with a project centred on child welfare, she underlines the flexibility and variability of family organisation both among West Indians in the Caribbean, and among West Indians and natives in Britain. There are, she notes, many differences between English and West Indian family styles although many of them are subtle and based on similar normative prescriptions. There are also considerable difficulties in comparing family life styles cross-culturally, particularly since it is extremely hazardous to try to allow for class and status differentials. Fitzherbert mentions a number of differences between English and West Indian family styles ranging from attitudes to family structure and instability, fostering and child care, and to education and child rearing practices. In addition, she notes differences in language, food and dress habits, religious practices, and attitudes to welfare services. Finally, there are differences in temperament and the degree of formality in friendship and sexual relations.

A number of factors influence variation in these patterns, including island of origin, class position, length and place of residence in Britain, age and sex differentials, etc. Similar differences exist, of course, among native British groupings. However, this is not to say that everything is relative. There appear to be important distinctions in family types, the classification of which would benefit from further research, particularly

106

into the everyday life of families over time. The interesting feature is to see how patterns of migration and settlement have influenced the structure of the West Indian lower class family as it has moved from a partly rural, peasant-based economy to an urban-industrial setting.

Robert Bell (1969) has compared lower class negro families in Philadelphia with a sample of West Indian families in Reading, Berkshire, and has drawn some interesting conclusions. He suggests, for example, that West Indian views on sex and marriage are moving towards an 'English' concept of monogamy. He also argues that, for both marriage partners, the West Indian family unit provides more meaningful roles than found in the family structure of a comparable American negro sample. Thus, the former incorporates roles which are more closely related to opportunities for the man to be a breadwinner and the wife expects certain rights because she, too, has economic independence. Bell concludes that West Indians generally have higher aspirations than American negroes. However, this is only an isolated study, the results of which have not been further researched. Therefore, one cannot draw concrete conclusions from it.

Sheila Patterson's (1965) profile of the Jamaican community in Brixton was also concerned with an analysis of family organisation and the changes produced by migration and settlement. The vast majority of migrants in her study were lower class, and consequently, family patterns tended towards 'maternal' and non-legal unions (1965:264). But this was an early study, carried out in the late 1950s and most of the West Indians who came under scrutiny appear to have lived in Britain for less than two years. It is unlikely, therefore, that such a period of settlement was long enough for many significant changes to have occurred. Nevertheless, Patterson notes a growing tendency towards a greater incidence of legal marriage. A trend also noted by Davison (1966) whose study, once again of Jamaicans, revealed that the proportion among his sample who were legally married had risen from 22 per cent to 52 per cent since migration to Britain. More recent research mentioned in Cross (1978:126), and a further study of Jamaicans in London (Foner, 1979), points towards an increase in legal marriage.

Further confirmation of this trend is provided by the present study, which is based on a sample that represents a greater range of Caribbean backgrounds than most of the studies discussed above. Therefore, it would seem that the trend towards legal marriage is general among West Indians in Britain and not simply confined to Jamaicans. As was noted earlier, the West Indian settlement in Easton has a relatively settled population. It is not surprising, therefore, that the majority of the 108 respondents in the sample had lived in the city for several years. In fact, 76 per cent had lived in Easton for at least eleven years and some had lived there for as much as sixteen or seventeen years. Out of a total of 68 residential units 59 were based on male-female unions. Of these, 47 involved legal marriages, and only 12, non-legal unions. There were, in addition, 4 women living with one or two children but without a male partner, and 4 men and 5 women who were living completely alone. Of the 47 married couples, 26 had married since arrival in Britain. In some cases, the couple had met for the first time in Britain, but in others, they had known one another in the West Indies. Often, one spouse came to Britain, became established, and then sent for his or her partner. Usually, this involved a husband sending for his wife or, if they were not yet married, an unmarried man sending for his girl friend or fiancee. For example, Mr. R., a Nevisian said:

> I came over in '61, and came to Easton because my brother was here though he's gone to Birmingham now. I stayed with him and his wife for a couple of years almost, had a good job at ... and getting some money together until I could get some rooms of my own. I sent over for my wife and she left the two kids with her sister until the year after when they came over and we was all together. We managed to scrape up enough for this house, so we're pretty settled now.

This was a fairly typical case, although in a number of instances a single man or woman had come to Britain with no relatives or friends and had married since his or her arrival. Thus, Mr. B., an Antiguan said:

> I worked for the railway in London when I arrived but I wasn't too keen on the conditions there. I shared a house with several other men and I had a friend in Easton who wrote and said the jobs and houses were easier here so I came up here and worked as a packer. I met my wife here soon after and we got married the year after and we've been here ever since in the same job, although I've moved house about three times.

Since several couples had maintained such unions since their arrival in Britain, many of the non-legal unions were apparently permanent. Moreover, the existence of a trend towards legal marriage was confirmed by informants from several islands who had lived in the area since the earliest arrival of West Indians in Easton. Discussions with local clergymen indicated that many West Indians had married soon after arrival in the city. They also suggested that legal marriage had become the norm for younger couples, particularly those who had been born or, more commonly, received most of their education in Britain. Unfortunately, owing to the lack of a statistically valid sampling frame, it cannot be stated that this trend towards legal marriage is representative of all West Indians in Easton (and certainly not in Britain) but it does seem to indicate a tendency in that direction among West Indians since their arrival in this country.

It is significant to recall in this connection that the sample was drawn mainly from West Indians with lower class origins in their respective islands. Comparatively few respondents could be placed, using occupational indices, within the middle classes. This raises the interesting possibility that settlement in Britain, at least in the urban area which forms the subject of this study, is leading the class differences in family patterns which exist in the West Indies to disappear. It may simply be the case that the migrant lower class is undergoing a process of internal differentiation as far as patterns of marriage and family organisation are concerned. Alternatively, what we may be witnessing is an upwardly mobile working class—upwardly mobile, that is to say, relative to the working classes in their islands of origin—and possibly even the incipient emergence of a migrant lower middle class.

Several factors are significant in such a process. The major one is the rise in economic status experienced by many West Indian individuals in Easton. The predominance of non-legal unions amongst the lower class in the West Indies was explained earlier by the existence of values in terms of which economic maturity is often a necessary precondition for entry into legal marriage. Thus, with a rise in earnings and greater material stability, (the majority of our sample claimed that they were 'better-off' or 'much better-off' in money terms in Britain), many West Indians see themselves as having risen in social status. This has meant that many older West Indians, who previously adhered to a non-legal union, now consider themselves to be in a position legally to marry, whilst many younger West Indians are in an economic position which enables them to enter a legal union immediately, or at least to change from a non-legal to a legal union at a much earlier age than their parents had done.

Among the other factors which have played a part in promoting the tendency towards legal marriage and in transforming some unstable unions into stable ones, the increasing financial independence experienced by many West Indian women in Britain is important. However, this trend towards greater financial independence on the part of West Indian women is not without its strains and stresses. The comments offered by Morris Freilich and Lewis Coser on the 'gratificatory system' (that is to say the system of negative and positive sanctions) within the Caribbean mating pattern are appropriate here:

> In view of their minimal rewards, women will gladly turn to
> alternatives if such should present themselves. They will have
> much to gain from modernisation which would offer them
> some means of reducing their dependency on their sexual
> partners. When forces of industrialisation or urbanisation

begin seriously to impinge on the system, the male-female relationship will emerge as one of the weakest links in the structure. Here, as elsewhere, exploitative relationships will be resisted, and strains towards complete reciprocity will emerge in full force once traditional impediments to equalisation have begun to crumble . (1972:20)

There is every sign that these 'traditional impediments' are crumbling (Foner, 1979:54) and that the process of migration from the Caribbean to Britain is akin to the processes of modernisation in so far as they are occurring within particular West Indian societies themselves (Cross, 1979:85).

The isolation of West Indian family units in Britain also promotes stability as the segregation of conjugal roles common to the West Indies may be broken down. Patterns of work, a lack of recreational outlets and a harsh social existence force many West Indian men to spend more of their time in the household with their wives than would be the case in the Caribbean. However, these changes in family relationships will depend very largely on the size of the local West Indian population and, more specifically, on the presence or otherwise of friends and kinfolk within a particular island grouping. In many ways the social community of West Indian village life, and the co-operative efforts of matrilineal kin, have been undermined in the sombre urban locations of Britain. Many West Indians, particularly the women, constantly reiterated the fact that the lively, outdoor and warm environment of their home town or village had changed to the indoor life of, at best, a warm fire, a few friends, and the television. At worst, it was a withdrawn, socially isolated existence amongst damp walls, paraffin stoves and overcrowded rooms.

Other influences in this trend have been the ratio of West Indian women to men in Britain, which tends to favour women rather more than is the case in the West Indies. This reduction in competition for males, reinforced by the fact that the availability of white women re-dresses the balance only marginally—there are strong taboos in Britain on interracial sexual unions—has helped family units to stabilise even further. More direct social pressures in British situations have also played an important part in producing this trend towards a greater proportion of legal marriages among West Indians. Local mores condemn non-legal unions far more strongly than their counterparts in the West Indies. Whilst, as has been shown, legal unions may be normatively aspired to in the West Indies, the extent of non-legal unions belies the existence of severe constraints in that direction. Moreover, contact between the middle and lower classes in the West Indies is not of a degree or type to permit effective censure. In any case, the retention, at least among middle class men, of forms of permissiveness akin to that which exists among the lower classes serves to dissipate even further social control of lower class sexual patterns from that source.

In Britain, however, West Indians are faced with the dominant value system of the host society which largely condemns non-legal unions. Even without a high degree of social contact between West Indians and local whites (a tendency firmly indicated in our survey) contacts with certain local institutions, such as schools, churches and welfare agencies, as well as the influence of the media, provide indirect social control in this area. Patterson has suggested, for example, that:

> Another powerful incentive may be provided when the migrant's children are sufficiently old to compare their own and their schoolmates family circumstances, and to exert pressure on their parents or parent to conform to local patterns. (1965:268)

All these factors, in isolation or combined, are likely to increase the proportion of legal marriages among West Indians in Britain. However, it should be noted that many West Indians in Easton were legally married before arrival in Britain. Although very few respondents could be clearly defined as middle class, many of them were upwardly mobile, skilled workmen and hence more likely to be in a legal union.

Patterson, (1965), whilst mentioning many of the points previously discussed in relation to factors producing more stable unions, also points out that certain of these factors could serve to fragment family units. Similarly, Sheila Allen (1971:83) has argued that whilst the urban location of West Indians in Western industrialised societies such as Britain tends to provide constraining influences towards legal unions, the nature of this urban existence means a slackening of internal social controls over certain types of non-legal union, controls which would be exercised in the communal closeness of a village or small town setting in the Caribbean.

It is important to stress once again that whilst forms of non-legal union are accepted among the lower classes in the Caribbean, this does not indicate an anarchic situation where 'promiscuity' and 'immorality' are the norm. Indeed, the values attached to non-legal unions by West Indians in the Caribbean are practically identical to those equated with legal unions. The urban situation in Britain places the West Indian in a social context which is confused and hence the indigenous family and kinship structures of the Caribbean are 'pushed and pulled' by their new cultural and social environment, often with paradoxical results. Thus, Sheila Allen perceives that family and kinship patterns among West Indian communities in Britain display:

> Two contradictory trends of greater degrees of legal marriage but less control over non-legal unions existing together and having to be seen in relation to a multiplicity of pressures

and counterpressures exerted on West Indian men and women in the context of British society. (1971:83)

The importance of these 'contradictory trends' for West Indian political organisation will be discussed later in this chapter. At this point, it should be noted that the greater economic 'stability' of West Indians in Britain compared with their situation in the Caribbean, appears to have influenced a trend towards legal marriage, but this economic improvement may also have the reverse effect and enable individuals, notably West Indian women, to break a legal, or perhaps more commonly, non-legal, stable unit and exist on their own resources.

We have seen that many West Indian women in Easton have full-time jobs (see Chapter 3). In the majority of cases, this is a necessity brought about by the perceived desire to supplement the income of the male partner in the family unit. The important thing to note in this connection is that, even the remuneration of lowly paid manual or unskilled work gives many West Indian women a degree of financial independence which they did not enjoy in their home island. The consequent lessening of financial dependence on men has enabled some West Indian women to sever 'marital' relationships with sometimes long-standing male partners. The availability of social security benefits in Britain has also contributed to this situation. There were some West Indian women in Easton, who voluntarily or involuntarily, were bringing up a family without a male partner. In many cases, this was because the women had been left to fend for themselves by a common-law partner, but several women had established independent households since arriving in Britain, breaking long-standing legal or more often common-law partnerships in order to do so. Nevertheless, this eventuality was relatively untypical in what has been shown to be a largely stable West Indian settlement.

The vast majority of formal associations established by West Indians in Easton, are dominated by men. Nevertheless, many West Indian women are influential in the informal organisation of their communities. For example, some West Indians have established rotating credit associations in their respective island communities. These are usually based on family and kinship networks and many of the 'bankers' are women. Many West Indians maintained that these financial associations are less prevalent in Britain than in the home island because of the greater availability of alternative financial organisations in this country. Consequently, they are able to use the economic outlets for saving or borrowing money provided by the host society or even, in some cases, those developed by the local South Asian communities.

However, rotating credit associations are fairly common, particularly among those West Indian communities which originated from the smaller islands. Several associations of this type were discovered, for example, in the Barbudan, Montserration and Antiguan communities. In most cases, these were based on two or three families who were closely related in kinship terms. It was difficult to ascertain why so many of the bankers in these associations were women, but many West Indian respondents argued that it was because the women in the household could be trusted and could therefore perform this kind of role which depended on a high degree of mutual trust among members. It has certainly been argued that the female is very influential in West Indian households generally. Therefore, the performance of 'banker' roles in these credit associations may be an illustration of her importance. Certainly it gives some West Indian women a degree of power which, due to their exclusion from formal leadership positions, is denied them within the wider community.

In addition to their participation in credit associations, some West Indian women were widely known for their provision of certain services for their communities. For example, one of the leading members of the BWIC owned a hairdressing salon which acted as a focal point for informal discussion among West Indians in Easton. Similarly, some women were well-known in the city for arranging weddings and Christenings for West Indians. These women would make wedding cakes and arrange for parties in the bride's parents' home after the marriage service. Other women ran dressmaking businesses in their spare time. These services were highly informal and often based on friendship or kinship relationships rather than impersonal financial links. They were invariably restricted to relationships between West Indian women, but often, homes where the woman provided an important service for her community or family network, served as common meeting places for both sexes. Furthermore, a few West Indian women in Easton who were 'bankers' in rotating credit associations or who were relied upon for 'social' occasions were highly influential within their respective island communities. Mrs A or Miss B was looked upon as an important individual and was often consulted on activities in the community which were not necessarily connected with her primary function as a provider of a particular specialised service. These women, in common with some of the men who were more formally recognised as 'leaders', for example, of a voluntary association established by an island community, were used as counsellors by other West Indians who required advice or information. The latter ranged from information about the whereabouts of a friend or relative, advice about arranging a wedding and so forth, to the passing on of gossip. Therefore, in a very restricted sense these women acted as 'information brokers' in their respective island communities, and by fulfilling this role they acquired a degree of authority within their community or family network which was denied them in more formal political roles within West Indian voluntary associations in the city.

However, it is important to note that these informal networks within West Indian communities were very restricted. Only an extremely small number of West Indian women were 'known' in their communities for the provision of some of the services which have been briefly described above. Similarly, comparatively few West Indians belong to credit associations. West Indian family and kinship networks, particularly in small island communities where informal relationships are highly intimate and still based upon social links maintained from the home island, must be seen as associations which perform important functions for their members and in some cases for the wider community. In addition to those functions which Rex (1973:15) has assigned to 'primary communities', these networks also perform certain functions which are more common to specialised voluntary associations. That is to say, in addition to the provision of such needs as are required by family and household members who are bound together by intimate personal ties, the informal friendship and kinship networks within West Indian communities also provide some of the specialised services required by the latter, and in addition, act as supportive agencies in conjunction with those voluntary associations established by West Indians in Easton. Finally, family and kinship networks enable certain individuals, in particular West Indian women, to participate in and occupy power positions of an informal kind within their respective island communities and possibly throughout the West Indian settlement in the city.

But, West Indian family and household networks do not embrace the multi-functional role common to the joint family systems of Indians and Pakistanis. South Asian communities are characterised by the existence of kinship systems which differ markedly from West Indian patterns of family and household organisation (Lyon, 1973). A comparative appraisal of South Asian and West Indian family and kinship patterns in this country would be a complex but rewarding exercise. At this juncture, following on from our earlier discussion of the limited political significance of the Caribbean household, it seems reasonable to suggest that West Indian family organisation lacks the system of mutual obligations which typifies the family in South Asian minorities (Khan, 1979; Ballard and Ballard, 1977). Within the latter, it is impossible to separate political and economic relationships from religious and kinship ties because they mutually interrelate with one another. The social network of a South Asian community consists of a number of multiple relationships in which economic goals are influenced by familial obligations. These obligations rest on the maintenance of authority relationships which stem from the home society and which are reproduced in Britain. This retention of indigenous familial obligations offers greater potential (than the more individualistic West Indian family structure) for communal

114

self-help and for the creation of institutions separate from those offered by the host society. This is demonstrated in the degree of financial interdependence within and among South Asian communities which exists on a far more sophisticated level than the limited West Indian credit associations.

The difference between West Indian and Asian family organisation primarily rests on the fact that the traditional joint family common to South Asian communities in Britain embraces a system of mutual interdependencies which typifies a form of family organisation which has escaped the peculiar stresses of slavery and consequent forms of oppression suffered by West Indian 'families' in recent centuries. Above all, Asian family organisation reflects the influence of tradition, and of a religious and political base which includes a common set of values unblemished by problems of ambivalence and inconsistency. The West Indian is unable to maintain an ethnically separate identity in the British situation without severe difficulties because, historically, there is no strict separation between the Western and non-Western features of his or her life situation. That is to say, there is a built-in ambiguity in the latter, reinforced by the co-existence of conflicting value systems which were maintained in the West Indies and which have now been transposed to the British migrant situation. Many Asians can maintain a separate identity in Britain because their traditional ties depend, not upon an artificially created colonial amalgam, but upon ancient norms and prescriptions which reach back into a cultural heritage established long before the British entered the Indian sub-continent. Historical and cultural differences such as these, in conjunction with a host of other social factors, produce a common Asian household pattern that leans towards a degree of collectivism and mutual interdependence which is often absent in the more individualistic West Indian family units. This brings us to the question of the links between family organisation and political association among West Indians in Easton. Two main sets of questions are raised in this connection: firstly, the significance of patterns of family organisation, both in the Caribbean and in Britain, for the formation of political associations by West Indians; and secondly, the significance of these patterns in producing individuals capable of adopting active roles either in forming or maintaining such associations.

The status attached to male and female roles is generally important when examining the relationship between 'leadership' within the family or household unit and activism in 'external', that is non-familial, associations. There is a close connection between the availability of leadership roles within the family, the learning processes which reinforce them in that context, and the possibility of transferring these roles to external associations in which such leadership roles may be reproduced. Many studies have questioned the availability of such roles to male partners within lower-class West Indian households (Smith, 1960:73). This leads us into the dangerous waters of male 'marginality' and 'instability' which were questioned earlier. Previously we noted the existence of parallel patterns of the ultimate legal and economic authority of the male *within* the household, and a common seeking of social status in 'friending' relationships with other women, and, above all, within male peer groups *outside* the family unit (Wilson, 1973). Thus, the prestige sought by many lower class men is often measured in social contexts peripheral to authority relations within the household.

In Britain, the admittedly fragmentary, evidence suggests that many West Indian men still seek a 'reputation' on the basis of sexual exploitation (Pryce, 1979) and their acceptance in an exclusively male camaraderie. However, considerable numbers of males have legally married and seek 'respect' in Britain. This aspiration, together with different work patterns and the possibilities of a reduced network of friends in the metropolitan society, makes the household far more central in their everyday lives. It might be assumed that this would strengthen the authority of West Indian men but this ignores the equally important changes in the status of West Indian women previously discussed. Foner (1979:78), in her recent study of Jamaicans, shows how the greater economic independence of women, in combination with their loss of aid from kin in the British setting, encourages them (often successfully) to make greater demands on their menfolk. The West Indian male in Britain tends to be caught between the mores which prevail within his own island grouping, the possibly contradictory norms surrounding the West Indian settlement as a whole—which may or may not be consistent with his own class and status position—and finally the forms of social control which emanate from the 'host community'. The latter, of course, may well be shaped by stereotypical 'labels' rather than by direct interaction between the different ethnic groups.

As Fitzherbert notes: 'The (West Indian) man in Britain has less flexibility ... he can be the 'family man' or the 'kickster' having a good time (but it is) very difficult to combine the roles' (1967:27). The lower-class female obviously faces the common deprivations of colour and class in Britain, but her greater financial independence further strengthens her role as mother within the household; a position which is positively sanctioned both within and outside her own community.

Not surprisingly, status conflict between West Indian men and women is common and it exercises an important influence on participation in associations outside the family unit. Paul Pollard, for example, in a recent study of the relationships between Jamaicans and Trinidadians in North London, observed that:

A man is made to look weak in front of a woman, for example, if both he and his wife are members of the same voluntary association, but the wife occupies the position of vice-chairman while his own position is that of general member. For this reason, and others, spouses rarely took up membership in the same organisations in the borough. (1972:377)

This is only one example of the separation of the sexes which still tends to be common in West Indian families, although the British settting promotes less segregation than in the Caribbean (Foner, 1979). Nevertheless, few first generation husbands and wives (in Easton), regularly attend recreational events together. The men still prefer to go to the pub, dances or a sports event in small groups leaving their wives at home or to visit other wives in the locality. In addition, division of labour in the home appears to be strict with many West Indian men expressing the view that most tasks within the home are 'womens' work. Whilst these observations are only relatively superficial they suggest a continuity between British and Caribbean patterns within the new boundaries set by metropolitan work conditions and changing marriage patterns.

Some younger West Indian couples who were newly married and more importantly, born in this country, appeared to be breaking away from these traditions. The husband would assist his wife with the housework and stay at home most evenings. This was in sharp contrast to many first generation West Indian homes where the husband was out every evening, perhaps only taking his wife with him at the weekend. Other young married men, however, continued the 'traditional' pattern and went around in small male peer groups.

This distinction between male and female roles tends to be influential in local West Indian voluntary associations in a number of ways. It prevented the amalgamation of the JWA and BWIC, for example, because of the suspicion which had arisen between the Jamaican men and the women who ran the British-West Indian Club. The JWA only co-operated with the BWIC when the latter was solely concerned with catering for 'social functions' (see Chapter 4). Women were encouraged to perform these kinds of duties but were dissuaded from taking any active part in the more 'serious' (as defined by West Indian men) business of policy making. Thus, many West Indian women who were better educated and more used than their male counterparts to adopting authoritative positions within the family, were denied access to most formal 'leadership positions' within the West Indian settlement.

The psychological and sociological implications of the relationship between parental roles in West Indian families and, in turn, the links between these roles and political activism require considerably more study and a greater depth of analysis than can be attempted here. Care is required in examining the problems of personality formation, socialisation patterns and their relationships to particular family structures or the parental roles within those structures.[3] Similarly, the importance of 'male marginality' and its links with leadership potential (or the lack of it) within the West Indian family, is an extremely delicate issue.

Although the personality level is undoubtedly important in measuring the relationships between family structure and individual responses to the political process, the complexity and in many ways ill-defined nature of the concepts used to define 'personality', preclude one from making more concrete statements in this context. Thankfully, we are on firmer ground when examining the overall social structural significance of West Indian family patterns for West Indian political organisation.

We observed earlier that the legal/non-legal dichotomy of West Indian family types broadly follows class lines in the Caribbean. Furthermore, the degree of family 'stability', including the tendency towards patriarchal leadership roles, varies directly with social class position. Consequently in common with the norm in the majority of Western industrialised societies, most political leadership roles in the Caribbean are dominated by middle and upper class individuals. Of course, family situation is only one of a number of factors which affect this situation. Economic stability, availability of time, educational attainment and so forth are all influential in this respect. However, at present we are primarily concerned with those features of West Indian family organisation which influence the degree of West Indian participation in associations and organisations, particularly of a political nature, which are external to the family unit.

Given the fact that the majority of West Indians in Britain are working class, one would not, perhaps, expect among them a high level of participation in political and other forms of voluntary association. However, their level of activity is low relative to that of other minority groups (and the indigenous white working class, although this is problematic). As we have seen, the greater economic security of West Indians in this country and the associated trend towards legal marriage means that many see themselves as upwardly mobile relative to the positions they held in their home islands. It may even be the case that a small proportion see themselves as becoming middle class. The increase of stable family units certainly seems to point in at least the former direction. Hence, the continued absence of participation is puzzling, for one might expect an increase in the number of higher status family units to be coupled with a higher level of political participation.

A number of factors account for the failure of the expected trend towards higher levels of political participation to occur. Firstly, although many West Indians have stabilised their position, they may still be affected by forms of socialisation and childhood insecurity which stem from their earlier low-class status. This may mean that personality difficulties are reproduced in the higher status position, or it may simply denote that a disinclination for activism is only a short-term phenomenon which will disappear with the increasing stability of the family unit. However, a number of factors negate this kind of reasoning.

If one examines closely those upwardly mobile West Indians in Britain who have adopted legal marriage, this, together with increased economic security, is the only feature which distinguishes them from West Indians who still retain non-legal forms of family organisation. Consequently many upwardly mobile families are unable to confirm their 'higher' status (and/or class) position by drawing on those ascriptive attributes, for example, phenotypical characteristics which are used in the Caribbean to indicate higher or lower class positions. Moreover, since most upwardly mobile West Indian families in Easton retain occupations, levels of educational attainment, modes of speech and dress, etc., which are indicative of lower class status, they do not comply, in achieved terms, with all the status requirements which are commonly attached to higher class positions in the Caribbean.

Furthermore, whereas in West Indian societies a high class position is often underpinned by acknowledgement from other strata, the status of upwardly mobile West Indians in Britain is undermined by the native population, who tend to subsume all West Indians under the negative 'coloured immigrant' label. Therefore, those West Indian families which raise their status relative to their position in their home island, may not do so in the eyes of other West Indians in Britain, not only because their position is not reinforced by those achieved concomitants of high status recognised in the Caribbean, but also because members of the host society fail to acknowledge this 'rise' in status.

A further feature of the wider society's influence is the fact that political activity on the part of upwardly mobile individuals is sometimes regarded, by the individuals themselves, as potentially damaging to their own or their family's 'respectability'. The aspiration towards high status (for example, a middle class position) among West Indians tends to take the form of aspirations towards European values and normative expectations. Consequently, even with a larger proportion of West Indians within legal family units, this may well negate rather than increase the likelihood of political activity, simply because the possibility of provoking negative sanctions from members of the host community is heightened by overt actions which may be interpreted (by majority members) as hostile.

Therefore, we can see that those upwardly mobile West Indians who do adopt activist roles, or possibly even contemplate such actions, are faced with severe problems of status ambiguity, both with regard to their position in West Indian groupings and with respect to their standing in the wider setting. Conversely, of course, the upwardly mobile may reject or ignore the problem of 'white acceptance' and thus increase their potential for political activism. But this potential may still be partially negated by the status distinctions within the West Indian settlement described above.

In addition, consideration must be given to the parallel existence in Britain of non-legal, fragmented West Indian household units which, because of the diffuse urban situation, are subject to a lower degree of social control from other West Indians. The presence of types of family organisation that are perceived, by members of the host community, as deviating from the normative expectations of family life current in Britain, may affect the general level of political participation among West Indians. The existence of 'deviant' family forms helps to produce or sustain negative images among the native population and these stereotypes, in turn, influence the degree of constraint under which all West Indians in Britain are forced to live.

Labels of 'promiscuity' and 'immorality' may be attached to West Indians generally because of stereotypes built on an inadequate knowledge of unfamiliar household types, derived from the media or local gossip channels. These images of deviancy cancel out, or indeed, completely transfigure the 'respectable image' sought by the majority of West Indians. Such attempts are ironically self-defeating since respectability is demonstrated by covert actions, for example, avoiding house parties and 'keeping oneself to oneself'. Such actions, because of the low degree of informal interaction between West Indians and other community members, are not readily apparent to the latter.

It is important to stress that the relation of family and social organisation to political activity is not simply a mechanical process whereby different forms of organisation within a 'family' structure give rise to a given potential for political activism. Nor is it merely a question of looking at the cultural background of a minority migrant group and then relating its social and cultural characteristics to those of the majority. If the latter perspective is adopted one becomes involved in the 'problems' of acculteration, assimilation and integration with their myriad connotations of mechanical lines of similarity and difference between host and migrant groups. What has to be considered is how contemporary minority/majority contact situations are related to the historical process of interaction between the groups involved, the emergent patterns of interdependence and of super- and subordination between them, and the belief systems which help to maintain this pattern.

The arrival of West Indians in Britain in significant numbers cannot be seen simply as a migrant, rural-based group settling in an urbanised, industrial setting with concrete cultural differences. The patterns of settlement and re-settlement of West Indians in Britain are merely one phase in the patterns of migration which have taken West Indians to the United States, Canada, Central America and now to Europe (Lewis,

1969). Settlement in Britain has re-emphasised the lines of white/black domination perceived in the Caribbean. The ambivalence produced by the conflictual nature of the relationships between white and non-white are an extension of colonial/historical relationships, not merely a 'new stage of development' in Britain set in motion by an incoming migrant group. The settlement of West Indians in Britain has produced different forms of relationships both within and between various groupings in the metropolitan society and it will inevitably produce different beliefs and sentiments which will in turn influence the forms of relationship and the patterns of modification which they undergo.

Flexibility in social relationships can be perceived as beneficial in adjusting to new situations and relationships and hence the West Indian 'family structure', in its various forms, may appear convenient for such a process. However, this is to forget that those historical contingencies which produced and changed this family structure were related to forms of subordination which were expressed in and through colonial patterns of domination. West Indians in Britain now find themselves in a situation where patterns of relationships and social situations may have changed, but for many, if not all, those patterns of domination associated with colonialism still remain and consequently the forms of subordination which have negated political expression until very recently are being reproduced in the metropolitan society. This reproduction introduces ambiguity and ambivalence within and between individuals and groups and into their perception of their situation to such an extent that it becomes extremely difficult for stable and on-going forms of political expression to be maintained. Nevertheless, changes can be discerned within West Indian communities in Britain which suggest a move towards consolidation and permanence in social relationships, changes which are reflected in the nature of West Indian family and social organisation in Easton and which point towards the possibility of political organisation occurring in the future. But the eventual outcome of these changes will be contingent upon changes in power relationships and in the degree of access to resources which the host society allows or, more likely, is forced to give up.

Patterns of West Indian family and social organisation not only influence forms of economic and political activity but also tend to promote certain beliefs and expectations within and between coloured minorities and the majority society. Such beliefs in their turn, influence relations of power and domination generally. These patterns of family and social organisation should be perceived, therefore, as one important feature in any consideration of the social relationships within West Indian communities, in the relationships between such groupings, and, finally, in those between the West Indian settlement and the wider community in Easton. This whole network of relationships is framed within the historical context of the on-going forms of subordination and superordination which initially shaped West Indian family patterns and social relations in the Caribbean. They now influence the existence of West Indian family and household units in Britain.

Having examined some of the relationships between West Indian family organisation and West Indian participation in other forms of association, the following chapter will explore, in similar fashion, the links between West Indian religious associations and politicisation.

Notes

1   For overviews of an extensive literature see Smith (1960), Lowenthal (1972) and Henry and Wilson (1975).
2   For a useful summary of competing perspectives on, for example, the survival (or otherwise) of African culture, see Morris (1979).
3   The relations between personality, culture and political behaviour are explored in Hsu (1966) and Mussen and Wysznski (1952).

6   Religion: West Indian participation

The majority of studies of West Indians in Britain have remarked upon the fact that Caribbean migrants tend not to form, join or become deeply committed to formal associations (see Introduction). Religious worship is the only exception to this general pattern. In this area of social life the levels of membership, participation and commitment are high. This is especially the case in the West Indies but, with one or two important modifications, the overall Caribbean pattern has been at least partly transplanted to the British setting. The following tables 6.1 and 6.2 provide a comparison between patterns of religious association in the home island and Easton:

Table 6.1

Religious affiliations of West Indian respondents

Denomination/Sect[1]	Caribbean			Britain (Easton)		
	Male	Female	Total %	Male	Female	Total %
Anglican	27	31	58 (53.7)	16	23	39 (36.1)
Methodist	6	6	12 (11.1)	3	2	5 (4.6)
Seventh Day Adventist	8	6	14 (12.9)	3	4	7 (6.5)
Pentecostal	2	6	8 (7.4)	3	13	16 (14.8)
Roman Catholic	3	3	6 (5.6)	0	1	1 (0.9)
Baptist	2	2	4 (3.7)	1	1	2 (1.9)
Other	3	1	4 (3.7)	0		(0.0)
No affiliation	1	1	2 (1.9)	26	12	38 (35.2)
			n = 108			n = 108

Table 6.2

Rates of attendance at religious gatherings

	Caribbean			Britain (Easton)		
	Male	Female	Total %	Male	Female	Total %
Every week	31	32	**63 (58.3)**	9	14	23 (21.3)
At least once a month	16	22	38 (35.1)	6	20	26 (24.1)
Less than once a month	5	2	7 (6.5)	40	19	59 (54.6)
			n = 108			n = 108

The above tables demonstrate that religious commitment, both in terms of membership and attendance rates, was extremely high among our sample prior to migration. These findings lend support to the view that: 'Of all forms of secondary association in the Caribbean, religious

123

institutions are numerically the most important' (Cross, 1979:93). Of course, patterns of religious participation and belief are not uniform throughout the West Indies. There is, as one would expect, considerable variation along class lines. The upper and middle classes belong mainly to the Anglican and Catholic churches. The lower classes, although Christian in a formal sense, not only belong to a number of the major denominations but also participate in sectarian forms of worship which often contain vestigial elements of magic and myth which originated either in the days of slavery or in Africa. As David Lowenthal remarks:

> Most working-class Creoles are no less formally Christian than the elite and middle class, but the institutional structures, systems of belief, and emotional significance of religious faith differ profoundly. Caribbean peasantries and proletariats combine traditional, evangelical, and fundamentalist forms of Christianity with revivalism and spiritualism. (1972:114)

Patterns of religious belief and practice in the West Indies are complicated even further by the existence of differences between the islands. These have arisen, by and large, because of their different colonial histories. Catholicism predominates in islands which were originally settled by the French and Spanish. This is the case even when such islands later came under British rule. Dominica and St Lucia are examples of islands in the British West Indies in which Catholicism is the dominant religion because they had previously been French or Spanish possessions. Islands, such as Barbados, which have been under British rule throughout all or most of their colonial history are largely Anglican.

West Indian societies are also notable for the multiplicity of churches and sects they contain. After emancipation, the Caribbean was subjected to a period of vigorous missionary activity. In the words of Sheila Allen:

> The intense missionary activity which began in the post-Emancipation period led to a multiplicity of Christian sects; Christian Science, Seventh Day Adventists, Society of Friends, Jehovah's Witnesses, as well as the splitting of the more conventional church into Baptists, Methodists, Congregationalists, and the like. (1971:99)

Nonconformism spread throughout the working classes, fostering beliefs which tended to promote material acquisition and individualism, as well as conferring respect on its adherents (Cross, 1979:97). In addition to the above, there exist, particularly in the more rural areas of the larger islands, certain cults and sects whose roots can be traced back to the shores of Africa. Among the most notable are the Shango cults in Trinidad and the Revivalist and Pocomanian movements in Jamaica. The membership of these cults is drawn mainly, but not exclusively, from the lower classes. The latter seek some solace from poverty in magic and mysticism, but, as Madeline Kerr has written: 'The middle and the rising middle classes will deny hotly that magic plays any part in their lives, yet in cases of breakdown, many people will revert to magical practices and healing' (Lowenthal, 1972:117).

It is difficult for West Indians in the Caribbean to avoid the social mores which dictate participation in some form of worship. Church membership is obligatory for upper and middle class West Indians because it is seen as an affirmation of their class and status position. Within the lower classes, religious worship is also expected, whether in formal church attendance or participation in sectarian or cultist activity.

In the British context the migration process has, not unexpectedly, transformed certain aspects of West Indian social organisation, including the nature of religious participation.

The Lowdale area, where most West Indians in Easton reside, contains a variety of churches and sects. There are four Anglican, two Roman Catholic, a Baptist and a Methodist church within its boundaries. In addition to these churches, there are several other religious associations in or adjacent to Lowdale. These include local branches of the Seventh Day Adventists, Jehovah's Witnesses, a Pentecostal and an Evangelical church. The proportion of West Indian members in particular congregations varied with individual places of worship, ranging from the few West Indians in most Anglican congregations to the exclusively West Indian memberships of the Pentecostal and Evangelical churches.

Tables 6.1 and 6.2 above, show that 106 respondents (98 per cent) reported some form of religious affiliation in the Caribbean compared with the 70 (65 per cent) in Easton. The figures on rates of church attendance are even more revealing. Whereas fewer than 7 per cent of the sample claimed to have attended a religious gathering less than once a month in their home island, the corresponding figure had risen to 55 per cent in Britain. Thus, consequent upon migration, a marked fall in both church membership and rates of attendance at religious gatherings had occurred. Therefore, the patterns of worship discernible among West Indians in Easton are consistent with those noted by other studies of West Indian settlement elsewhere in Britain.[2]

It is interesting to note that the drop, both in levels of membership and rates of attendance, was lower for women than for men. In the Caribbean, the men and women in the sample were approximately equal in both of these respects. In Easton, however, 26 out of a total of 52 male respondents claimed that they were no longer members of a religious association, whilst 44 of the female members of the sample claimed that they still belonged to a church. Similarly, 34 West Indian women claimed that they attended their place of worship at least once a month, whilst only 15 men made such a claim.

The rise in West Indian membership of Pentecostal churches in Easton compared with the membership level claimed in the Caribbean, is also significant. The number claiming to belong to this type of religious organisation in the city was double the number making such a claim with respect to their period of residence in the West Indies. The importance of the growth of West Indian Pentecostalism will be discussed in some detail later in the chapter.

Religious participation is such a widely accepted and expected form of activity in the Caribbean, that it was to be expected that most West Indian migrants would, on arrival in Britain, seek to join a church in their new area of settlement. However, many West Indians have met with mixed receptions in British churches ranging from condescending acceptance to outright rejection (Hill, 1963). Furthermore, even if West Indians did not meet or overcome these affronteries, they often left local congregations because of what are, to them, the dull and lifeless forms of worship in most churches in Britain. In the West Indies, services, including many within the major denominations, tend to be more spontaneous and livelier than their counterparts in the host society.

A number of factors such as these have combined to lead many West Indians in Britain to change their patterns of religious affiliation and church attendance. They have either turned to alternative forms of religious expression, for example, Pentecostalism, or have adopted the pattern of non-attendance common to the majority of members of the host society. Whether or not they maintained religious affiliations, many members of the West Indian population in Easton disapproved of the low level of church going in the white community, expressing their dismay or disgust at the seemingly 'un-Christian' trend towards secularisation. The following comment by a Nevisian respondent was typical of many West Indians in the area: 'I wish that people realised that there is a God ... that more people would go to church and get love in their heart'. Similar sentiments were expressed by an Antiguan: 'People here don't go to or worship in the church like in the West Indies'. And a Jamaican woman said: 'In Jamaica everyone used to go to church sometimes two or three times on a Sunday. Here (that is to say in Easton) they find all things to do except worship the Lord. I fear for my children that they will go the same way'.

These views underline the fact that many West Indians were surprised to see their traditional white rulers, who so firmly avowed the need for Christian principles in their teachings in the West Indies, seemingly ignoring them in Britain. Even more inexplicable to them was the rejection or avoidance from white churchgoers which many West Indians encountered in local churches. Apparently church fellowship halted at the boundaries of skin colour in the mother country. Thus, many respondents recounted how they had joined a congregation in Easton but had soon left because of the 'reception' which they received from white parishioners. Often the condescending manner with which West Indians were picked out as our 'black brothers' by members of the clergy or congregation annoyed them more than when local whites refused to sit in the same pew in church. A Barbadian who had been an active member of his church in the West Indies, described the latter reaction when he recounted how:

> When I first came to Easton we went up to St ... in our first few weeks. We had been told not to expect opening arms from my cousin who was here but I suppose it was a matter of pride and not really believing. I find it difficult to describe what it was like ... the service seemed to take days and my wife was in tears when we came away. It was like you were being stripped naked by all those eyes and some of them were not just curious but really disliking us there. I went for a few weeks and some of the people were very nice but it was like being in the zoo with all that staring, you just got too uncomfortable to stay.

There was no discernible pattern of acceptance or avoidance among the different denominations in and around Lowdale. In some Anglican churches, a small number of West Indians, noticeably better off than many of their fellows, were accepted within their respective congregations. These West Indians were middle or upwardly mobile working class and this factor presumably compensated partly for their colour.

In other local churches, the attitude of the minister towards the migrants was very influential. One Anglican minister, in particular, had made deliberate attempts to encourage West Indians into his church. In the early 1950s, when West Indians began to settle in Lowdale in not inconsiderable numbers, several Caribbean migrants came to his church, St John's. The initial reaction from the white congregation was ambivalent, a mixture of curiosity and hostility. However, during this early period when only a few West Indians joined the congregation, most of the white parishioners continued to attend services. When the numbers of West Indians increased there was a virtual exodus of white members which the Minister described as 'very disconcerting'! Nevertheless, despite his dwindling congregation, he continued his 'open door' policy towards the West Indians in his parish. By 1960, very few white members remained in the congregation but the numbers of West Indians who regularly attended St John's continued to rise. This trend persisted until the late 1960s when the church had gained a reputation in Lowdale as a 'black church'. A small number of whites continued to attend but the congregation was predominantly West Indian. However, in recent years, the numbers attending St John's have declined quite significantly, leaving only those West Indians whom the Minister described as 'hardened' in their religious convictions. The Minister attributed the decline in church attendance to the fact that many West Indians, particularly younger, second generation West Indians, were adopting the secular habits of the majority of the local white community.

The experience of West Indian attendance at St John's indicates that some caution is required in approaching an explanation of West Indian patterns of religious association. If nothing else, it points towards the dangers of attributing these falling levels of membership and rates of church attendance among West Indians solely to rejection by the host community.

Social changes common to West Indian communities in Britain, have also played an influential part. Thus, forms of social control which constrain West Indians in the Caribbean to engage in certain types of social participation, including church attendance, have been loosened or destroyed by the process of migration to Britain. For example, the falling-off of West Indian involvement in indigenous religious organisations in Easton may reflect a change in the degree of internal social control within the West Indian settlement and hence a loosening of the prescriptions surrounding religious membership and attendance. This could account for the move towards secularisation rather than increasing religiosity among West Indians in Britain.

The performance of official roles in religious associations is often conducive to the learning of administrative skills, and the confidence to use them, and these skills may be transferable to other associational settings (Lazerwitz, 1962). Therefore, since religious participation appears to be the most common formal associational activity among lower-class West Indians, both in Britain and the Caribbean, the level of 'activism' in 'official' church/sect positions which they display could be significant for leadership in other associations. The following tables, 6.3 and 6.4, show the number of respondents in the sample who were, or had been, church/sect 'officials' in the West Indies or in Easton, and the nature of the 'official' positions held:

Table 6.3

Number of respondents who held 'official' positions
in a church or sect

In the West Indies	No.	%	In Britain	No.	%
Officials	19	(17.6)	Officials	8	(7.4)
Non-officials	87	(80.6)	Non-officials	99	(91.7)
Not given	2	(1.9)	Not given	1	(0.9)
	n = 108			n = 108	

Table 6.4

'Official' positions mentioned

In the West Indies	No.	In Britain	No.
Church Council	2	Church Council	2
Sidesman	3	Sidesman	1
Choir Member	14	Choir Member	5
	n = 19		n = 8

Tables 6.3 and 6.4 reveal that the number of respondents holding 'official' positions in religious organisations is small. This pattern is roughly the same for the West Indies and for Britain, particularly if one separates choir membership from the occupancy of more important positions in the church. However, the figures for the Caribbean may have been depressed somewhat by the fact that some of the respondents would have been too young when resident in the West Indies to be considered for official positions in their churches.

It is interesting to note that whereas the figures for the Caribbean include 'official' positions in a number of different denominations, the Easton figures relate to only two churches, both of them Anglican. In fact, 7 of the 8 'official' positions mentioned by respondents in relation to Easton were positions in St John's. Sex differentials were not significant in either the West Indies or Easton. Thus, in the Caribbean, the majority of choir members were women whilst all the respondents who claimed to be sidesmen or on the church council were men. A similar pattern was observable in Easton where only one choir member was male and no women were on church councils. The tentative conclusions which can be drawn from the above figures point towards the fact that very few West Indians in Easton occupy 'official' positions in local churches and, hence, this kind of participation may be relatively unimportant as a means of providing leadership for other forms of formal association. Nevertheless, this only relates to the present situation. The future implications of religious association for other forms of participation will be discussed later in the chapter.

To summarise the pattern of religious participation among West Indians in Easton at this point, one can see that there is a tendency for West Indian church membership to be high in the early days of settlement in Britain. However, for a variety of reasons, both membership and attendance declined until only limited numbers of West Indians are to be found in the local congregations of the major denominations. Conversely, membership and attendance in exclusively West Indian Pentecostal churches are rising. The figures for West Indian membership of indigenous sectarian organisations in the city are still lower than for their counterparts in the Caribbean but they are significantly higher than the corresponding figures for West Indian membership in traditional church denominations in Easton.

I mentioned earlier that 'sects' like the Seventh Day Adventists and the Jehovah's Witnesses are accepted as churches in the West Indies. Both of these religious organisations are represented in Easton and have several West Indian members. Attendance at the meetings of these groups is small compared with the major denominations but it was noticeable that the proportion of West Indians in their 'congregations' is considerably higher than in most of the Anglican churches in and around Lowdale. The Seventh Day Adventists, for example, had a large number of Antiguan members. Adventism is particularly strong in Antigua and hence it was not surprising to find that the sizeable Antiguan population in Easton was well represented in the local Adventist branch. The Jehovah's Witnesses also had some West Indian members, most of them from Jamaica and Montserrat.

Unlike the major denominations, these sects did not experience a significant loss of white members when West Indians joined them. This is primarily due to the fact that sectarian forms of worship are perceived as separatist, fringe activities within the wider community. Thus, white members of the sects in Easton may not have perceived the admission of West Indians to their organisations as endangering either their status or their 'respectability'. Furthermore, both the Adventists and the 'Witnesses' are openly evangelistic in their aims and this would tend to assist the entry of migrants into their organisations.[3] Their more informal types of worship would also be more attractive to many West Indians than forms of worship in more traditional churches and this would have further encouraged a higher West Indian membership. Thus, the high incidence of West Indians in those sects in Britain can be seen partly as a reflection of Caribbean patterns of religious association, but the deprivations of metropolitan existence are also highly pertinent (Theobald, 1974).

Despite the importance of West Indian membership of indigenous sects, previous researchers have been most concerned with the establishment and growth of black (that is to say West Indian) Pentecostal churches in Britain. There were two 'churches' of this type in Easton at the time of the present research. Both held meetings in large, terraced houses in Adelaide Street, Lowdale. One, the 'New Testament Church of God', was a local branch of a church which has grown throughout the West Indian population in Britain. The other, the Evangelical church, was a branch of West Indian Pentecostalism which was growing in the Midlands. The leader of the Evangelical church lived in Easton, whilst the pastor who usually led the meetings of the New Testament church, lived in a nearby town. Both ministers were Jamaican.

The form of worship in these churches is markedly different from the traditional forms of worship in the major British denominations. There is an emphasis on the spiritual, for example, the 'speaking of tongues' where a 'disciple' in the congregation takes possession of the Holy Ghost. At Pentecostalist meetings, members may enter this spiritual state and thus transfer the words of the Apostles to fellow 'saints' (Pryce, 1979). Pentecostalist meetings are richly spontaneous, the minister delivering loud exhortations which are returned by the congregation with ritualistic replies. The Pentecostalists believe that a direct connection between the Deity and themselves is established during their meetings. This peculiar combination of spontaneity of response and ritual shouting bears little resemblance to services in traditional British churches. Commenting on Pentecostalism in the West Indies, Lowenthal states:

> Their deity is accessible to direct persuasion. They believe both in salvation by faith and in a spirit world where the dead possess supernatural powers and mediate among the living ... Their rites frequently generate intense emotions, often culminating in group-induced spirit possession and public conversion. (1972:115)

Like their white counterparts, these Pentecostal groups tend to be highly puritanical. In fact, in all these sects there is a strict disavowal of wordly pleasures and the outward display of material wealth. Tobacco and alcohol are forbidden and sexual abuse is severely frowned upon. The West Indian Pentecostal churches encourage legal marriage and faithfulness between marriage partners. However, they are attuned to family mores within the lower classes in the Caribbean and, therefore, their attitudes are in some ways flexible. Nevertheless, promiscuity or immorality as defined by these churches is forbidden.

The reasons for the establishment and growth of black Pentecostalism in Britain has been the subject of some debate. Most writers agree that these churches provide certain supportive functions for their West Indian followers who commonly occupy positions of social deprivation in the metropolitan society and in the Caribbean. Thus, in the West Indies these forms of worship are exclusive to the proletariat and the peasantry, although, as has been mentioned, the middle and upper classes may secretly subscribe to some of the magical beliefs contained in sectarian and cultist worship.

The vast majority of West Indians in Britain are from the working classes in the Caribbean and hence it has been argued that the establishment and growth of Pentecostalism among West Indian settlement in Britain is not unexpected. Malcolm Calley (1962, 1965), for example, views the growth of black Pentecostalism as a reflection of the large numbers of lower class Jamaicans in Britain. He suggests that this growth reflects a need felt by many lower class West Indians in Britain to practice forms of worship which guard against the harshness of their lives in the host society. Moreover, Kiev (1964) has argued, that Pentecostalist beliefs can have a cathartic, psychotherapeutic effect on those—the groups described by Niebuhr (1957) as 'the dispossessed'—who adhere to them. Pentecostal worship, that is to say, by providing forms of spiritual release, can compensate for the deprivations of worldly existence.

The growth of black Pentecostalism can, in part, be explained by the fact that entry to these churches only depends on the acceptance of the doctrines preached within them and the adoption of a life style which is shaped by these doctrines. The format of Pentecostalist meetings does not require high levels of literacy or verbal facility from participants. Similarly, membership does not depend upon the class, status and colour prescriptions which tend to restrict entry to the major denominations both in Britain and the Caribbean. All these factors tend to encourage attendance from lower class West Indians.

A further reason for the high memberships and rates of attendance in black Pentecostal churches applies to religious participation among West Indians generally. Religious worship provides many West Indians with an opportunity to enjoy themselves, to become the centre of attention, to dress in their best clothes and communally take part in an activity which can include the whole family. Every Sunday morning in Lowdale, a stream of West Indians can be seen walking along Adelaide Street. The women and the children in neat and brightly coloured clothes, the men in more sober but still stylish suits. This sight stands out in sharp contrast to the drabness of the physical surroundings.

According to Clifford Hill, the growth of black Pentecostalism in Britain has to be explained largely in terms of factors inherent in the host society. It is not, in his view, a simple extension of religious practices from the West Indies but a response to 'deprivation' and 'racialism'. As he puts it:

> Deprivation has the effect of driving together in social solidarity, members of the pariah group (that is to say West Indians in Britain). Thus the rapid rise in membership of immigrant organised religious sects may well be a response to the experience of social deprivation ... a rise in congregations is equated with a rise of racialism. (Hill, 1971:187)

Hill points out that the composition of Pentecostal congregations in Britain is different from that of their counterparts in Jamaica. There are, he argues, proportionately higher numbers of men and better-off West Indians in the British congregations, whereas, in the Caribbean, the membership of these churches is almost exclusively lower-class and female. Hill traces the rise of Pentecostalism in West Indian 'communities' in Britain back to the 1964 General Election when, he argues, 'race' became, for the first time, a national issue. He counters the argument that women still predominate in these churches in Britain and that therefore, the growth in Pentecostalism can be seen as an extension of Caribbean norms, by pointing out that, proportionately, women made their biggest contribution to total migrant numbers in the early years of West Indian migration to Britain. The rapid rise in black Pentecostalism, however, has occurred in the last few years when male migrants have been proportionately more significant. Thus, Hill argues, if the proportion of women in the migrant population is an important cause of the growth of Pentecostalism, this rise should have occurred much earlier than in fact it did. Hill explains the increase in male membership in these churches by arguing that West Indian men suffer from a greater sense of status loss in Britain than West Indian women. This loss of status forces them into Pentecostalism which is the only religious outlet in Britain which offers them support against status deprivation and discrimination.

Michael Banton has recently called for a more detailed examination of the internal structure of black Pentecostal sects so that some of the arguments regarding their establishment and growth in Britain can be resolved (1972:152). For example, what is the island and class composition of the Pentecostal congregations in Britain? Do they, in fact, draw their memberships from predominantly lower-class, female Jamaicans, which would support Calley's argument, or do they show a widening of island, class and sex affiliations which may point towards greater validity for Hill's thesis?

The present study does not purport to reconcile these contrasting points of view in any definitive sense. It has been concerned with several aspects of the social organisation of West Indian groupings in only one urban location in Britain and has not been focused solely on religion. Nevertheless, the following appraisal of black Pentecostal churches in Easton does contribute to the debate, lending support to some earlier interpretations whilst, at the same time, detracting from others.

Both of the black Pentecostal churches in Easton were established in the late 1960s. The New Testament Church was formed in 1969, whilst the Evangelical Church was established in the following year. The establishment of both churches coincided with the settlement of larger numbers of West Indians in Easton, most of whom resided in Lowdale. However, it should be pointed out that at least 6,000 West Indians lived in Easton prior to the mid-sixties. Thus, it could be argued that sufficient numbers of West Indians were present in Lowdale from the early 1950s to support the establishment of a Pentecostal Church in the area. The recency of the formation of these churches in Easton could lend weight to Hill's argument, which stresses the importance of what he takes to be the rise in 'radicalism' in Britain in the late 1960s in explaining the

133

establishment and growth of black Pentecostalism in the host society.

It was difficult to ascertain the island composition of the Pentecostal congregations because records had not been kept since their inception either of total memberships or of island affiliations. However, by questioning many members and past and present ministers of both churches, a rough indication of the numbers and composition of their respective congregations could be established. Meetings in the first year of formation in both churches averaged an attendance of between twenty and thirty members. These figures had grown steadily until, at the present time, attendances were consistently averaging between sixty and seventy members.

In contrast to many other West Indian settlements in Britain, Easton is interesting because the Jamaican community, whilst significant, does not form an overwhelmingly large proportion of the total number of West Indians in the area. The Antiguans are the largest group but there are many other islands with sizeable numbers in the city. The island composition of the local West Indian settlement in Easton is crucial to those arguments which attribute a growth in Pentecolstalism to the presence of substantial Jamaican communities in Britain. The late establishment of the Pentecostal Churches in Easton detracts from the latter argument somewhat. The pattern of West Indian settlement in the city clearly shows that the Jamaicans were among the earliest migrants to settle in Lowdale. But the Pentecostal Churches were formed at the time when much larger numbers of West Indians from other islands were settling in the area. If the establishment and growth of these churches is to be explained solely by the presence of Jamaicans, the evidence from Easton would appear to indicate otherwise. Pentecostalism should have been established much earlier, when the Jamaicans were the largest West Indian community in the city. Furthermore, Pentecostal membership would not continue to rise after the arrival of other island groupings, particularly when this arrival was not in any way paralleled by a continued expansion of the Jamaican community.

However, to redress the balance it must be pointed out that both congregations had significant numbers of Jamaican members. Whilst exact figures were unavailable, the proportion of Jamaicans attending services in both Pentecostal Churches in Lowdale was estimated at not less than one third and, on many occasions, more than half of the total membership present. These figures show that the Jamaicans formed a significantly higher proportion of both congregations, despite the size of the Jamaican community in relation to other West Indian groupings in the city. The evidence from this study appears to lend support to both Calley and Hill, who put forward alternative explanations for the establishment and growth of black Pentecostal Churches. Therefore, it can be suggested that both local and national contingencies should be considered when examining the establishment and growth of black Pentecostalism in Britain. If this perspective is adopted, it is possible to equate the establishment of black Pentecostal Churches in Easton with the expansion of this type of religious organisation at a national level in Britain, a process which is heavily influenced by the substantial numbers of Jamaicans in the host society. However, when examining the growth of Pentecostal Churches in Easton, the increasing numbers of West Indians from islands other than Jamaica who are joining these congregations, must be accounted for. Nevertheless, the Jamaican community still provides the largest proportion of saints in the city because of the predominance of this type of worship within this island society in the Caribbean. Thus, the pattern of establishment and growth of black Pentecostalism in Easton would appear to reconcile the opposing theses of Hill and Calley. If both local and national contingencies are considered their alternative explanations are not necessarily incompatible.

It was difficult to observe whether the majority of saints in Easton were drawn from the poorer sections of the West Indian communities in the city. But it was noticeable that none of the middle or upwardly mobile working class West Indians in the sample, who were active in non-religious formal associations were saints. Similarly, none of the sample who had intermediate or professional occupations claimed membership of Pentecostal Churches. Nevertheless, those respondents (16 in all) who were saints were not significantly different socio-economically from the rest of the sample. A questioning of saints and local Pentecostal ministers substantiated the fact that very few 'better-off' West Indians regularly attended meetings. Most of the congregation were no different from the majority of West Indians in Easton. That is to say, they were mostly skilled and semi-skilled manual workers who lived in or adjacent to Lowdale. However, it should be noted that the number of unskilled West Indians was comparatively low and that, similarly, the nature of West Indian migration has necessarily altered the composition of black Pentecostal Churches in Britain.

Previous research indicates that the majority of West Indian migrants in this country are drawn from those sections of the Caribbean population who, in the West Indies, do not usually participate in sectarian and cultist forms of worship (Hill, 1971; Calley, 1965). In other words, the rural peasantry are not well-represented in many West Indian communities in Britain, including Easton. Therefore, it is to be expected that black churches in Britain will reflect these features of the migrant population. However, it would appear that the lower stratum of West Indians does provide the largest proportion of saints in Britain. Relatively speaking, although most saints in Britain are higher status West Indians than would be probable in the Caribbean, they still occupy the lowest positions within their respective communities in the metropolitan society.

There is also some consistency between the social background of saints in Britain and the Caribbean in terms of sex. Women form the highest proportion of black Pentecostal congregations both in Britain and the West Indies (Henry and Wilson, 1975:189). Within the sample in Easton, 13 of the 16 respondents who claimed to be saints were women. On those occasions when Pentecostal meetings were attended, the predominance of females in the congregations was marked. Members of both Pentecostal Churches in Lowdale confirmed that this was a consistent pattern and that very few West Indian men attended their meetings. Calley (1965), too, shows that West Indian women predominate in Pentecostal meetings but he also argues that the proportion of West Indian men in these congregations has increased. This rise in male membership is attributed to the fact that West Indian men suffer from a greater sense of status loss than West Indian women in the metropolitan context. Implicit in this argument, however, is the assumption that West Indians in Britain measure their status solely in relation to members of the host society. Thus, Calley states:

> Membership in a sect compensates the individual for the inferior status assigned to him in society. West Indian piety is fixed on the next world. (1965:64)

Similarly, the life styles which are governed by Pentecostal beliefs are also looked at in relation to the attitudes of the white community. Again, Calley points out:

> Because the sects take up a great deal of their members' time and specifically forbid their taking part in the 'affairs of the world', members are prevented from participating in English social life ... the insistence of the sect on members leading a clean life, and on their being legally married and faithful to their spouses, might be expected to engender respect for them in the white community and so assist assimilation. However, they are not visible to the white community. (1965:64)

The interpretations which white members of the host community attach to forms of West Indian religious association are a most significant area for further research. However, it is equally important to consider the attitudes which West Indians, who do not conform to these forms of religion, have towards other West Indians who are saints. This is particularly crucial in the area of status evaluation and the formation of status groups within West Indian communities such as those in Easton. For example, some saints may find that the status that is accorded to them within a Pentecostal congregation will be higher than that accorded to them by members of the host community. This is extremely likely because skin colour will not be socially disadvantageous in black churches but it will certainly be so as far as the majority of local whites are concerned. However, the saints are also labelled as 'lower class' and accorded low status by many other West Indians who are not Pentecostalists. Thus, it would appear that membership of a black Pentecostal Church can be socially disadvantageous for saints in relation to their position within the West Indian population as well as in the wider host community. This is because the life styles and beliefs of saints are unacceptable to many West Indians (Pryce, 1979:229). Local whites often made disparaging remarks about the saints in Easton. Indeed, many West Indians criticised the black churches and their members in Easton for much the same reasons as the local white population. The following comments from West Indians are typical. A Barbudan railway porter, for example, commented:

> These hot gospellers give us a bad name. You walk up Adelaide Street and the singing and shouting comes right down the street. No wonder we are seen as peculiar by some people.

The Secretary of the JWA said that:

> Anyone has a right to have their own religion but these people don't contribute to the community. They are told you can't do this and that and they just go back to their homes and rest easy in their beliefs without coming out to us.

Another Jamaican said:

> They're just a lot of simple minded people, what do you expect. At home they don't do no harm but some whites think all Jamaicans act like that.

These comments demonstrate that black Pentecostalism is viewed with suspicion and hostility not only by local whites but also by many West Indians. Therefore, saints may find that their religious affiliations do act as a supportive agency against the hardships of everyday life in the host society, but they also isolate them from large numbers of fellow 'migrants'. Pentecostal doctrines do not only inhibit participation in 'English social life'. They also tend to isolate the saints from many forms of recreation established by fellow West Indians. The abstemiousness of the life styles of the saints may inspire respect from some West Indians but others view it as a form of 'stand-offishness' or priggishness. This withdrawal from both the host community and other West Indian communities may present the saint with considerable problems of adjustment, both social and psychological. This point has been emphasised by Leonard Bloom, although he does not specifically mention relationships between West Indians when he discusses the implications of Pentecostal membership for saints. He argues:

> This retreat tends, moreover, to be cumulative, which

effectively prevents communication with other groups. This in turn encourages uncertainty about the meaning and motives of the behaviour of other groups, because only with contact can come understanding. There thus develops a spiral in which lack of contact exacerbates fear, anxiety and a sense of threat, and this inhibits contact ... (Bloom, 1971:148)

We can see that the life styles connected with black Pentecostalism can command respect from members of West Indian communities and the host community, by, for example, the encouragement of legal marriage and 'clean living', but the adoption of these life styles also involves separatism and isolation from other groups in Easton. Hence the 'respectability' of certain actions of the saints may not be directly visible to those individuals who are not black Pentecostal members. Non-West Indian groups in the city, moreover, have little or no direct knowledge of the saints beliefs or life styles. The West Indian communities may be in a similar position, any knowledge often being based upon gossip rather than direct observation. Only the saints themselves are direct observers of their form of worship but certain forms of display which precede and follow Pentecostal meetings are observable to outsiders. At the same time, however, the content of much of the ceremony within meetings is audible to a much wider audience.

Any person who strolls along Adelaide Street on a Sunday morning when Pentecostal meetings are taking place may form distinct negative impressions from the loud music and shoutings which emanate from these 'churches'. The loudness and brashness of their services gives no indication of the extreme sobriety of the beliefs which are being expressed. Similarly, the sight of many saints in bright clothes may also be viewed as an unsober expression of religious beliefs. These supposedly loud, spontaneous and brash displays are often perceived as highly deviant forms of behaviour by both whites and other West Indians because they appear to contradict their expectations of what should constitute religious participation. Local whites frequently express fear or hostility because of the sight of sizeable numbers of West Indians forming a coherent, highly visible group. Black Pentecostal worship is one of the very few occasions which presents West Indians in this way. Members of the host community tend to base their criticisms of this form of worship on its cultural strangeness. Other West Indians who criticise the saints also centre on its deviant character when compared with more traditional forms of worship which they subscribe to but they also perceive that the deviant actions of a specific group of West Indians could be transformed into general labels which are ascribed to all West Indians or 'coloured people' by other groups in the city. Therefore, many West Indians criticised the saints because they not only stood apart from the rest of the West Indian population in Easton but also threatened to disrupt black and white relations in the city through their separatist and 'deviant' or 'strange' activities. Paradoxically, the retreatism of the saints intruded into the life situations of other West Indians and this was widely resented by them.

It can be seen that there is a direct link between religious beliefs, acts of worship and concomitant life styles for West Indian Pentecostalists. Black Pentecostalism provides both a *Weltanschauung* and distinct way of life for its believers. In common with a majority of the host community traditional religious affiliations, that is those in the major denominations, do not affect most West Indians in this way. Religious participation is perceived as just another form of action in a whole complex of single stranded relationships. In short, for many individuals, religious belief is separated from other areas of everyday life. An interesting illustration of this phenomenon emerged from the data drawn from the Easton sample. It was noticeable that a number of West Indians had changed their religious affiliation since arrival in Britain. There appeared to be no consistent pattern in these changes. Some respondents who had been, for example, Anglicans in their home society, had changed to Methodism in Easton. Others had swung from Anglicanism to Pentecostalism, or from one particular denomination to another. There was, it appeared, a random change from one form of church allegiance in the home island to another form in Britain. This would seem to raise the possibility, that for some West Indians, the observable act of participating in religion is more important than the specific doctrinal beliefs.

Factors such as the degree of receptivity towards migrants of indigenous churches in the host society probably have some significance in reinforcing or changing religious affiliations among West Indians. This appears to borne out by many of the reasons given by respondents for their change of religious affiliation. It was frequently mentioned, for example, that they often met with a cool reception in the local branch of the church they had supported in the Caribbean. Undoubtedly, this has contributed to the fall in church attendance of West Indians in Britain. However, some West Indians when confronted with rejection in one church moved to alternative places of worship, in some instances, of a different denomination. In many cases, the move was prompted by a friend or relative of a different religious persuasion who 'recommended' their own church. It would be interesting to discover whether this is a common feature of West Indian religious affiliation in Britain. At this juncture, however, it can only be suggested that many West Indians appear to view the social attributes of participation in any form of 'respectable' (as opposed to non-respectable Pentecostalism) religious organisation as more important than the doctrinal beliefs which underpin memberships of particular forms of worship.

Having analysed certain forms of religious membership and participation among West Indians in Easton, the links between religious and other forms of associational activity can now be briefly examined. The wider implications of black Pentecostalism and its recent growth in Britain are an obvious starting point. Calley has suggested that West Indian sects:

> Impede assimilation because they are almost exclusively West Indian in membership ... they emphasise a solidarity based on a manner of worship which is typical of some of the larger West Indian islands but appears exotic to the English. (1965:63)

I have argued that Pentecostalist beliefs and the life styles which stem from them, should be acceptable to many members of the host society and hence might assist assimilation. But it has also been demonstrated that the performance of Pentecostal forms of worship partly negates the acceptability of the values inculcated in this form of worship. This leads the saints to:

> Retreat into a self-imposed ghetto (which) may be the only psychological defence against the unbearable pain of the abrasions of hostile social contacts, but it is dangerously easy for this self-defensiveness to merge into a state that is close to paranoia ... (Bloom, 1971:148)

Therefore, despite the solidaristic nature of these forms of religious association and the apparent acceptability to the majority society of the values expressed within them, the separatist nature of black Pentecostalism inhibits accommodation. In addition, because the saints are isolated from many other West Indians, black Pentecostalism also inhibits group solidarity at a wider level among West Indians in Easton. It reinforces in-group/out-group distinctions both between and within themselves from those West Indians who do not subscribe to the puritanical life styles which are requested or enforced by sectarian allegiance. Separate attendance of traditional and sectarian forms of religious association tends to fragment the West Indian settlement because both forms of worship portray a form of 'respectability' which precludes others who do not adhere to such standards. The first type of respectability, which is largely found in the traditional forms of worship like Anglicanism, can be called status respectability for it uses church attendance as a criterion for status reinforcement. The second type, broadly equated with sectarian forms of worship, is more aptly termed doctrinal respectability because it uses the values inculcated in the member to reinforce sectarian positions. Both these forms of respectability are separatist because they reinforce in-group/out-group distinctions among West Indians.

These distinctions may also explain why some West Indians change from their religious affiliations in the Caribbean to alternative denominations in Britain. If religious association is seen by some West Indians as a form of activity which reinforces one's class or status position, or as an acknowledged form of participation which raises the latter, general participation may be more important than specific beliefs. Therefore, some West Indians will be prepared to change their religious affiliation to a different form of worship if they meet rejection in Britain. Changes in doctrine may be less important than the act of worship and hence a change of affiliation can be reconciled with the benefits gained from participating in some form of worship rather than none at all.

Those West Indians, who for a variety of reasons, may feel the deprivations of life in Britain rather more than some of their peers will perhaps seek solace in sectarian forms of religion which provide a set of beliefs and a regularised life style. Adherents to the value of status respectability are concerned with the present world and their status in it *vis-a-vis* other West Indians and the host society. Adherents to the value of doctrinal respectability, however, have shifted their emphasis towards a retreat from the present world and are seemingly quite prepared to weigh the benefits of this retreat against their isolation from the wider community and many other West Indians.

The separatism of sectarian forms of worship and the fragmentary nature of West Indian traditional religious participation may be only transitory. Both sectarian and traditional forms could encourage other forms of communal association among West Indians in Easton. It has been argued, for example, that the lines of religious conflict within West Indian communities are much more subtle and less intrusive than those which separate South Asian migrants in Britain. Banton, for example, has suggested that:

> The West Indian groups differ from the Asians in that they do not show the same mixture of political, religious, economic, kinship and other ties. They do not, as a rule, have to bother so much about maintaining a good reputation with relatives and former neighbours in their district of origin, or among their fellows in Britain. They are more ready to keep separate different kinds of relationship as the English do. Thus, they lack the multi-purpose associations based on origin which have helped the first-generation Asian migrants. (1973:147)

The central point concerning the contrast between Asian multiple and West Indian single stranded relationships is well taken. Within the South Asian communities in Easton, the temple, mosque and gurdwara act as community centres as well as specialised religious institutions. These places of worship are multi-functional and they can be used for political meetings and so forth. Religious affiliations do factionalise Indian and Pakistani communities but they also provide a basis for solidaristic

141

group formation (Allen, 1971:88).

Unlike West Indian groupings, South Asian communities are held together by a set of multiple obligations which cut across kinship, religious, economic and political relationships. Hence, religious affiliations are not perceived as separatist and individualistic forms of social participation. Religion and kinship ties commonly provide the basis for financial cooperation, for example, group house purchase or they can encourage the formation of political associations. At present, there is little evidence to suggest that the religious associations formed by West Indians are similarly multi-functional for their communities. As Banton (1972) suggests, West Indians tend to treat religious membership and attendance as a social activity which does not necessarily cross-cut kinship ties or economic and political relationships within West Indian communities. This would certainly apply to the majority of West Indians in Easton who are members of major denominations in the city. However, black Pentecostalism may be an exception, for this form of worship does embrace the whole life style of its followers. Compared with Asian religious affiliations, black Pentecostalism is still a minority form of worship which at present affects only a limited number of West Indians in the city. Thus, the importance of, for example, the possible economic and political benefits derived from religious association are strictly limited by the exclusivity of Pentecostal membership. Indeed, such exclusive benefits may be an important reinforcer of disharmony within West Indian settlements.[4] The South Asian groupings in Easton are dominated by major religions which affect the lives of the majority of Indians and Pakistanis. The Hindu, Sikh and Moslem religions which embrace the multi-functional relationships referred to previously, are majority forms of worship. Consequently, they provide a solidaristic basis for large, coherent social groups in contrast with the small, fringe associations which are the norm among the West Indian communities in the locality.

Nevertheless, it would appear that religious membership and participation among West Indians may have important repercussions for other forms of associational activity. This applies to both traditional and sectarian forms of worship. The experience gained by West Indians in occupying official positions within religious associations could provide the knowledge and, more importantly, the confidence, for participation and leadership in other forms of activism. This has been demonstrated in Easton where one or two West Indians who were members of local church councils, later became committee members of a housing project in Lowdale. Similarly, as one of the few forms of West Indian association which is not purely recreational, religious associations provide a formal context where West Indians from different islands and differing class and status positions can meet and exchange ideas. Church membership may perform a useful function in promoting group solidarity in this sense.

However, individual ministers and congregations in their respective churches will be a crucial factor in this respect. One Anglican minister in Easton openly encouraged West Indians to take an active part in the organisation of his church. Furthermore, West Indians were also encouraged to participate in the running of youth clubs and welfare agencies connected with this church. These activities provided some links with associations outside of strictly religious affiliations. But it should be remembered that such a level of West Indian participation within a traditional, indigenous church in Easton was exceptional. At present, the policy of the major denominations depends on the attitude of particular ministers and their congregations and many are apathetic if not hostile towards the issue of the integration of the West Indians in their parishes.

Gus John (1970) has argued, quite forcibly, that most churches and their members merely reflect liberal patronage or rejection in their attitudes to local black populations. He argues that the major denominations in Britain are too benign in their attitudes towards the social deprivations which many of their parishioners, especially black people, encounter in their daily lives. John calls for the churches to speak out against forms of oppression, racial or otherwise, and goes on to suggest that churches should 'fertilise the seeds of discontent' among West Indian adolescents instead of merely promoting 'moderate' sports and youth clubs. He points out that the church is in a unique position of being able to offer ample premises and financial aid to local self-help groups. The church, he says, could encourage a 'theology of revolution' (John, 1970:346). However admirable these suggestions might be, they appear little more than utopian at present since John misses the vital point: namely, that it is likely that the majority of West Indian church members would reject this 'radical expression' by the church.

The majority of West Indians who are members of the major denominations in Easton stem from the upwardly mobile working class in the local West Indian communities. These churchgoers are more conscious than most West Indians of their status and the 'respectability' upon which this status rests. It is likely that if traditional church members do enter other forms of association, particularly those of a political nature, they will adopt 'moderate' rather than 'radical' forms of action and belief. Hence, it is likely that reformist rather than revolutionary movements will originate from religious affiliation to the major denominations in Britain. However, traditional church participation, by possibly promoting West Indian activism in reformist associations, may lead to more radical alternatives. Perhaps even a 'theology of revolution' will be created in the future. In addition, sectarian forms of religious association, for example, black Pentecostalism, may take on a millenarian character in which religious fervour may be transformed into political activism. This last prediction is particularly pertinent if race relations in Britain are in any way comparable to the United States or the Caribbean or whether future changes in the metropolitan society may make it so.

In a recent book, Chris Mullard (1973) compares the race relations situation in Britain with previous 'stages' in the development of race relations in the United States. He argues that events in Britain are closely following the 'racist spiral' which is observable across the Atlantic.[5] The lines of conflict between black and white, he suggests, are becoming more and more tightly drawn. More specifically, Mullard equates the growth of black Pentecostalism among West Indians in Britain with the same conditions which produced organisations like the Black Moslems in the United States. Speaking of West Indian Pentecostalism in Britain, Mullard argues:

> These sects are completely insular, all black, the energy providing machine for struggling through another week of hostility. At the moment they are non-political but if the American experience is any indication of future trends they could become the nucleus, indeed the leadership, of a quasi-political movement. (1973:139)

There are also possible parallels between black Pentecostalism in Britain and certain religious movements in the Caribbean, for example, the Rastafarian cults in Jamaica.[6] Research carried out in the 1950s tended to dismiss the political potential of the Rastas. Rastafarianism was perceived at this time as a form of religious revivalism remote from political expression. Thus, George Simpson (1955, 1956) argued that Rastafarians were more concerned with providing a limited kind of economic co-operation among the many thousands of urban poor in Kingston than with encouraging political change. Rastafarianism, he suggested, only provided an escape from social deprivation. It did not involve a deliberate attempt to eliminate such poverty by political action. Indeed, Simpson noticed a marked tendency among the Rastafarians to reject any kind of formalised political activity. He argued:

> Because Rastafarians distrust all who are associated with politics and government, they say it is useless to attend political rallies, accept political assignments or vote. (1955:146)

A more recent study by Barrett (1968) also tended to depict the Rastas as a religious movement whose apolitical stance was more likely to sustain rather than change the *status quo*. Nevertheless, current events in Jamaica suggest that the Rastafarians have modified their views considerably. The Rasta groups were very influential in the election of Michael Manley to the Jamaican premiership in 1972 (Kuper, 1976:104). Manley subsequently used the Rastafarians as an effective 'voice' among the urban poor in Kingston and Rasta leaders have successfully maintained their position as one important set of political spokesmen for the urban proletariat in Jamaica to the present day. Rastafarianism, moreover, has become steadily more influential in the British context, particularly among second generation West Indians, both as a focus for identity formation and religio-political expression (see Postscript).

Rex Nettleford (1970) confirms that the Rastafarians are something more than a separatist, revivalist cult. He claims that Rastafarianism is becoming a revolutionary rather than a retreatist force and that its aims are positively political rather than strictly religio-separatist. The Rastas are now looking inward to seek change in their own society rather than continuing to look exclusively beyond the shores of the Caribbean to salvation in Ethiopia. Nettleford sees some similarity between the Rastafarians and Black Power groups in Britain in their common display of condemnation and fear of white oppression. However, at present, black Pentecostalism in Britain is not directly linked with black power groupings. At least this was the case in Easton. Indeed, all forms of 'traditional' religious affiliation among West Indians in the city were firmly separated from any thoughts of 'black power'. The local BPG were seen as highly disreputable by church and sectarian worshippers alike. Much of this antipathy is based upon inter-generational conflicts which pervade the West Indian communities. Religious affiliation is predominantly a first generation West Indian form of association. Black Power is very much associated with the second generation at present. Consequently, in order for religious activism to be transformed into political action among West Indians, particularly through any connection with 'black power', numerous residual conflicts within West Indian communities in the city will have to be resolved. At present, it is rather difficult to envisage the puritanical Pentecostalist making the leap into the youthful 'counter-culture' which is embedded in the black power ethos!

Much will depend upon the rapidly changing climate of racial or ethnic relations in Britain and how West Indians in general will interpret their situation. There may be some points of comparability between Rastafarianism, both in Britain and the Caribbean and the rise of black Pentecostalism in Britain. The most crucial one is the fact that their doctrines and forms of association have grown out of a common attempt to give some meaning and voice to the reactions of the dispossessed and powerless. Continued economic and social pressure may, therefore, promote a new political assertiveness within the black Pentecostal movement in Britain (Pryce, 1979:274). However, the present study indicates that, at the moment, this expression of discontent is being voiced within separate enclaves within the West Indian population in Easton. Patterns of religious affiliation among West Indians in the city reveal that religious associations form yet another feature of the internal divisions within and between West Indian communities. West Indian religious affiliations reinforce class and status distinctions in similar ways to those which family and household patterns have been shown, in the previous chapter, to do.

It has been suggested that status groupings are forming within the West Indian settlement in Easton and hence intra-class distinctions among West Indians in Britain are broadly following the inter-class distinctions which exist, or have existed, in the Caribbean. Thus, 'traditional' forms of worship still remain the prerogative of upwardly mobile West Indians who are still concerned with trying to establish a foothold within the limits placed on them by the host society, whilst sectarian forms of worship are the province of those West Indians who have opted out of the present world and seek solace in the thought of compensation in the next.

The discussion in the preceding pages indicates that the relationships between religious affiliations and class and status distinctions within West Indian communities have some important implications for membership and attendance of other forms of association. Similarly, patterns of West Indian religious association may have both present and future influences on political activism among West Indians in the city. These implications will be examined in greater detail in the following chapter which will be concerned with a detailed analysis of political activism among West Indians in Easton.

Notes

1   It is important to note that many religious organisations that are accepted as 'churches' or 'denominations' in the Caribbean would be defined as 'sects' in Britain, in terms of their styles of worship and lack of hierarchically organised structure. In the present context, noting the cross-cultural problems of definition, commonly used British conventions will be followed for stylistic convenience—see Wilson, (1959).

2   See, for example, the striking consistency between immediate post-war studies—Little, (1947); Banton, (1955); and more recent studies—Richmond, (1973); and Lawrence, (1974).

3   On the capacity of some types of sect, particularly Adventist, to proselytise whilst at the same time maintain their exclusive basis of commitment, see Wilson, (1961).

4   For an interesting comparative study which illustrates the political implications of this form of religious separatism, see Roberts, (1967/8).

5   Other writers have seriously questioned the parallels between race relations in Britain and the United States, for example, see Rex and Tomlinson, (1979:6).

6   For a useful overview of the literature on the Rastafarians in Jamaica, see Owens (1977/8).

7 The dynamics of West Indian activism

A point has now been reached where we can pull together the separate strands of analysis relating to localised West Indian political activism presented to date. The exploratory nature of this study dictates caution so some degree of tentativeness must be expected in the final analysis. Nevertheless, there would seem to be a number of significant features of West Indian social organisation, both in Britain and the Caribbean, which at least partially explain the pattern of formal associational fragmentation which we have observed in Easton. However, before discussing these features in some depth, let us return to some of the 'explanations' that were mentioned at the beginning of the book.

One possible explanation for the low level of associational activity embraces the notion of culture shock. To reiterate the point briefly, West Indians arrive in Britain bringing with them a set of cultural norms from the Caribbean which conflict with those encountered in the host society. In its most dramatic portrayal, the initial experience of a West Indian migrant might be likened to an 'illiterate, rural peasant' confronted with the hustle and bustle of the sophisticated urban milieux of the Western, industrialised, metropolitan society. Such a picture is at best stereotypical, with only a marginal essence of truth attached to it. If it is accepted that the social structures of Caribbean societies have been shaped by a colonial history of plantation economies, the West Indian does not fit easily into categories such as 'rural' and 'peasant' (Frucht, 1967). Nevertheless, despite the partially pronounced urban and Westernised characteristics of many West Indian migrants, their arrival in Britain was often traumatic.

Many West Indians in Easton admitted that their expectations before arrival in Britain were utopian. They were often surprised and horrified at the coolness of the welcome extended to them by the 'mother country'. The difficulties of cultural adaptation, compounded by the problems of finding jobs and houses in a possibly hostile community, may provide sufficient evidence to explain the dearth of communal associations of a formal nature among newly arrived West Indian migrants.

However, many West Indians in Easton did not meet such severe problems when they arrived in Britain. Most of them acquired jobs and accommodation relatively easily. Furthermore, West Indian groupings in the city were well established and most West Indians had lived in the locality for some years. Consequently, it seems reasonable to argue that the initial problems of settlement of migrants in Easton should have receded and any cultural adaptation to a new environment should have been at least partially accomplished.

The notion of culture shock is often linked with the additional problems of social deprivation. Consideration of the latter concept introduces the argument that certain groups in Britain, notably black minorities, face considerable day-to-day problems in simply maintaining a subsistence level of living. The hardships of daily existence largely negate the possibility for communal association. Poverty, with all its social repercussions, for example, unemployment, sub-standard housing, family 'disorganisation', etc., dehumanises the individual to such an extent that any expectation of high levels of social participation in communal associations is quite unrealistic.[1]

This argument has great validity when applied to a number of British cities where many West Indians are faced with these kinds of social problems and in consequence their social organisation no doubt reflects such poverty. But, this proposition has much less weight when applied to the Easton situation. The majority of West Indians in the city are not faced with harsh levels of poverty and deprivation. Nevertheless, they can be seen as relatively deprived when their position is contrasted with that of other groups in the city. West Indians are one of the most deprived groups in a highly affluent city where the types of social problems encountered by urban dwellers elsewhere in Britain are less severe. West Indians in Easton occupy some of the worst housing, and many are less favourably employed than the majority of residents in the city. In addition, the rapid erosion of previously existing 'favourable' housing and employment conditions; the presence of highly organised and vocal anti-immigrant associations, numerous apparent and/or alleged conflicts between the police and West Indian youth and frictions between immigrants and local Council housing and welfare policies, all served as constant reminders of West Indian subordination. Thus, one cannot simply explain the paucity of West Indian political associations by the absence of local issues or debates. In short, it is important to make a distinction between areas of social deprivation *per se,* with all their connotations of subsistence living standards, and the relative deprivation of West Indians in Easton which compares quite favourably with the social situation of many West Indians in other areas of settlement in Britain.

One might have thought that the more favourable position of West Indians in Easton would encourage the formation of voluntary associations and possibly political activism. Freed from the constraints of extreme poverty but perceiving their relatively inferior position *vis-a-vis* other groups in the city, the local West Indian population might have been expected to seek changes in their life situation through communal action. Indeed, many West Indians in the city did express considerable discontent which arose from their perceptions of their relatively deprived positions compared with the life situations of many local Asians and whites. However, the absence of West Indian political associations and the ephemerality of those associations which did exist belies the permanence and stability of local West Indian groupings. This suggests that explanations of the former must include social factors in addition to culture shock and social deprivation.

A further possibility that can be largely discounted is the proposition that high residential mobility, coupled with the temporary nature of West Indian migration, does not encourage high levels of associational activity. It could be argued that West Indians do not establish their own formal associations because they view their migration to Britain as transitional. In addition, a high rate of geographical mobility among West Indians would further reduce the probability of their forming permanent associations in a particular locality. Once again, the evidence as far as West Indians in Easton are concerned, casts doubt on these explanations. Most West Indians revealed a low level of geographical mobility; many of them had lived solely in Easton since their arrival in Britain some years ago. Residential mobility within the city was somewhat higher, but the majority of West Indians lived within restricted areas and thus formed a reasonably compact settlement.

The argument which stresses the temporary nature of West Indian settlement in Britain confuses a desire among migrants to return to the Caribbean with the likelihood of this eventuality. The majority of West Indians questioned in Easton expressed such a desire but most of them accepted that an early return to the West Indies was unlikely, at least in any permanent sense. There was little evidence to suggest that many West Indians saw a forthcoming re-migration to the Caribbean as a panacea for any social ills they suffered from in Britain.

A further factor that could inhibit the formation of associations designed to develop the interests of West Indians in Britain, centres on how they perceive their position in the metropolitan society along the lines of separatism or non-separatism. This question involves a consideration of a number of somewhat contentious terms, namely 'assimilation', 'accommodation' and 'integration' (Banton, 1972:52). These terms have generated considerable controversy because of the wide disagreement about the nature of West Indian intentions in Britain. The debate rests on the desired degree of contact between West Indians and local whites as perceived by both sides. Initially, most West Indians arriving in Britain wished to establish amicable social relationships with members of the receiving society which they were entering. However, this does not imply that West Indians wanted to become totally absorbed into the host community, either culturally and/or biologically in the near or more distant future. Assimilation implies that West Indians would gradually throw-off those cultural differences that distinguished them from the host community until they had become fully 'acceptable' to local whites. There is also, as hinted above, the possible implication that a process of cultural homogenisation would lead ultimately to widespread miscegenation and eventual biological integration of black minorities and the white majority.

The present study does not support the assimilationist-integrationist hypotheses, in part because most West Indians have voluntarily retained much of the culture of their Caribbean background. This culture is embedded, for example, within family and household structures, kinship and friendship relationships, distinctive cuisines, patterns of recreation and the social organisation of West Indian associations. There is a pattern of settlement among West Indians in Easton which is partly separatist and partly accommodative. On the one hand, most West Indians seek to maintain cultural links with the Caribbean whilst, on the other, they wish to form compatible social relationships with the indigenous population in Britain in a variety of situations; economic, political and recreational.

Unfortunately, this desire on the part of West Indians to accommodate themselves partially to the expectations of members of the host community has often been met with rejection. In a variety of social contexts, West Indians have been unable to establish on-going social relationships with local whites or Asians. These social contexts range from formal work situations or common church attendance to the more intimate areas of friendship and inter-marriage. This is not to suggest that all West Indians do not achieve some degree of rapprochement with these groups. Most West Indians mix peacefully enough in the factory or in church, but outside of these formal contacts they live somewhat separate lives. This is partly by choice, but often because there is little opportunity for more intimate social relationships with other groups in the locality.

Therefore, irrespective of the desires of West Indians to 'assimilate' or 'integrate' they are compelled to fit into a quasi-separatist position where the arenas for social interaction between black and white are laid down by the latter. This also applies to any social contact between West Indians and Asians which in many ways is even more restricted. The relative social isolation of West Indians tends to shape associational formation among them in a number of ways. It may tend, for example, to make many West Indians more self-aware in a negative or positive way. In a negative sense, this will involve a retreat behind any number of social or psychological barriers. In some cases this can mean a very real fear of venturing over one's own doorstep. More commonly, West Indians live out their daily lives within their own homes, providing their own entertainment and restricting their social networks to fellow West Indians. In a minority of cases this social isolation (*vis-a-vis* non-West Indians) encourages the formation of united, cohesive associations which seek to encourage some form of political action. Most West Indians, however, have chosen, or have been forced to choose, the second option, retreatism; whilst only a few have sought to establish and maintain some form of communal action designed to change the life situation of their communities.

The relationships between West Indians and members of the receiving society are governed by those sanctions placed upon them by the latter which encourage separatism within well-defined formal boundaries. This separatism is also perceived within West Indian groups to a certain extent. The 'individualism' of West Indians was commented upon at an earlier point in the study. I mentioned that it has often been seen as a psychological phenomenon that centres on an 'individualistic personality' which encourages self-hate, marginality and negates the formation of meaningful group identities which, in turn, encourage communal association. Whilst I argued that the study of personality formation, particularly within the context of colonial history, was a fascinating and possibly rewarding area for further study, it was stressed that individualism would be used in a sociological sense within the present context. Thus, it was viewed as a type of social organisation which may or may not have intrinsic links with what might be called an 'individualistic personality'.

Within this context, individualism has to be seen as a social phenomenon derived from a colonial history of slavery and deprivation which is still nurtured within the Caribbean by neo-colonial constraints. It can be further argued that these deprivations have been maintained by the metropolitan society since the earliest settlement of West Indians in Britain. Hence, there is an ever-present link between the past and present. Dilip Hiro, discussing the effects of slavery in relation to the present position of West Indians in British cities, demonstrates that there is a historical continuity to colonial policies of divide and rule:

> The (inter-mixing of tribes in the West Indies) ... dramatically ruptured the continuity of their social order, and destroyed their communal way of life. It also tended to encourage a 'go-it-alone' attitude among the slaves, though the cruelty of the system periodically brought them together to revolt.
>
> The West Indian community in modern Britain manifests similar tendencies in a different context. In normal times, individualism among West Indians and the absence of tradition of following a recognised leader—tribal, communal or caste—which occurs in the settled societies of Asia and Africa, make it difficult to organise the community for the purpose

of pursuing such positive objectives as, say, establishing community centres. (1971:82)

This 'go-it-alone' tendency among West Indians has been mentioned by several writers. Donald Hinds, for example, says:

The average West Indian is a 'go-it-aloner'; despite the fact that he probably lives in close proximity with fellow migrants, he prefers ... to fight racial prejudice as he meets it in everyday life as an individual citizen, rather than to help form a nation-wide movement after the American pattern. (1966:136)

Most West Indians in Easton fit this description. They are primarily concerned with their own families and view any problems encountered locally in a personalised sense rather than within a broader, 'West Indian' communal categorisation. Moreover, individualism is demonstrated in the way that so many West Indians impute motives of personal gain to local West Indian activists rather than accept any claims of altruism from the latter.

The 'go-it-alone' tendency is also apparent in the lack of commercial organisation among West Indians in the city. In sharp contrast to their South Asian neighbours, there are few examples of West Indian owned shops, businesses, or lending institutions, etc. Those economic associations which are present (for example, credit associations) are highly informal and restricted to small kinship and island groupings. Thus, it can be seen that the social organisation of the West Indian settlement stresses individualism rather than mutualism and that this tendency does not lend itself to widespread formal associational activity within or between Caribbean groupings.

Where associations are established, they are influenced by a number of subtle cross-cutting lines of conflict. These conflictual divisions include length of residence, generational differences and island and regional separation. Under-pinning these bases for factionalism are class, status and colour distinctions reflected in religious and family organisational differences and consequent patterns of political allegiance.

The length of residence of West Indian groups and individuals in Easton was an important determinant of associational activity. The pattern of West Indian settlement in the city has been briefly described and it has been shown that, whilst a number of West Indians settled in Easton immediately after the Second World War, the vast majority of migrants from the Caribbean settled in the locality during the late 1950s and early 1960s. The arrival of these migrants was perceived with mixed feelings by the earliest West Indian settlers. These 'old-timers', were pleased to see the arrival of West Indian 'newcomers', especially if they included among them family and friends from the home island, but there were also many regrets and fears that this 'mass settlement' might be met with hostility from the white community. Any degree of acceptance which old-timers may have achieved, they felt, might be jeopardised by the arrival of so many newcomers. Furthermore, many of these newcomers were not from the same islands as the old-timers; nor were they, in the main, from the same perceived class background. Most of the early West Indian settlers in Easton were from Jamaica and Barbados. The arrival of so-called 'low-class, small island people' was often not welcomed by old-timers for these reasons. Length of residence, in isolation from other factors, does not necessarily produce conflicts within West Indian groupings but reinforced by, for example, island or class distinctions, it is an important source of division between them. There were many instances when West Indians who had resided in Easton for some years expressed considerable regret that the racial harmony which they believed existed in the city in the early post-war years, had been ruined by too many newcomers who were 'less accommodating' than themselves. The 'shortcomings' of those West Indians who were recent arrivals were often ascribed by the old-timers to the 'ignorance' or 'couldn't care less' attitudes of the newcomers. Such attitudes, it was held, were what one would expect from 'illiterate', 'low-class', 'small-island' West Indians.

Age distinctions within West Indian groupings are also potentially divisive. Many younger West Indians, particularly those who have been born or spent the greater part of their lives in Britain, may not accept status distinctions, acknowledged by first generation West Indians, which are based upon forms of prestige bestowed on individuals in the Caribbean. First generation West Indians commonly attribute status on the basis of kinship links, colour, occupation, education and other criteria which were established in the West Indies and still have some credibility among other West Indians. Young black Britons, with little or no experience of the Caribbean, however, often refuse to acknowledge these status distinctions and the consequent withdrawal of prestige is resented by older West Indians.

Similarly, younger West Indians tend to be more radical than their older counterparts in their attitudes towards white society. In part, this is due to their greater separation from Caribbean backgrounds which stressed the importance of European influences and the desirability of 'whiteness'. The experiences of young blacks within the British educational system are different from those which West Indians educated in the Caribbean encountered. Moreover, the social inequalities between black and white are often more sharply experienced by second generation West Indians. The latter tend to compare themselves with their white peers who have better perceived life chances and this creates much resentment among West Indian youth. Many first generation West Indians have more limited aspirations and interpret the resentment among

154

young blacks as a feature of their youth rather than as a result of discrimination. Second generation West Indians, furthermore, are more affected by restricted job opportunities and spiralling house prices because their education has prompted higher aspirations than those originally held by their parents. These aspirations conflict with the restricted opportunities met in areas of employment which are adjudged by white employers as unsuitable for black workers. Older West Indians may have initially expected equal job opportunities but have long since become reconciled to restricted areas of employment, in part because the financial rewards from these jobs are often better than those received in the Caribbean. Younger West Indians do not have this sort of perspective and can only compare their present position with their white and South Asian contemporaries. Whilst the comparative data on the aspirations and attainments of white, South Asian and West Indian youth is far from conclusive; reflecting, for example, differences in sampling and regional variations, most evidence suggests that second generation West Indians often fare particularly badly in the linked areas of education and employment (Dex, 1979; Driver, 1979; Rex and Tomlinson, 1979). Second generation West Indians also face the additional problems encountered in an economic climate which has deteriorated over the years of West Indian settlement. Easton in the 1950s and 1960s might not have offered West Indians equal opportunities with all other groups in the locality, but jobs and houses were available. In more recent years, the housing and employment situation in Easton has rapidly deteriorated and, in a period, where all groups find difficulty in acquiring cheap housing or plentiful job opportunities, young blacks are seriously disadvantaged.

The generational conflicts within many West Indian families have been exaggerated and the whole question of relations between and within generations requires far more serious study (Foner, 1979). But, undoubtedly some West Indian parents display a Victorian authoritarianism towards their children which often leads to serious inter-generational rifts within the family. These problems are exacerbated by 'permissive' forms of discipline within the educational system in Britain which stand in sharp contrast to the often punitive forms of control common to some West Indian homes.

Second generation West Indians also face identity problems in Britain which are often more acute than those faced by their parents (Weinreich, 1979). It has been shown that most West Indians desire acceptance in Britain but that they also seek to retain links with their islands of origin. The retention of these Caribbean roots, albeit highly problematic ones, still affords some focus of identification. If the first generation West Indian was not treated as a black Englishman in the metropolitan society, he could at least still call himself a Jamaican or an Antiguan and so forth.

The second generation, however, brought up in Britain, mixing with white peer groups, often speaking with an 'Easton' rather than a 'West Indian' accent, have to reconcile the loss of their Caribbean roots with the refusal to be admitted as an 'Englishman' by their white contemporaries (Mullard, 1973; Midgett, 1975). This reconciliation means dealing with the conflicts between home and school, the problems of colour and discrimination and those misplaced aspirations alluded to above. Failure to resolve these social pressures has led many black adolescents into aimless unemployment, homelessness, and forms of radical political expression like the BPG, which are unacceptable to most whites and many older West Indians. Many of these youths in Easton belong to a subculture which incorporates a type of life style which is utterly rejected by the majority of first generation migrants.

This overt life style, which includes distinctive fashions, speech patterns, musical forms and a leaning towards political militancy is seen by older West Indians as a form of expression likely to exacerbate relations between all West Indians and the wider community. These generational differences have an important influence on formal associational activity. First generation West Indians have tended to form moderate, a-political associations whilst more radical groups are invariably dominated by second generation West Indians. Hence these generational differences must be related to varying forms of political expression. A point we will return to later in the chapter.

One of the most important divisions between West Indians in Easton is their island of origin and regional differences within their respective island groupings. First generation West Indians see themselves first and foremost as Jamaicans, Antiguans, Barbadians, etc., and their common Caribbean background is seen as a somewhat secondary feature. Most West Indians in Easton had migrated directly from their home island to Britain and few had been to other West Indian societies before migration. Consequently, it is not unusual for West Indians from different islands to have little knowledge of one another's societies. Geographical remoteness (Kingston, Jamaica is as far from Port of Spain, Trinidad, as London is from Moscow) and a West Indian educational system which stresses the links between individual Caribbean societies and Britain rather than those between the former, are important sources of island insularity. A recent history of island nationalism has reinforced this form of separatism. Island distinctions are typified by stereotypes used widely among West Indians to describe individuals from islands other than their own. Among them, the large island/small island distinction is the most pronounced. In addition to inter-island distinctions in the Caribbean, there are also differences between city and town dwellers and those West Indians who have a more 'rural' background. These differences are most apparent in Jamaica or Trinidad. The town dweller in Port-of-

Spain, for example, will often refer to 'country bookies' who live in the 'bush'. These stereotypes are comparable to the caricatures drawn in British culture which portray the countryman as a 'backward yokel' with 'quaint' customs and dialects compared with the sophistication and modernity of his urban counterpart.

These island and to a lesser extent regional differences, are pronounced among West Indians and they form a most important basis of conflict within and between their communities in relation to associational activity. Island differences were one of the most important problems encountered by those activists who sought to establish communal associations among West Indians in Easton. For example, the earlier noted difficulties met by the JWA when the mere labelling of this group as 'Jamaican' effectively reduced support from a wide section of the West Indian settlement. West Indians from other, smaller societies, interpreted the formation of the JWA as an example of Jamaican status-seeking. Members of the JWA in turn saw these criticisms as illustrative of small island pettiness.

The pattern of voluntary association formation among West Indians in Easton confirmed that most formal associations and many informal groupings were established within island delineations. The only exceptions were those associations formed or partly established by second generation West Indians who were less concerned with island and regional distinctions. Those associations formed by mainly first generation West Indians which had memberships drawn from a number of islands invariably had formal committees composed of members with similar island origins. Thus, the JWA and the West Indian Sports Association which preceded it, plus the majority of recreational associations had committees which were island exclusive even if the 'paper membership' showed that the membership was drawn from a wider island base. The BWI club was the only formal association which had a mixed committee (in terms of island affiliations) but this group managed to maintain itself solely because of the informal and non-political nature of its activities and aspirations.

At the informal level, island distinctions were less important. The realisation of common deprivations gradually cements closer relationships among West Indians of differing backgrounds in the British context (Midgett, 1975). Most West Indians discounted the importance of island affiliations in forming friendships with fellow migrants, but 'closer friends' were invariably drawn from the same island background. Despite this evidence of a breaking down of island parochialism, such distinctions were swiftly redrawn in situations requiring some degree of trust and/or deference. For example, relationships involving financial transactions or individual and group attempts to claim political standing tended to be most successful within island delineations. Consequently formal associations among West Indians are generally island exclusive, and island and regional differences are crucial to the explanation of the lack or ephemerality of formal communal associations which attempt to transcend these distinctions.

Class, status and colour divisions are also important among West Indians, both in Britain and the Caribbean. In the West Indies societies are stratified by highly complex class and colour lines. Similarly, status distinctions are also intricate and based upon innumerable criteria. In general it appears that class, status and colour distinctions based upon the Caribbean pattern are broadly reproduced in Britain, although with some important modifications (Foner, 1979). Class distinctions appeared to be less important in Easton because most West Indians originated from the same, lower class background in the Caribbean. This in turn tended to reduce the importance of colour distinctions between West Indians in the city. Phenotypical features and colour gradations are still used as forms of status assessment but they appear to have diminished in importance as status attributes because of the common class position of most West Indians in the city. Local whites, for example, are often unaware of the sophisticated phenotypical distinctions used by West Indians to differentiate themselves and label all Caribbean migrants as 'coloured' or 'black'. Consequently, many West Indians recognise that they do occupy a common position as far as outsiders are concerned and this lessens the importance of very subtle colour divisions between them. However, less subtle distinctions are still important and a lighter skin is often accorded a higher status in Britain than a very dark complexion, particularly among older West Indians.

An additional reason for the lessening importance of colour gradations among West Indians in Britain also stems from the sharp distinctions made between white and black by local whites. Many West Indians stress the greater degree of racial harmony in the Caribbean as compared with Britain and this also tends to decrease the importance of colour distinction within West Indian groupings in Britain. It should be noted that this image of racial harmony is essentially mythical. The Caribbean is not a racial paradise; it is merely the setting for a sophisticated pattern of colour distinctions that contrasts with the rather more 'crude' pattern of colour divisions in Britain. This is well illustrated by Gordon Lewis's remarks that:

> The racial harmony of West Indian islands is a myth. What takes place, is not that the migrant comes from a harmonious race relations system to a system of incipient racialism but that, rather, he moves from a classificatory system based on the fine detective recognition of 'shade' to an English classificatory system that has taken over the American black-white dichotomy; so much more brutal and insulting. (1969:81)

However mythical the view of racial harmony might be among West Indians in Britain, it is a belief which is widely held. Many West Indians in Easton described the 'openness' of their islands in glowing terms. The retention of this myth does decrease the importance of colour distinctions among West Indians in the British setting but it also places those few middle class migrants in a very ambivalent position.

In the Caribbean, at least at the time of migration in the 1950s, a middle class position was equated with light skin colour and 'good' (that is near European) facial features. It was also connected with skilled and professional occupations and consequently with higher levels of educational attainment, income and wealth. Using all these criteria, there were very few West Indians in Easton who would have been accorded a middle class position by other West Indians in the Caribbean. Thus, those few West Indians who did have middle class jobs and a higher standard of living than their fellows, were in a marginal position between the host community and the majority of black workers. In most cases, local whites would not accept any West Indian as middle class because of his colour. Other West Indians might also refuse to acknowledge the higher class position of a fellow migrant because transfer to Britain is often seen as altering the class distinctions that were used in the Caribbean (Foner, 1979:134). Similarly, 'lightness' of skin may not automatically place an individual in a higher status position among West Indians in Britain because of the changes in the assessment of colour gradations within the West Indian settlement described above. Thus many lighter skinned West Indians face acute problems of status deprivation in Britain because of the withdrawal of prestige from both the host community and fellow West Indians. This will be seen to have great importance for community leadership when this problem is discussed later in the chapter.

Class distinctions within West Indian groupings in Easton are relatively unimportant because of the common class position of the vast majority of West Indians in the locality. Whether class is measured 'subjectively' in terms of how West Indians perceive their own or other migrants' class position, or 'objectively' by an observer, most West Indians in the city would be categorised as 'working' or 'lower' class. However, one of the most significant social processes to be considered is the formation of status groups within this common class base. Status groups may be formed on the basis of length of residence, age, island and regional background, occupation and education, etc. Life styles attributed to certain types of family structure and particular forms of religious worship are also important indicators of status amongst West Indians. I have suggested in this respect, that changes in the household and family structure of many West Indians in Britain indicate a move towards *intra-class* divisions in the metropolitan society that are comparable to *inter-*

159

class divisions in the Caribbean. For example, in the West Indies stable, legal family units are connected with a higher class life style whilst more loosely structured family units correspond to a lower class position (see Chapter 5). In Easton, stable or 'unstable' family units accord with higher or lower status positions within a common class base. Such status groups are formed along the lines of 'respectable' or 'non-respectable' life styles. A position within a stable family unit will accord with the former designation and therefore a high status position whilst a non-respectable background in an unstable household is congruent with a lower status evaluation. Respectability is equated with a legal marriage partnership or a permanent common-law partnership which is expected to lead to eventual legal marriage. Non-respectability is defined in accordance with those negative prescriptions assigned to ephemeral sexual partnerships that are formed outside of a formal family or household unit. Such views are further strengthened by condemnatory attitudes from local whites and Asians, many of whom tend to label loosely structured family units as indicative of the 'immorality' or 'promiscuity' which they often believe are typical of all West Indian sexual relationships. Therefore, respectability and non-respectability are measured (by West Indians) not only in relation to the social mores within West Indian groupings but also in terms of external evaluations of certain West Indian life styles by local whites (and possibly Asians).

Patterns of religious association also influence the formation of status groups. Distinctions are made within West Indian groupings between those individuals who are members of 'traditional' churches and denominations and those who belong to more sectarian religious associations. Membership of traditional churches and denominations is connected with status respectability. Religious membership of this kind is equated with high status and complements other prestigious pre-requisites which may include light skin colour, possession of educational qualifications, a skilled occupation and residence in a 'better' area, etc.

Sectarian forms of worship, for example, black Pentecostalism, are more concerned with doctrinal respectability, which accords with a low status position among most West Indians (see Chapter 6). Religious beliefs for the 'saints' were not additional status factors but *the* status factor which shaped their whole life style. In this sense, the saints are comparable to black power adherents who also adopt life styles which place them in low status positions as far as the majority of West Indians are concerned. However, the position of black power activists and the saints is somewhat ambiguous as far as the overall status system (if one can talk in such terms) within the West Indian settlement in Easton is concerned. Whilst it could be said that, for example, a dark skinned labourer, living in the heart of Lowdale in a loosely structured family unit, would be accorded a low status position by the majority of West

Indians; this individual would be accepted within the status system of the West Indian settlement in Easton. However, despite the fact that most saints and black power activists would be assigned low status positions by other West Indians, these two groups would be separated from the overall status system. Both the saints and the black power group had separate life styles which stemmed from their own particular world views.

It would simplify matters if West Indians could be placed within a dichotomy of respectability/non-respectability. There would be positive attributes connected with the former and negative attributes connected with the latter. Individuals could be placed in a high or low status position within their common working class category. But this assumes that there is one status system within the West Indian community and that individual attributes tend to be congruent with the dichotomy outlined above. That is to say, stable family units correspond with traditional religious membership, skilled occupations, some formal education, etc. and unstable family units are similarly aligned with sectarian worship, unskilled jobs and a lack of education. Possession of the former set of attributes would typify a high status 'respectable' position in the West Indian communities, whilst possession of the latter set would indicate a low status, 'non-respectable' position.

Whilst it is true to say that many West Indian individuals did approach one polarity or the other, therefore suggesting this model has some heuristic value, there are several points which make a dichotomy of this kind far too simplistic. One problem is concerned with the fact that status groups measured in terms of attributional criteria are not necessarily consistent with status groups measured interactionally. Invariably those status groups which could be defined according to 'objective' and external factors introduced by the observer did not always remain congruent with status groups defined on the basis of which individuals interacted with others of a similar life style within West Indian groupings.

Furthermore, if island affiliations are introduced, it can be seen that these cross-cut status lines. West Indians in Easton can be placed in attributional status groups irrespective of island affiliations, but interactional status groups must be seen to form within island groupings. An additional problem is centred on formal association membership and participation. Status formation among West Indians in Easton was exceptionally fluid and inconsistent. Both membership and participation in formal associations tended to blur status distinctions even further. Apart from specific sectarian forms of religious association and the BPG, there were no West Indian formal associations in the city which corresponded totally with status distinctions along the lines of respectability/ non-respectability. Activism in formal associations together with island affiliations blurred consistent status lines that could be drawn across

West Indian groupings.

For example, the committee members of the JWA were middle aged, long term residents. They lived within 'stable' family unions and those who were church-goers attended non-sectarian places of worship. One or two committee members resided in 'better areas' and were representative of the very small number of middle class West Indians in Easton. All of these members would accord with a high status, 'respectable' position measured in terms of these attributes. But the act of participation in the JWA was perceived as 'non-respectable' by many West Indians because of the supposed political nature of the association.

JWA committee members were adjudged as respectable within their own island community but they were often viewed as non-respectable political activists by first generation West Indians from other island groupings in the city. Political activism was non-respectable because it was seen as a form of activity which might endanger harmonious West Indian/host community relations. Thus, we can see that the status position of these activists is highly ambiguous because of inter- and intra- island distinctions.

The presence of recreational associations also tended to blur status distinctions. Most West Indians in Easton either chose or were forced to organise their own forms of entertainment. This meant that dances and sports activities were attended by a range of individuals who may not have mixed socially in the West Indies. Apart from the shebeens and some commercial parties which were generally seen as non-respectable forms of entertainment, most forms of recreational association cut across lines of respectability/non respectability. The more informal the interaction, the less important status distinctions appeared to be. In recreational settings, all the lines of conflict previously described may be important, for example, island exclusivity may be maintained but within these delineations the informality of the occasion appears to break down status differences.

This lack of recreational facilities for local West Indians appears to create a situation where status distinctions are partly ignored. If separate recreational associations could be provided by each island community, or by status groups within them, informal associations might be as divisive as formal associational activity. Certainly it would appear that, as soon as associations become formalised, they take on a degree of importance among West Indians which re-introduces status distinctions. These distinctions must be seen together with other factors as being a crucial explanation for the lack of formal association among West Indians generally. The complexity and divisiveness of the status systems within West Indian groupings reduces, at least at present, the potential for establishing permanent communal formal associations. The inconsistency of many status distinctions further restricts the possibilities for solidaristic group formations.

If a dichotomous status system existed along the lines of respectability/non-respectability, this might encourage the establishment of on-going formal associations because of strong in-group/out-group feelings between 'respectable' and 'non-respectable' members of the West Indian communities. Consistent, albeit conflictual, associations could be developed within these polarities. But West Indians in Easton could not be placed within a single coherent status system. Status group formation operated within a number of systems, both inter- and intra-island distinctions being particularly important. This inconsistency nullified the possibility of coherent associations being established along status lines.

Status competitiveness, combined with the individualism of West Indians also had significant implications for the scarcity of 'leaders' within the West Indian communities. The paucity of individuals who were able to establish on-going formal associations is another important reason for the limited political organisation among West Indians in the city. The middle classes dominate formal association leadership in the Caribbean but there are very few middle class West Indians in Easton. However, the noted presence of upwardly mobile individuals might be expected to counteract this deficiency. Certainly, within high status groups, some West Indians have moved towards middle class positions within their respective communities. Therefore, it might appear that these individuals could provide some leadership potential.

At this point, it will be useful to mention certain studies which have been concerned with black leadership in Britain. Sydney Collins (1957), for example, distinguished between what he called 'instrumental' and 'model' leaders within black minority groups in Britain. The former combine authority and control over fellow migrants based upon traditional authority ascriptions derived from the society of origin. Instrumental leaders are also those individuals who occupy formal authority positions within local migrant associations in Britain. Model leaders on the other hand exert no direct control through the occupancy of formal positions of authority in such associations. Their 'leadership' is based upon the influence they exert through their possession of prestige which is derived from their social position in society at large. Collins mentions the importance of black politicians, sportsmen or film stars as role models for the 'leaders' of coloured minorities in Britain. Thus, black individuals who occupy high status positions, in any society, may influence leadership patterns among migrant groups in Britain. Collins' leadership typologies lose some of their usefulness when it is realised that they are supposed to relate to all black and coloured minorities in Britain. It appears unlikely that similar leadership models can be used to explain leadership patterns within West Indian and South Asian groupings because of their cultural diversity and the distinctiveness of their respective colonial histories.

For example, it is difficult to utilise the concept of instrumental leadership among West Indian groupings in Britain because West Indian societies do not contain the religious and political 'traditional' patterns to such a marked extent as those which typify leadership in South Asian communities in India, Pakistan and Bangladesh. Similarly, it is also questionable whether instrumental leaders will have authority which is recognised throughout West Indian communities. Invariably 'leadership' within West Indian formal associations in Easton is only likely to be recognised within the different island groupings. Furthermore, whilst members of formal associations may occupy positions of authority within particular associations, it remains problematic whether such authority is acknowledged outside of the structure of the formal association in question, even within an island grouping.

The idea of 'model' leadership is an interesting one but again it appears somewhat misplaced as far as West Indians in Easton are concerned. There seems to be some confusion of leadership *per se* with the influence of a role model that may inspire leadership in others. West Indian cricketers, African politicians, American negro civil rights leaders and the growing numbers of black British athletes and soccer players may be seen as role models for West Indians in Britain. These individuals can project feelings of negritude or black self-esteem which stem from their accomplishment in a particular field of endeavour, whether in a political or sporting arena. This level of achievement could inspire leadership among other black men throughout the world; but even Collins acknowledges that there is no direct link between the role model and 'immigrant leaders' (or potential leaders) and therefore it is difficult to equate this type of influence with 'leadership'. It would appear completely fortuitous whether the prowess of the 'role model' is transformed into localised political activity within black communities. Nevertheless, it would seem profitable for further research to be carried out to examine the links between 'model leaders' and localised political activism.

Manderson-Jones (1971) in a more recent study[2] criticised Collins for similar reasons to those given above. He partly rejects the notion of 'leadership' within West Indian groups mainly on the grounds that the concept of 'leadership' was overwhelmingly rejected by his sample of West Indian political activists. Manderson-Jones equates leadership with positions of authority within formal or semi-formal associations and therefore argues that, because most West Indian political activism takes place outside of such associations, the concept of 'leadership' is misplaced. He states that:

> A considerable amount of the main current of West Indian
> dialogue—not only the interchange of ideas but practical

organisation and planning for action—occurs outside the major formal and semi-formal structures and within small, completely informal groups, either locally closed or drawing together people with common interests from widely separate areas. (1971:198)

Despite some reservations, Manderson-Jones suggests that West Indian leadership in Britain can be viewed as forming within two opposing ideological positions—the militant-radical and the conservative-moderate. The militant-radical position is typified by those West Indian political activists who reject European and white influences and align themselves with an international 'black cause'. Historical links with Africa and the universality of negritude are emphasised and thus the position of West Indians in Britain is seen to be directly comparable with, for example, the contemporary position of blacks in the United States. Finally, militant-radicals do not rule out the use of violence in the quest for black equality in Britain.

The conservative-moderate occupies a position in polar opposition to militant-radicalism. West Indian activists of a conservative-moderate persuasion partially accept European influences and do not rule out the assistance of whites in their associations. They tend to view West Indian activism within a national rather than an international context and the use of violence is firmly disavowed.

Manderson-Jones's study provides much useful material in a neglected research area but his militant radical-conservative moderate dichotomy is rather simplistic. Certainly our findings in Easton point towards this conclusion.

It is possible to place the Black Power group and West Indians who actively support its ethos within the militant-radical position. Similarly, the JWA could be placed within the opposite ideological category. Nevertheless, this does simplify the concreteness of these ideological positions and the supposed firmness of the links between them and particular West Indian formal associations. A more useful approach would be to examine the inter-meshing of these ideological standpoints. I would suggest that this interpenetration of ideologies further exaggerates the ambivalence of most West Indian associations (both formal and informal) in Easton and the individual members within them. The position of middle class or upwardly mobile working class West Indians is a case in point.

We noted that all West Indians face problems of identity, both in Britain and in the Caribbean. This is related to the historical and contemporary culture clash of African and European inheritances, their relation to the social structure of West Indian societies and the social organisation of West Indian groupings in Britain. The way in which West Indians evaluate their own and other West Indians' status and class position is a graphic illustration of this 'cultural ambivalence'. West Indians in Britain must decide whether to measure their status in relation to other West Indians, the host community or both.

Middle class and upwardly mobile West Indians in Britain face the most acute problems of identification because they occupy social positions of the greatest status inconsistency. Thus, for example, high status may be acknowledged by the West Indian settlement (or at least an island group within it) but not by local whites. In addition, status inconsistency is related to political activism or formal association membership in a number of ways which tend further to confuse the status position of the individuals concerned. Middle class and upwardly mobile working class West Indians may decide to measure their status in relation to local whites and this will tend to reduce the possibility of their involvement in political activity. This is because the host community often perceives political activism among such West Indians as a sign of hostility towards them and they will therefore not acknowledge a higher status position. With this eventuality middle class and upwardly mobile working class West Indians are unlikely to participate in any associational activity which they believe to have any radical political connotations. Indeed, they may withdraw both socially and residentially from any contacts with other West Indians who are seen by them to be from a lower class or status position.

However, it is problematic whether this type of separation or political moderation will result in upwardly mobile West Indians being accepted by their white neighbours. In which case these West Indians may react by involving themselves in political activity, even to the point of militant-radicalism. Paradoxically, this overt political activism may be viewed as a 'non-respectable' activity by most other West Indians and this will result in further status loss. Consequently, the majority of middle class and upwardly mobile working class West Indians disassociate themselves from participation in any type of formal association except those highly informal recreational associations in which status distinctions tend to be less important.

Militant-radical associations are labelled as deviant by the vast majority of local whites and by many West Indians, particularly first generation migrants. Therefore, at present, political associations of this type are few and tend to be even more fragmented than more 'moderate' West Indian associations. Faced with hostility from local whites and, at best, merely token support from West Indian communities, the difficulties of formation and maintenance of militant-radical associations are acute. Similarly, the number of West Indians who are prepared to adopt 'leadership' roles within militant-radical associations and face such hostilities, is, not surprisingly, small. However, the position of second generation West Indians in Easton is highly significant for future political activism and this will be briefly discussed in the following, concluding chapter.

The presence of other ethnic groups in Easton also has a marked influence on associational activity among West Indians. The substantial South Asian communities in the city are particularly pertinent here. South Asian groupings are cross-cut by numerous national, regional, linguistic and religious differences to name only a few major divisions within them. However, the degree of social interaction between Asians and West Indians in Easton is extremely limited. In consequence, these internal divisions within the erroneously described 'Asian community' are not readily apparent to West Indians. Hence, the general stereotypes that West Indians commonly use to describe Gujaratis, Punjabis or Mirpuris tend to emphasise the closeness and solidarity of the South Asian communities. The profusion of Asian commercial enterprises and places of worship tends to reinforce these beliefs, as the communal organisation reflected by these activities is readily visible to the local West Indian population.

The apparent success of Asians in establishing numerous organisations and associations stands in sharp contrast to the dearth of West Indian associations. This situation reinforces the feelings of inferiority which many West Indians experience. These feelings are quite visible, for whilst many West Indians expressed a considerable hostility towards Asians in general, there is also an undisguised admiration of the degree to which South Asian communities were able to organise and provide numerous facilities for themselves. For example, whereas the West Indians were still struggling to attain some unity which could enable them to establish a community centre for themselves, the South Asian communities had long since acquired several premises for this purpose, in addition to the elaborate buildings which were used for religious ceremonies and recreational activities.

The demise of West Indian formal associations and the lack of success in establishing a community centre became a self-fulfilling prophecy for many West Indians in Easton. Associations were not formed by West Indians because it was felt by them that they would inevitably fail. If associations were hopefully established, they were often dissolved through lack of communal support. Support was not forthcoming because so many West Indians foresaw failure! Thus, there existed a cycle of associational fragmentation which was partly generated by the lack of confidence which many West Indians had, either in their own or in other West Indians' ability to form on-going associations. The presence of other ethnic communities in Easton who had established a wide range of such associations, despite being faced with similar types of rejection in the city, compounded West Indian beliefs in their own inferiority and reinforced the fragmentary cycle within the West Indian settlement. Recognition of this cycle turned many West Indians towards self and group deprecation which further reinforced the type of psychological and social individualism previously described.

We can see that the formation of West Indian formal associations in Easton is rendered highly problematic by a number of social contingencies. These contingencies which influence communal formal association must be viewed within the contemporary and historical framework within which West Indians and other members of the metropolitan society are placed. Some of the social dimensions which have shaped relationships between Britain and the various West Indian societies have been briefly described throughout this study. It has been constantly stressed that the social configurations embedded within these societal relationships have had a profound effect on the structure of relationships between and within West Indian groupings in Easton, between West Indians and adjacent ethnic minorities, and between West Indians and the host community.

The twin heritages of Africa and Europe have historically shaped societies in the Caribbean which are still seeking to forge their own unique identities. The social organisation of West Indian groupings in Easton reflects this quest and the innumerable complexities surrounding it. It would be erroneous to state that patterns of association among West Indians in Britain are simply a reproduction of Caribbean forms. What has occurred is an inter-penetration of social factors which partly originate from the Caribbean cultural background and partly stem from those contingencies which West Indians are confronted with in the metropolitan society. Most of the problems which surround West Indian formal associations arise from this inter-meshing of cultural differences and the continuation of a colonial relationship between Britain and the West Indies which has rendered many West Indians powerless both within their societies of origin and in Britain.

The history of the black lower classes in the Caribbean has been marked by a tendency towards informal association and spontaneous uprisings rather than formalised political activism. In the present century, whilst the lower classes in West Indian societies have maintained a vigorous interest in political change, they have only comparatively recently been enfranchised and the leadership which originally came from white elite members is still largely within the hands of those coloured middle-class elites which replaced the latter. The past two decades have seen striking changes in the old traditions of negative status evaluation and very recent signs of greater lower class political awareness (see Chapter 2). Nevertheless, despite the close links between the Caribbean and West Indian migrants in Britain, most black workers in Easton came out of island societies in the 1950s when the traditional impediments to formal political participation were still firmly entrenched.

168

In Easton, West Indian social organisation is primarily informal and largely characterised by primary rather than secondary associations. Leadership patterns reflect differing styles of politics that stem from distinct class backgrounds in the Caribbean and consequent attitudes to European 'white respectability'. Most formally organised West Indian political associations in Easton are modelled on middle class forms of voluntary association common to Britain and the West Indies. They have recognised offices, rules and procedures and seek at least some minimal incorporation into the local political system. Many West Indians who occupy official positions in these associations are able to legitimate themselves as 'leaders' in the eyes of local white politicians and government officials, but their following within the West Indian settlement is usually far more tenuous. For these 'leaders' the very assumption of a leadership position militates against the competitive egalitarianism among West Indians. The 'respect' gleaned from a relatively small number of West Indian and white fellow participants must be set against a general pattern of scepticism and allegations of self-seeking. In essence, the limited authority of the majority of West Indian activists in formally organised associations in Easton, stems from their occupance of an official position rather than legitimised personal attributes.

Other 'leaders' do not belong to associations, but have a following through an acknowledgement from others of personal skills. The good talker, stylish dancer, outstanding domino player or successful hustler, acquires a reputation in a specific area of everyday life without aspiring to general political leadership and, therefore, endangering his personal status.

This delicate balance between respectability and reputation has been eloquently described by Peter Wilson (1973) specifically in relation to competing modes of social organisation (see Chapter 5). These inter-dependent 'complexes of value, behavior, and relationships ... (are) expressed in a continuous dialectic of action and reaction, of imposition and erosion, of boasting and gossiping, of climbing up and pulling down' (Wilson, 1973:222-3). Respectability stems from middle class West Indian evaluations which tend to rank others according to their indivi-dual attainments in Western terms. The occupancy of bureaucratic offices, educational achievement or acceptance in the 'right' circles are examples which come to mind here. Reputation, far from being based on externally imposed status criteria, emerges from assessments drawn exclusively from within the black community; whether it be personal mannerisms, sporting achievement, sexual prowess or whatever. The crux of the matter rests with the relationship between respectability and reputation, particularly the way in which one system of evaluation acts as a self-sustaining defence against the other. As Wilson perceptively remarks:

> Reputation tends to stress the equality of human inequalities, whereas respectability seeks to rank them. Reputation recognizes personal attainment and differentiation and it sanctions personal competition. It prizes in particular those talents and skills which bolster a self-image by putting down, undermining, and ridiculing respectability. As a system of rewards, reputation sustains a community whose measures of personal worth are an intrinsic and self-adjusting part of the community itself rather than coming from the outside. (Wilson, 1973:223-4)

Wilson suggests that West Indian societies have to throw off the externally imposed colonial and neo-colonial shackles of 'respectable' evaluation by adopting those measures of reputation intrinsic to the black masses. The recent loosening of traditional forms of status evaluation in the Caribbean no doubt demonstrates some moves in this direction. However, migration to Britain places the West Indian within a metropolitan context where 'respectability' is widely sanctioned and thus a new set of constraints mirror those embedded in the Caribbean context. The complexity of status systems operating within West Indian communities is one of the most striking impediments to political leadership in Easton. Any move into the formal political arena in the British context necessitates some form of reconciliation between competing modes of social acceptance. In order to be accepted by 'white society' some degree of respectability must be attained but often at the price of derogation from one's (West Indian) fellows. Conversely, if one adopts a life style that militates against metropolitan constraints, these actions may acquire one a specific reputation, although the generality of acceptance throughout the West Indian settlement is problematic. But such actions are likely to provoke retaliation from the 'host community' in any number of guises from legal constraint to personal avoidance. Faced with these competing demands, most West Indians seek modest reputations in social arenas divorced from the dangers of political action. For aspirations towards political participation, particularly leadership, inevitably place one at the point of tension between forms of external constraint and the subtleties of internal derogation.

The links between systems of reputation and respectability are a further example of what I would describe as cultural ambivalence. West Indians, that is to say, are in a state of 'social tension' in the way in which they symbolise the world and place themselves in discrete social categories. The West Indian both in Britain and the Caribbean must consciously or unconsciously make decisions about himself and others in terms of a set of competing conceptualisations of the social world. For example, in the way in which he measures his own or others' status position, in the way in which he accords or withdraws prestige, a set of criteria exist that reflect the Euro/Afro dynamic. This particular form of marginality[3] has obvious allusions to personal identity and these, in turn, are related to certain types of social correlates, for example, 'individualism'.

The ramifications of cultural ambivalence lie at the heart of the differences in social organisation and consequent patterns of leadership among West Indians and South Asians. South Asian communities are by no means free of organisational factionalism, inter-generational conflict and the presence of self-appointed political leaders (Ballard and Ballard, 1978; Khan, 1977, 1979; Ballard, 1979). But the systems of reciprocity and mutual obligation encompassed by the hierarchical forms of authority common to South Asian communities, ensures some semblance of traditional patterns of leadership within village-kin networks. These traditional bases for authority are often challenged in the metropolitan situation, not least by a South Asian second generation who may find familial demands as restrictive as they are protective. But patron-client relations operate within established rules of deference, which despite the possibilities of new conflictual definitions emerging in Britain, provide a ready framework for political organisation or mutual assistance at home and work (Khan, 1979; Brooks and Singh, 1979). For a Sikh or Gujarati, and more pertinently his or her children, residence in Britain poses the problem of retaining one's own ancient and honoured culture or the adoption of British social mores. For the West Indian, particularly young blacks, the 'choice' lies between some accommodation with the metropolitan society or the redefinition of one's own less prestigious cultural background. The nub of this dilemma lies in the fact that historically both 'minority' and 'majority' cultures are inextricably linked and the opprobrium of one is dependent on the pervasive coercive quality of the other. Hence, the difficult task of formulating totally new identities.

West Indians in Easton also occupy marginal positions because of the nature of black-white relations in Britain. The 'colour line' in this country is not totally rigid and hence some degree of limited upward mobility in terms of education, employment, etc., is possible. Whilst West Indians are culturally distinct from the indigenous white community in Easton they are sufficiently similar in language, dress and customs, for example, to afford some West Indians the possibility of achieving a degree of social acceptance which enables them to cross the 'colour line'. Thus, West Indians have to decide whether they wish to aspire towards white acceptance or concentrate on forging a separate 'West Indian' or 'black' self-identity. Complete rejection by the host community would encourage the latter but the likelihood, albeit a limited one, of some mobility across the colour line tended to reinforce the marginal position of West

Indians in the city.

A further major problem for West Indians is their occupancy of a marginal position between the indigenous white population and the migrant South Asian communities in the city. West Indians and Asians occupy similar minority positions *vis-a-vis* the majority, as most local whites tend to perceive all black workers as 'coloured immigrants' and therefore both groups are subsumed under the same label. However, we have seen that West Indians and Asians are culturally distinct and that social interaction between them is extremely limited. Consequently, they rarely assist one another in forming joint representative associations. As a result, the West Indians in Easton occupy a minority position within the much wider migrant-indigenous, black-white dichotomies which describe social and colour divisions in the city. The West Indians are a minority within a minority.

West Indians and South Asian communities are in direct competition for scarce resources; for example, housing, employment and recreational facilities. The social organisation of West Indian groupings does not lend itself to the formation of communal 'self-help' associations whilst the structure of South Asian communities would appear to do so. As a consequence, West Indians are rendered relatively powerless, not only by actual or believed acts of discrimination on the part of the white community, but also by the presence of neighbouring, ethnic minorities, whose social mores favour communal rather than individualistic types of association and place them in a more advantageous position than their West Indian counterparts.

The implications of relative power distinctions within the supposed 'black community' in Easton will be remarked on in the concluding chapter. At this juncture, the present chapter can be brought to a close by briefly illustrating how the nature of West Indian formal association relates to those very limited opportunities which the receiving society provides for the amelioration of the social problems encountered by black minorities in Britain.

For a number of reasons, West Indians do not perceive the trade union movement or the political party system in Britain as representative of their needs. Consequently, the formal political machinery of local government or local trade unions in Easton are, in the main, not seen by West Indians in the city as possible avenues for West Indian political expression. The only alternative organisation provided by the host community is the local Committee of the Community Relations Commission and its officers. The shortcomings or otherwise of this body have been described elsewhere (Abbott, 1971; Katsnelson, 1973; Pearson, 1976). The sole purpose of this brief examination of the position of the Community Relations machinery in Easton is merely to describe the relationship it had to local West Indian groupings and how it influenced their associational activity. This is best illustrated by returning to the difficulties which West Indians encountered when attempting to establish their own community centre in Easton. This was briefly touched upon earlier when the activities of the JWA were described. The Community Relations Council and its related committees represent one of the very few platforms where West Indian and South Asian 'leaders' meet each other in Easton. However, it has already been established that, at the time of the research, only the JWA were represented on the Board. This meant that only a small section of the West Indian population in Easton was seen by other West Indians to be represented, namely the Jamaicans.

The non-representativeness of the JWA was also recognised by the local Community Relations Office but it took the view that some West Indian representation was better than none at all! Paradoxically, the 'egalitarian' policy of the Easton City Council and the Community Relations Council towards local black communities seriously disadvantaged the West Indian settlement. Both the Council and the Community Relations Office claimed to treat all groups equally but this tended to ignore the fact that there were distinct inequalities between Asians and West Indians in the city. For example, West Indians were not able to rely upon separate commercial and financial organisations such as had been established locally by the South Asian groupings, but West Indians and Asians were treated equally with regard to housing provision and so forth by the Easton City Council.

The significant point to note here is that many West Indians in Easton believed that the Council did not take note of the respective, differing needs of Asians and themselves in the city. They were acutely aware of the self-sufficiency of local South Asian communities in contrast to their own difficulties and felt that the Council should compensate for this by giving them more assistance than their Asian neighbours. The Council's refusal to adopt this kind of policy was seen as directly discriminatory by the West Indian population.

The Council did not appear to be aware that West Indians had unique problems of organisation which prevented them from achieving the same degree of communal association as other groups in the city, both black and white; although the island distinctions within the West Indian settlement were certainly visible to the City Council because the application of the JWA for financial assistance towards the building of a community centre was rejected on the grounds that this association (quite correctly) was unrepresentative of all West Indians in the locality. The Council took the view that, if Indian and Pakistani communities, to say nothing of other minorities in the city were able to establish their own community centres without financial assistance from them, the local West Indians should be able to do so the same.

Whether by accident or design, this policy of the Council placed West

Indians in yet another vicious circle. Many West Indians felt that a community centre would be highly desirable because it might encourage some degree of unity among the various island communities. But it was recognised that West Indians, on their own, could not possibly raise the necessary finance for such a project hence the application to the Council for assistance. Such assistance required evidence of West Indian unity before sanctioning the financing of a community centre which was designed to bring about this kind of unity!

The majority of local West Indian activists interpreted this position as confirming their belief in the obstructive and discriminatory nature of Council policies. They also rejected the Community Relations Office because it was seen as either supporting the Council or seemingly incapable of altering the policies of the latter on their behalf. This lack of rapport between West Indian leaders and the Council effectively ruled out any assistance from official bodies in the city in the early 1970s. The desirability of internal West Indian political associations was never more graphically illustrated than by the recognition among West Indians that they would have to organise themselves in the face of little outside aid.

We can see that a number of factors prevent or inhibit the formation of formal communal association, particularly of a political nature, among West Indians in Easton. These factors include the external contingencies that West Indians are faced with in Britain, the internal divisions within West Indian groupings which take a number of forms, and above all, the subtle and complex ways in which these external and internal contingencies inter-penetrate and, in turn, produce additional constraints on formal associational activity. Thus, it becomes apparent that, despite the fact that many West Indians have achieved a standard of living which lifts them above the harshest levels of social and economic deprivation; despite the existence of upwardly mobile West Indians who might act as leaders of political activism; and, above all, despite the expressed desire for change among West Indians in Easton, this inter-penetration of social contingencies has so far produced few results in the way of political association.

Notes

1   It should be appreciated that social deprivation affects the associational activities of not only black minorities but also large numbers of the white population in Britain. Similarly, the structural placement of black workers is part of a much wider spectrum of deprivation among many migrant workers in Western Europe, both white and black. The latter point is well illustrated by Gorz (1970) and Castles and Kozack (1973). For material on social deprivation among the white and black

population in Britain see, for example, Coates and Silburn (1970); Harrison (1973) and Townsend (1979).

2   Manderson-Jones' data are drawn from a London sample and are based on activists from those few West Indian associations which purport to be nationally based. It is interesting to note that the present study which only attempts to examine a localised example of West Indian associational patterns, nevertheless appears to correspond with Manderson-Jones' main findings.

3   It is important to distinguish between the terms cultural ambivalence and marginality used here. Marginality frequently alludes to a social position and/or set of psychological dispositions which stem from the occupancy of two or more contradictory social positions or a form of, for example, 'racial hybridization'. Cultural ambivalence relates to a form of social and psychological tension, emanating from the Caribbean colonial experience, which incorporates racial, social and psychological features. These in turn influence the marginal social position of the West Indian in Britain wherein he has to reconcile his composite identity to the metropolitan situation. Thus, a 'marginal' cultural amalgam is confronted with the marginal (in a traditional sense) immigrant position in the British context.

4   This became the Commission for Racial Equality in 1977.

8 Postscript

In 1978 I returned to Easton for a brief, three month visit. Much remained unchanged but some new developments were observable in the local scene. Most striking were the visible signs of South Asian business expansion in Lowdale. The Gujarati and Sikh populations, in particular, had demonstrated their entrepreneurial skills from the earliest days of Asian settlement in the city, but by the end of the 1970s the traditional corner shop was joined by Asian owned chain stores and supermarkets. Stimulated by the injection of additional skills and capital from recently arrived migrants from East Africa, the South Asian business sector now controlled a wide range of retail and wholesale outlets, finance houses and even factories. Hence, the diverse local Asian population, now grown to approximately 50,000, had further revitalised the inner city through ethnic enterprise.

Compared with the growth and successful economic diversification of at least a significant minority of the South Asian population, the local West Indian settlement displayed few overt changes. Indeed, one might be forgiven for initial feelings of *deja vu*. But the black communities in Easton found that increasing economic and social pressures promoted new forms of unity. In particular, a local model of South Asian achievement, growing fears for black youth and the vigour of anti-immigrant political groups welded together disparate factions into some form of an alliance which succeeded in getting a Caribbean community centre project off the ground.

In Chapter 4 we recounted the series of events in 1973 and early 1974 that led to the JWA's plans for a community centre being thwarted. A combination of island insularity, city council inflexibility and lack of funds spelled initial failure, but changes in local attitudes and national policies eventually provided a more positive climate. It was very evident to West Indian activists in Easton that they had to mend their differences and present a common front if they were to achieve anything. In the latter part of 1974, the various West Indian associations in the city met once again to discuss the community centre project. Island and other differences were still visible, but a federation of local black organisations was suggested so that funding applications could be made on the basis of a representative West Indian platform. This proposal was finally agreed upon and an umbrella-like organisation, the Combined Caribbean Association (CCA) was established.   West Indian

176

association in the city was asked to nominate two representatives onto a general management committee and places were allocated to other individual members.

This bureaucratic arrangement could hardly be expected to erase old conflicts overnight, so in some ways divisions between the various associations were simply replicated within the new organisation. This was inevitable because the personalities involved in West Indian associations prior to the formation of the CCA, were still present in the new organisation. But those activists still influential in the JWA, the BWIC, the island development associations and the sports clubs, were now joined by newcomers on the local political scene. Most notably, a London based community worker, also attached to Easton University, who was able to advise on national funding schemes for community projects.

If the impetus for acquiring a West Indian community centre sprang from new attempts at co-operation at the local level, eventual success in obtaining finance for a suitable building and staff emanated from the national policies of successive British governments responding to increased racial conflict in the 1970s. The success of the National Front, measured in terms of an effective symbolisation of anti-immigrant feelings if not parliamentary gains, illustrated the presence of fear, suspicion and hostility about colour and cultural differences which was evident in many urban areas. Furthermore, the growing alienation of black youth was widely publicised in a series of 'moral panics' (Cohen, 1973) about mugging, street crime and hostilities with the police (Hall, 1978). A scenario of violent political demonstrations, numerous hostile acts towards West Indian and South Asian communities from Brixton to Southall, from Handsworth to Brick Lane; and confrontations between the police and young blacks at the 1976 and 1977 Notting Hill Carnivals, merely provided visible signs of group conflicts that had been recognisable in more covert forms for many years. The response to these events was a process of continual refinement of the bureaucratisation of race (Mullard, 1973). By the mid 1970s this was demonstrated by a profusion of government funded minority self-help projects.

In Easton, the CCA took full advantage of this political climate and successfully applied for a grant from the Community Relations Commission to establish a community centre. In 1978 the project was nearing completion in an old building close to the city centre. Four full-time workers were attached to the scheme, one of whom supervised young unemployed youths who assisted with internal renovation. The Centre has not been entirely free from factional disputes, and recent financial difficulties were only alleviated by additional funds from the city council. Nevertheless, the project heralds a new attempt at consensus among the various West Indian communities in the locality. The proposed programme of youth work, cultural activities and black studies, as well as the provision of a recreational centre, follows a pattern replicated in most cities with substantial West Indian settlements. It is a form of self-help which strikes a continuity with the moderate forms of political activism and recreational association observable in Easton since the earliest days of black immigration. However, the current scene reflects an attempt at rapprochement between moderate and more militant aims, particularly a quest for greater self-determination.

Undoubtedly, this recent demonstration of greater co-operation among West Indians is a reaction to economic recession and social unrest. In the 1950s in Easton, West Indian recreational associations sprang up to service small, disparate primary groupings. The growth of these communities over the years led to island exclusivity and the duplication of many associational forms. At the present time this factionalism is still evident, but greater communality has arisen in classic fashion from a crisis situation. One of the most significant facets of this crisis is the growing concern among West Indian parents about the uncertain future for their children. Unemployment is widespread among the unskilled; particularly school-leavers, and black youth is proportionately over-represented in the jobless statistics (Smith, 1977:71). A mismatch between aspirations, educational achievement and job opportunities, and the crushing experience of growing up in an often alien white society, has produced new forms of social expression among young 'West Indians'. A recently formed youth subculture based around distinctive speech patterns, appearance, fashion and music forms, now provides the possible foundations for an emergent ethnicity centred on the commonalities of colour, culture and shared disadvantage (Miles and Phizacklea, 1977). This form of identification establishes a boundary between black youth and their South Asian and white peers. It also represents a potential or real barrier between the generations within the West Indian settlement (Lago and Troyna, 1978).

However, the so-called gap between first and second generations has still to be rigorously researched, so claims of wholesale disaffection should be viewed with caution. The majority of West Indian families in Easton are relatively close-knit and parents and children are mutually supportive. Nevertheless, the clash of values between one West Indian generation still prepared to 'make the best of a bad job' and another increasingly viewing such complacency with distaste, cannot be ignored. Consequently, the West Indian Community Centre in Easton must be seen, in part, as an attempt by older West Indians to provide their children with a focus for a 'respectable' identity. As Mike Phillips (1978) has noted, there are a growing number of West Indian clubs in Britain formed by parents to provide an alternative to 'the reggae/weed way of life'. Phillips concludes that:

> The West Indian clubs are part of an increasingly coherent
> drive to erect institutions which will serve to communicate
> the values which older West Indians regard as important.
> Their significance, at this moment, is that they are among
> the few public institutions which operate as a link between
> the generations. (1978:586)

It remains to be seen whether the CCA and the newly opened community centre in Easton will successfully bridge competing viewpoints within the local black communities. These conflicts are no longer, if they ever were, a simple reflex of different generations and the traditional moderate and militant strands of West Indian local politics. First generation activists now appear more militant in their rhetoric and there is far less deference to white liberals and cross-cultural window dressing. But the majority of leaders still work within the system because they are reliant upon external funding and support. Furthermore, the CCA is by no means exclusively dominated by the 'oldtimers', as younger West Indians from the sports clubs and what used to be the Caribbean Cultural Group, have been drafted onto the Centre committee. So if we are defining the moderates as those activists still prepared to seek some, albeit severely reduced, accommodation with the 'host community', the majority of local activists, young and old, fall within this category.

Of course, this raises the question of representation and the current legitimacy of West Indian 'leaders' within their own communities. An impressionistic glance at the local scene suggests this remains a major problem for black activists, because so many West Indians continue to seek individual solutions to current problems, or they cling to forms of communality which are clearly separatist within the local black population as a whole. The continued importance of black Pentecostalism and the nascent forms of Rastafarianism in Easton are cases in point.

The Ras Tafari movement represents a new pervasive influence among black youth, but there is a clear continuity between this contemporary social movement and earlier forms of political and socio-cultural expression among West Indians in Britain. Most notable is the sustained commitment to some vestiges of a Caribbean past in the metropolitan society. For the first generation, this involved a retention of a sense of home on the basis of island affiliation and the maintenance of subtle but distinctive cultural patterns. Such linkages proved both divisive and cohesive depending on the level of identification. The greater the communality at the island level, the weaker the identification with an all-embracing 'West Indian' label. For most of the second generation an island identity is indistinct and the harsh realities of present existence remain unsoftened by visions of a return to a Caribbean home. The shared experience of being black, of being alienated from school, work and possibly one's family, and a common perception of a racist society symbolised by police/black relations, merely required a catalyst to produce a newly emergent focus for group solidarity.

In the 1960s and early 1970s the more militant strand of West Indian politicisation sought to provide a positive framework for black communities by borrowing from the Afro-American experience. Much of the political rhetoric and organisation at this time had only limited appeal for most young West Indians. The BPG, for example, was too elitist and remote from the everyday experience of the majority of black youth in Easton. But the links between radical black thought in the United States and the Caribbean had been established to a point where it became inevitable that movements akin to Rastafarianism in Jamaica, would be reproduced in the back streets of London, Birmingham and Manchester. The crucial elements in this reproduction were a recognition of social deprivation in both geographical contexts, and the transference of a social, religious and political message through mediums which were already firmly rooted within the black communities. Jamaica, the British West Indian society which first experienced the traditions of black Zionism, through the early influences of Garveyism and the subsequent religio-political revivalism of the 1930s, has provided over half the Caribbean immigrants to Britain since the late Forties. Consequently, the likelihood and persistence of a transfer of a social movement from the urban poor in West Kingston (Jamaica) to the British black population, was heightened by the existence of substantial Jamaican settlements in Brixton, Handsworth and Moss Side. In these areas a trans-Atlantic blend of Afro hairstyles, soul music and a North American inspired black political rhetoric, was readily displaced or supplemented by a Caribbean religio-political expression that also provided a positive world view and highly visible life style. But this new subcultural outgrowth was specifically Jamaican (and later black British) in origin and contemporary form.

The move from a strictly sectarian minority following to a broader pattern of allegiance was achieved through the mediums of music, style and verbal exchange, which were already the hallmarks of reputation among many sections of the black communities in Britain. Rastafarianism, therefore, succeeded in gaining support not only through its ability to compensate for and explain life in the urban diaspora but also because it was shaped within the conventions of a lower class West Indian life style. For example, we noted earlier that one of the major impediments to West Indian political organisation is a pervasive social individualism. The Ras Tafari movement in Britain is communal in the sense that it grew out of loosely organised youth peer groups and a

180

common adherence to shared experience, but it is basically individual-istic and lacks formal organisation.[1] Cashmore, for example, relates how the Rastas developed some semblance of an organisational structure in England but he stresses that: 'It was this lack of personal focus and the concomitant lack of discipline which helped promote the enormous interest in Ras Tafari which followed'(1979:309). Cashmore argues that the growth of the movement was made possible by the existence of a young black population with similar life experiences, who were open to a world view which offered a coherent explanation for their deprivation. Rasta beliefs presented a positive and elitist conception of blackness, transmitted through the patois laden forms of reggae music, that promo-ted an inclusive ethnic boundary.

Hence, the growing exclusivity of important sections of black youth in Britain, Rasta or otherwise, represents an affinity with earlier discus-sed notions of status reputation (see Chapter 7). Status within many second generation peer groups is not based on the acceptability of one's behaviour or beliefs to external evaluations of respectability widespread among their parents and white society. Indeed, the strictly non-respec-table connotations of Rasta and 'Rude boy' images, in the eyes of local whites and many older West Indians, strengthen in-group identification. Reputation for a Rasta rests on the ability to reason, to debate, to make sense of the present world in his own terms. Group cohesion arises, therefore, from a flexible *individual* acceptance of a common basis of belief, rather than leader/follower authority relationships. Where autho-rity exists this appears to be more dependent on the reputation of charismatic personalities than the respect of office (Owens, 1977/78).

The possibility that these beliefs will become sufficiently ubiquitous and politically organised to pose a real alternative to more traditional West Indian associations remains a matter for conjecture. An appraisal of the current Easton scene suggests three quite distinct forms of adher-ence to Rastafarian influence. A very small number of second generation West Indians have adopted a fully religious expression. These black youths live together, adopt strict habits of custom and dress, and spend considerable time 'reasoning' and examining biblical texts. Another minority of local black youth represent a current extension of earlier forms of political militancy previously illustrated by the BPG. A loose grouping of young activists have assimilated various Rasta conventions of speech, fashion and appearance; the locks, patois, ganja smoking and hatred of Babylon being readily recognisable as a logical continuation of earlier separatist rhetoric and life styles. If this political strand of a highly disparate movement becomes more widespread, the possibilities for political mobilisation among black Britons will significantly increase. But the ultimate strength of political commitment will depend on the degree of susceptibility of Rastafarianism to a more organised form of political expression among black youth. Any moves towards a formalised leadership structure may well re-introduce the traditional problems of leader/follower relations discussed in the previous chapter.

At present the most common form of adherence to Rasta beliefs appears somewhat nebulous. Many of the youths who may be seen in the community centre, the Adelaide Street youth club or simply around town, have locks, wear red, yellow and green tams (woolly hats) and intersperse conversation with Rasta phrases drawn from reggae lyrics. But whether this outward display is a question of fashionable convention or a more deep-seated religious and/or political commitment, is difficult to assess. As Troyna recognises:

> The levels of commitment which can be observed are as diverse as the movement itself. Whilst for some the attraction of adopting Rasta symbols, emblems and language is in keeping abreast of current fashions, others consider the movement as symbolically representing their discontent with their actual social situation in contemporary Britain. By promoting the black identity, Rastafarianism inverts the norms and values of a racist society. (1978a:20).

Whatever form of commitment is expressed, it is relevant to stress the fact that external pressure is likely to reinforce the separatism demonstrated by the movement. One of the most striking features of the Rasta phenomenon is its visibility and well publicised alleged and actual connection with social deviance. Once again we have an illustration of British patterns partly replicating those previously observable in the Caribbean. In both contexts, the Rastamen evoke negative images of criminal violence and drug abuse. A stereotype compounded by bizarre appearance and an exotic life style which instils fear, suspicion or anger in the unbeliever. On the one hand, as noted earlier, external negativism reinforces in-group solidarity and reaffirms the failings of Babylon and of those West Indians who still respect it. On the other hand, the exclusivity of the Rasta movement and its equation with the militancy of black youth promote new divisions within West Indian settlements.

In common with past fears of 'black power', this most recent display of subcultural separatism finds a less than easy acceptance among first generation West Indians. At best, it strikes familiar chords of protest among some older migrants now more prepared to sympathise with a less passive political voice. At worst, it symbolises a gaping divide between generations socialised in different geographical and social climes. Many older Jamaicans remember the violence associated with the 'Rude boys' in Kingston in the 1950s and find it equally difficult to accept them in the contemporary British situation. For other island groups the Jamaican connection merely strengthens other negative

thoughts of a foreign social manifestation. At the heart of many generational differences, however, is a clear value contradiction between alternative philosophies. Not least is the problem of reconciling black Zionist
beliefs with the Judaeo-Christian ethic embedded in first generation West
Indian values (Hebdige, 1976:138). Irrespective of the signs of secularisation among West Indians in Britain (see Chapter 6), the rejection of
'conventional' Christian teachings by Rastafarians is unpalatable to
many older migrants. Somewhat ironically, there are two pervasive forms
of retreatism within West Indian settlements at the present time, which
seek alternative millenial solutions. The black Pentecostalist and follower
of Ras Tafari share a belief in future salvation for the dispossessed. Both
movements are based on fundamentalist biblical interpretations and
often espouse strict codes of self-denial. Ultimately, both seek escape
from a hostile world by constructing alternative conceptions of reality
that incorporate promises of future release. But Ras Tafari represents
a different textual interpretation, a different conception of the Kingdom,
and although certain forms of sobriety are shared (for example, an aver-
sion to alcohol and gambling), other beliefs are in sharp contradiction.
The Pentecostalist form of puritan austerity, exemplified by sober dress,
habits and beliefs in strict work habits, hardly squares with the stereotypical or actual exotic display of Rasta emblems and life styles; particularly when the latter have become inextricably linked with the firmly
irreligious and non-ascetic forms of diluted 'pseudo-Rasta' adherence
which many devout Rastafarians disavow. The creation of stereotypes
which readily equate the display of locks and tams with ganja smoking
and street crime, distort the multi-stranded nature of Rasta allegiance
and conflate often quite separate religious, political and strictly 'fashionable' forms of observance (Miles, 1978:25). These stereotypical images
not only promote negative responses within local white and South Asian
communities, but also nullify any possibilities of acceptance among a
broad section of the black population. The traditional subtle rift between the saints and more secular West Indians, has, therefore, been
further complicated by the emergence of an additional form of religious
retreatism.

　　If Rastafarianism demonstrates a growing influence among black
youth and some older West Indians, Pentecostalism also shows few signs
of losing support within the black communities in Easton. The Pentecostal churches examined in Chapter 6 are still thriving and have expanded
their community activities within their congregations. But, significantly,
they too are introducing youth programmes, and many saints voice fears
of their sons, if not daughters, drifting into what they perceive as disso-
lute and ungodly ways of life. Many parents are perplexed that some
adolescents are seeking strategies of self-help which involve a sharp rejection of Church teachings. As Louden notes: 'Most adolescents

consider the Church to have fostered a false and unattainable value system, i.e., that of work, co-operation, fair play, family, and fellowmen' (1977:50). This creed seems to bear little relation to the present world as many young blacks see it and they have little faith in passive otherworldly solutions.

At present, three general trends are observable in Easton which replicate, to a greater or lesser degree, similar processes observable in other cities with sizeable black populations. Firstly, a majority of first generation West Indians and many of their children, still appear to be fatalistic about present social and economic conditions. Most older West Indians may have lost hope of significant changes in their life situation, may even have rejected utopian thoughts of a return 'home', but remain politically quiescent. A large section of black youth, perhaps the majority in Easton, are considerably more disillusioned and/or resentful than their parents, but they still hope things will improve. Perhaps the economy will eventually pick up, that apprenticeship could come through or one's present job will not prove to be a dead-end. Secondly, however, it is indisputable that a growing number of black Britons are totally dispirited or have angrily rejected those limited opportunities offered by what they see as a malevolent society. Many of these young blacks are in the lower streams of local secondary schools, or are unemployed and have few or no educational qualifications to offer in the labour market, even if there were job vacancies. Some youths are homeless because of family situations where parents or other kin have interpreted group disaffection as an individual display of laziness or a refusal to work. It is this group which meets the full glare of media publicity and bears the brunt of academic scrutiny; this group which has shaped an emergent ethnicity around the symbols of Rasta, reggae and rebellion; and this group which has prompted the creation of moral panics, which in turn, strengthen peer group boundaries and re-vitalise a militant subculture.

Such moral panics shape public opinion and policy formation and underline a third pervasive trend. In the early 1970s, Katznelson, drawing attention to what he perceived as successive British governmental attempts to construct a series of 'racial buffers' between black activists and the wider polity, argued that:

> In the critical period of migration of Third World people to Britain, the most critical structural decision made was the establishment of national and local institutions outside of the traditional political arenas, to deal with the issues of race. The structural arrangements announced by the political consensus White Paper[2] did not integrate the Third World immigrants into the politics of institutionalised class conflict that characterize the liberal collectivist age, but

rather set up alternative political structures to deflect the politics of race from Westminster to the National Committee for Commonwealth Immigrants, and from the local political arenas to voluntary liaison committees. As a result the Third World population has been structurally linked to the polity indirectly through buffer institutions. (1973:150)

More recent commentators on this institutionalisation of political consensus suggest that the process is almost complete. Sivanandan (1976), for example, responding to more recent refinements in race relations and immigration legislation, and the plethora of projects funded by the CRE and the Urban Aid programme, concludes that: 'In terms of the larger picture, what has been achieved in half a decade is the accommodation of West Indian militant politics within the framework of social democracy'(1976:365). Whether one accepts a liberal social welfare model, or a more radical conspiracy thesis to explain this trend, the fact remains that the incorporation of most forms of West Indian political expression within a format of conciliation agencies and funding dependence, has raised a number of paradoxes. One major example being the nature of the choices open to both 'moderate' and 'militant' West Indian activists. The moderates heighten the possibilities of support from a still passive but more politically responsive section of the first generation, and the 'race relations industry', by maintaining a basically accommodative stance. But this strategy involves a dependence on external funding, of which even moderate West Indians are increasingly mistrustful. Any visible evidence of accommodative strategies, moreover, further threatens the traditionally uneasy relationship between the liberal and radical political associations within black communities. For example, the eventual success of the community centre project in Easton will undoubtedly depend on a reconciliation of those sections of the community who perceive it within recreational and social welfare terms and those with more overt political aims.

The direct successors of the BPG are freed from some of the predicaments of compromise faced by the moderates. Yet the militant-radical stance adopted towards black youth, who represent the most fertile ground for non-passive political strategies, is not unproblematic. In one sense an uncompromising black response which rejects menial labour for a wageless, subcultural existence, appears eminently susceptible to the overtures of more radical associations. But the long-term political ramifications of this kind of liaison are complex. This is firmly recognised by Hall *et al* (1978) in their recent perceptive analysis of the dilemma faced by black associations and activists who see revolutionary potential in the current disaffection of black youth. The authors recognise the obvious political attractions of a rebellious section of the West Indian second generation, but they recognise the dangers of a firm identification with this group:

> For the moment black organisations and the black community
> defend black youth against the harassment to which they are
> subject, they appear on the political stage as the 'defenders of
> street criminals'. Yet not to defend that sector of the class
> which is being systematically driven into crime is to abandon
> it to the ranks of those who have been permanently criminal-
> ised. (Hall, 1978:396)

Any firm alignment with street crime as a politically acceptable form of
behaviour threatens to alienate a substantial number of West Indians who
still cling to the virtues of employment, and what they see as a respectable, law-abiding lifestyle. Furthermore, such a strategy is unlikely to
gain support among the South Asian communities and certainly not
local whites.

The greatest paradox is that any support for 'social deviance' inevitably strengthens the moderate stance. The moral panics surrounding
mugging, the Rasta movement and other features of 'black rebellion'
have already attracted considerable government attention. One result
of their concern has been a bolstering of moderate West Indian associations and the official legitimation of 'leaders', self-appointed or otherwise. Therefore, despite the growing militancy of black rhetoric, despite
the increase in West Indian political co-operation, and despite the recur-
rence of events prompting what Rex has described as policies of defen-
sive confrontation within black settlements (Rex, 1979), there remains
a major question-mark over the future shape of black politics in Britain.
That question-mark centres on the possibilities for cohesive, on-going
political organisation as opposed to what Hall *et al* (1978:397) describe
as 'proto-political consciousness' and individualistic, spontaneous forms
of activism.

This brings us back to a brief, concluding re-appraisal of the political
options available to racial and ethnic minorities discussed in the Introduction. It will be remembered that Miles and Phizacklea (1977) introduced three alternative strategies which they described respectively as
the class unity, ethnic organisation and black unity processes. The
current situation in Easton tends to support their conclusion that the
class and black unity processes are not viable at present. Easton has
never had a strong history of unionisation and the bonds between black,
brown and white workers are somewhat tenuous. West Indians are not
strongly represented in the local labour movement, although there are
individual links between particular black activists, white trade unionists
and Labour councillors. The South Asian communities have developed
informal networks in particular factories, where Asian shop stewards
act as official or unofficial job brokers and worker representatives.

Furthermore, the Indian Workers Association is well organised and has a sizeable membership, particularly since a number of successful strike actions in the mid-1970s strengthened their position. Local (white) trade union support was hardly in evidence on these occasions. More significantly, whilst some black organisations from London and Birmingham sent money for the Asian strikers, the local West Indian population, including the vast majority of activists, stood aloof from the industrial dispute. Nevertheless, some links between the South Asian and West Indian communities have been forged. Firstly, between those 'leaders' who act as representatives for their associations on the local CRC committees and other local bodies established on a multi-ethnic basis. The legitimacy of these activists in the eyes of those they purport to represent always remains problematic, so the political efficacy of this kind of unity is frequently illusory. Secondly, more viable bonds have been established by associations, such as those formed by black teachers on both a national and local basis.[3] Here there is a specific problem, namely the educational needs of ethnic and racial minorities, which provides an immediate focus shared by South Asian and West Indian teachers alike. These types of association are relatively influential because their members are articulate, have access to professional resources and often have political contacts beyond the orbit of parochial interests. But their numbers are small and their influence highly specialised. The third level of black unity is more spontaneous and arises from periodic signs of direct external threat. The most graphic illustration of this kind of co-operation is the local response to the National Front. The Front has always been very active in Easton; a city which has one of the earliest established branches in Britain. In the 1976 local council elections, National Front candidates gained almost a third of total votes cast in the city and the party only failed to acquire a seat on the council by a handful of votes. The visible threat of a very active anti-immigrant organisation certainly promoted some degree of co-operation between the various ethnic communities in Easton. Hence, multi-ethnic associations were at least partly instrumental in reducing the National Front vote in the 1979 local elections, although other national factors must be taken into account.[4]

Despite some signs of unity on the basis of colour and minority status, the fact remains that there is still very little contact between the South Asian and West Indian groupings. Consequently, relationships between the various ethnic populations range from an uneasy co-existence to outright hostility. Not least because the increased size and relative success of the South Asians in Easton has promoted further Asian autonomy and mild or less mild West Indian resentment. By 1978, in addition to the visible signs of Asian business activity previously described, the local South Asian population had succeeded in voting an Indian onto the Easton City Council and the number of Asian associations registered by the CRC office had reached the one hundred mark. Many West Indians continue to view this level of organisation as indicative of Asian exclusivity and political strength; although, in truth, such an array of associations is also a symptom of internal division and the result of considerable factionalism within the diverse South Asian communities. As a consequence of often subtle but politically important inter-ethnic divisions, the possibilities for black unity rest on a small and often unrepresentative number of activists and the continuance of external pressures, rather than any natural affinity among culturally and socially diverse groupings.

This leaves us with the question of ethnic organisation within the West Indian settlement. Currently, there is evidence of greater unity symbolised by the community centre project, a narrowing of the gulf between moderates and militants as the former grow more responsive to radical solutions, and a common awareness of the problems of black youth. But a number of underlying contradictions within the West Indian communities still remain unresolved. Most West Indians remain highly individualistic and basically unimpressed by organised political overtures. Many black activists are still self-appointed messiahs and many associations are paper organisations without rank and file members. The competing demands of reputation and respectability remain; shaped within the contrast between what Pryce (1979) has defined as the expressive-disreputable and stable law-abiding orientations which run like divisive threads through the West Indian settlement. Often this division corresponds with inter-generational differences, but it should be remembered that the second generation is also heterogeneous and still beset by the problems of cultural ambivalence. A growing body of research reveals that black youths may seek an identity for themselves in a variety of individual ways (Weinreich, 1979:102). For example, second generation young women may not replicate the patterns observable among male peer groups. In addition, those youngsters who do achieve more than their fellows at school may still seek white acceptance instead of a stake in the separatism of black subcultures (Troyna, 1978b). There is even evidence to suggest that island differences have not been entirely dissolved among younger 'West Indians'(Driver, 1979), and hence primarily Jamaican inspired cultural innovations may not have the same appeal for all black youth.

Faced with this degree of complexity and social confusion any attempt at a prediction of future political eventualities is misplaced. The majority of West Indians in Britain can be viewed as a collectivity facing similar structural conditions in various urban contexts within a common historical colonial framework. But just as the Caribbean has traditionally presented a multi-faceted visage of similarity and difference, each city in

Britain has its own ethnic mix, history of ethnic and racial relations, and local social, economic and political contingencies. One suspects, therefore, that the future pattern of relations between black, brown and white in Britain will be as varied as the historical paths which led them to their present situation.

Notes

1   This is evident in the Caribbean and British literature on the Ras Tafari movement. See, Owens (1977/8); Miles (1978) and Cashmore (1979).

2   The White Paper cited here is *Immigration from the Commonwealth*, Cmnd.2739, HMSO, London, 1965.

3   The Association of Teachers of Ethnic Minorities is a prominent example of this type of organisation.

4   The nation-wide failure of the National Front in the 1979 General and local elections, has been attributed to the apparent immigrant control lobby within the Conservative Party, which drew many of the votes from potential Front supporters. See, for example, the argument put forward by Husbands and England (1979).

Research appendix

The dividing line between one's research and other autobiographical details is always somewhat arbitrary. No more so than when field research is the main method of investigation. In one sense, therefore, this book grew out of my residence in Easton between 1969 and 1973, supplemented by frequent visits in early 1974 and a three month sojourn in late 1978. However, the most intensive period of fieldwork took place between October, 1971 and July, 1973. My research at this time was based on three broad areas of study.

First, all West Indian voluntary associations which had been formed prior to, or during, the period of fieldwork were studied intensively. This involved participation and/or observation in these associations and their various activities. I attended committee and general meetings, examined the records of associations (if such records were kept) and participated in the recreational life of the respective groups. Dances, parties and sports events were attended on a great number of occasions. In addition, all committee members who were prepared to co-operate, and many general members of these associations, were interviewed extensively.

Interviews were conducted informally and were largely unstructured, although certain topics were focussed on with all interviewees. Some activists were interviewed on only one or two occasions, for periods of at least an hour, but many people were questioned many times throughout the period of fieldwork. Interviews were held in peoples' homes, in pubs, and in other recreational settings. Some interviews were tape-recorded where informants became very well-known to me and notes were taken during interviews whenever this was possible. But in the majority of cases, research notes were written-up immediately after the interview.

The second area of research was a sample survey of West Indian households. This technique was used in order to study a number of West Indians who might not be active in voluntary associations. Respondents who were active in voluntary associations were not assumed to be 'representative' of all West Indians in the area. Thus, activists in the West Indian settlements could be compared with non-activists. In common with previous studies of ethnic minorities in Britain, it proved difficult to find a suitable sampling frame from which respondents could be randomly selected. Electoral Registers, street directories etc., were either inappropriate (these lists do not indicate birth-place or nationality) or unavailable (for example, Council housing or rating lists).

A sample was finally constructed by using the files of a local vicar and a list of West Indian parents which was obtained from a local junior school. The vicar had frequent contacts with many West Indians in the city, both parishioners and non-parishioners. The headmaster of the junior school was a Jamaican and was able to provide the addresses of all West Indian parents who had children at his school. All these parents were contacted, so no selection procedure was utilised. The addresses from the vicar's files were selected randomly with the exception of island of origin. Previous knowledge of the area and advice from informants enabled some attempt to be made to allow for the differences in size between the various West Indian communities in Easton. West Indians from the larger communities, for example, the Antiguans, therefore formed a greater proportion of the sample than West Indian households from smaller communities.

Each household was sent a letter either from the vicar or the headmaster, introducing myself and briefly explaining the proposed research. The letter was followed by a visit from the researcher, accompanied by either the vicar, the headmaster, or another West Indian who was known to the household. At this meeting, further explanations were given for the nature of the research and each member of the household over the age of 18 was asked to complete a short questionnaire. These questionnaires were collected a few days later and, on this visit, all respondents were asked whether they were prepared to be interviewed. A very high response rate was obtained by these methods. Initially, 83 houses were visited. Only 7 outright refusals were encountered, but in 28 households one or more persons refused to complete a questionnaire, in many cases on the grounds that the questions would be duplicated if all members of the household completed them. However, all of the non-respondents agreed to be interviewed. A further 8 households could not be contacted because they had moved away from the area. The combined refusal and non-contacted total of 15, left a sample of 68 residential units, 43 from the headmaster's addresses, the remainder from the vicar's list.

Interviews were informal but more structured than those with voluntary association members. Questionnaire responses were used as the basis for interviews, although many discussions covered a very broad area. Many interviews were group affairs with, for example, both husband and wife present. However, no rigid pattern was adhered to because many household members were not available at the same time. Indeed, some households required constant re-visiting. No attempt was made to use a tape-recorder or to take notes during these interviews. Notes were written up immediately after an interview had been conducted. Most interviews lasted at least an hour, but many were prolonged. Several respondents were interviewed on a number of occasions as we became better acquainted.

The final and most important part of the research programme was concerned with participation and/or observation in and around the Lowdale area. Throughout the period of fieldwork many hours were spent in pubs, clubs and cafes, on street-corners and in peoples' homes. Research was not restricted to West Indians but included discussions with many other local residents, for example, Asians and local whites. In addition, local councillors, local government officials, social workers, teachers, journalists, etc., were consulted and interviewed at various times. In short, the classic tenets of field research were adopted. In 1978 some informants were re-visited, changes in local associations were noted and local reports, newspapers, etc., were studied. No one of the techniques used throughout the study could be said to be adequate in itself, but taken together, they enabled me to construct a composite picture from the inter-related data acquired.

Bibliography

Abbott, S. (ed), *The Prevention of Racial Discrimination in Britain*, Oxford University Press/Institute of Race Relations, London, 1971.

Allen, S., *New Minorities, Old Conflicts*, Random House, New York, 1971.

Allen, S. and Smith, C., 'Race and Ethnicity in Class Formation: A Comparison of Asian and West Indian Workers', in Parkin, F. (ed), *The Social Analysis of Class Structure*, Tavistock, London, 1974.

Arensberg, C., 'Methods of Community Analysis in the Caribbean', in Rubin, V. (ed), *Caribbean Studies*, University of Washington Press, Seattle, 1960.

Aurora, G., *The New Frontiersmen*, Popular Prakashan, Bombay, 1967.

Ayearst, M., 'A Note on Some Characteristics of West Indian Political Parties', *Social and Economic Studies*, vol.3, no.2, September 1954, pp.186—97.

Ballard, R., 'Ethnic Minorities and the Social Services', in Khan, V. (ed), *Minority Families in Britain*, Macmillan, London, 1979.

Ballard, R. and Ballard, C., 'The Sikhs: The Development of South Asian Settlements in Britain', in Watson, J. (ed), *Between Two Cultures*, Basil Blackwell, Oxford, 1977.

Banton, M., *The Coloured Quarter*, Cape, London, 1955.

Banton, M., *Racial Minorities*, Fontana, London, 1972.

Banton, M., 'Rational Choice: A Theory of Racial and Ethnic Relations', Social Science Research Council, Research Unit on Ethnic Relations Working Paper, no.8, 1977.

Barrett, L., *Rastafarians: A Study in Messianic Cultism in Jamaica*, University of Puerto Rico, Rio Pedras, 1968.

Beckford, G., *Persistent Poverty*, Oxford University Press, New York, 1972.

Beetham, D., *Transport and Turbans*, Oxford University Press/Institute of Race Relations, London, 1970.

Bell, R., 'The Lower-Class Negro Family in the United States and Great Britain', *Race*, vol.XL, no.2, October 1969, pp.173—83.

Bell, W., *The Democratic Revolution in the West Indies*, Schenkman, Cambridge, Mass., 1967.

Best, L., 'The February Revolution', in Lowenthal, D. and Comitas, L. (eds), *The Aftermath of Sovereignty*, Anchor Press, New York, 1973.

Bloom, L., *The Social Psychology of Race Relations*, Allen & Unwin,

London, 1971.

Bracey, J. *et al.* (eds), *Black Nationalism in America,* Bobbs-Merrill, New York, 1970.

Braithwaite, E., 'The "Coloured Immigrant" in Britain', *Daedalus,* no.96, 1967, pp.416—512.

Braithwaite, L., 'Social Stratification in Trinidad', *Social and Economic Studies,* vol.2, no.2, 1954, pp.5—176.

Braithwaite, L., 'Social and Political Aspects of Rural Development in the West Indies', *Social and Economic Studies,* vol.17, no.3, 1968, pp.264—75.

Brathwaite, E., *The Development of Creole Society in Jamaica, 1770—1820,* Clarendon Press, Oxford, 1971.

Brooks, D. and Singh, K., 'Pivots and Presents', in Wallman, S. (ed), *Ethnicity at Work,* Macmillan, London, 1979.

Calley, M., 'Pentecostal Sects among West Indian Migrants', *Race,* vol.III, no.2, May 1962, pp.55—64.

Calley, M., *God's People,* Oxford University Press/Institute of Race Relations, London, 1965.

Campbell, A., 'St. Thomas Negroes: A Study of Personality and Culture', *Psychological Monographs,* vol.LV., no.5, 1943.

Caplan, N., 'The New Ghetto Man: A Review of Recent Empirical Studies', *Journal of Social Issues,* vol.26, no.1, Winter 1970, pp.59—75.

Carmichael, S. and Hamilton, C., *Black Power,* Random House, New York, 1967.

Cashmore, E., 'More than a version: a study of reality creation', *British Journal of Sociology,* vol.XXX, no.3, September 1979, pp.307—21.

Castles, S. and Kosack, G., *Immigrant Workers and Class Structure in Western Europe,* Oxford University Press/Institute of Race Relations, London, 1973.

Coard, B., *How the West Indian Child is Made Educationally Sub-Normal in the British School System,* New Beacon Books, London, 1971.

Coates, K. and Silburn, R., *Poverty: The Forgotten Englishmen,* Penguin, London, 1970.

Cohen, S., *Folk Devils and Moral Panics,* Paladin, St. Albans, 1973.

Cohen, Y., 'The Social Organisation of a Selected Community in Jamaica', *Social and Economic Studies,* vol.2, no.4, 1954, pp.104—33.

Collins, S., *Coloured Minorities in Britain,* Lutterworth, London, 1957.

Cross, C., *Ethnic Minorities in the Inner City,* Commission for Racial Equality, London, 1978.

Cross, M., *Urbanization and Urban Growth in the Caribbean,* Cambridge University Press, Cambridge, 1979.

Cumper, G., 'The Jamaican Family: Village and Estate', *Social and Economic Studies*, vol.7, no.1, March 1958, pp.76–108.

Cumper, G. (ed), *The Economy of the West Indies*, Institute of Social and Economic Research, Jamaica, 1960.

Daniel, W., *Racial Discrimination in England*, Penguin, London, 1968.

Davison, R., *Black British*, Oxford University Press/Institute of Race Relations, London, 1966.

De Kadt. E. (ed), *Patterns of Foreign Influence in the Caribbean*, Oxford University Press, London, 1972.

Desai, R., *Indian Immigrants in Britain*, Oxford University Press/ Institute of Race Relations, London, 1963.

Dex, S., 'A Note on Discrimination in Employment and its Effects on Black Youths', *Journal of Social Policy*, vol.8, no.3, 1979, pp.357–69.

Driver, G., 'Classroom Stress and School Achievement' in Khan, V. (ed), *Minority Families in Britain*, Macmillan, London, 1979.

Fanon, F., *Black Skin, White Masks*, Paladin, London, 1970.

Fitzherbert, K., *West Indian Children in London*, Bell and Sons, London, 1967.

Foner, N., *Jamaica Farewell*, Routledge and Kegan Paul, London, 1979.

Freilich, M. and Coser, L., 'Structured Imbalances of Gratification: the Case of the Caribbean Mating System', *British Journal of Sociology*, vol.XXIII, no.1, March 1972, pp.1–19.

Frucht, R., 'A Caribbean Social Type: Neither "Peasant" nor "Proletarian" ', *Social and Economic Studies*, vol.13, no.3, 1967, pp.295–300.

Glass, R., *Newcomers*, G. Allen and Unwin, London, 1960.

Gorz, A., 'Immigrant Labour', *New Left Review*, no.61, 1970, pp.28–31.

Gosden, P., *Self-Help—Voluntary Associations in the Nineteenth Century*, Batsford, London, 1973.

Greene, J., 'A Review of Political Science Research in the English Speaking Caribbean: Towards a Methodology', *Social and Economic Studies*, vol.23, no.1, March 1974, pp.1–47.

Hadley, C., 'Personality Patterns, Social Class and Aggression in the British West Indies', *Human Relations*, vol.II, no.4, October 1949, pp.349–63.

Hall, D., 'Slaves and Slavery in the British West Indies', *Social and Economic Studies*, vol.II, no.4, December 1962, pp.305–18.

Hall, S. *et al.*, *Policing the Crisis*, Macmillan, London, 1978.

Harrison, I. (ed), *The New Poor: Anatomy of Underprivilege*, Peter Owen, London, 1973.

Hausknecht, M., *The Joiners*, Bedminster Press, New York, 1962.

Hebdige, D., 'Reggae, Rastas and Rudies', in Hall, S. and Jefferson, T. (eds), *Resistance through Rituals*, Hutchinson, London, 1976.

Heinemann, B., *The Politics of the Powerless*, Oxford University Press/ Institute of Race Relations, London, 1972.

Henry, F. and Wilson, P., 'The Status of Women in Caribbean Societies: an Overview of their Social, Economic and Sexual Roles', *Social and Economic Studies*, vol.24, no.2, June 1975.

Hill, C., *West Indian Migrants and the London Churches*, Oxford University Press/Institute of Race Relations, London, 1963.

Hill, C., 'Pentecostalist Growth—Result of Racialism', *Race Today*, vol.3, no.6, June 1971, pp.187—90.

Hindess, B., *The Decline of Working Class Politics*, Paladin, London, 1966.

Hinds, D., *Journey to an Illusion: The West Indian Comes to Britain*, Heinemann, London, 1966.

Hiro, D., *Black British, White British*, Eyre and Spottiswode, London, 1971.

Hsu, F. (ed), *Psychological Anthropology: Approaches to Culture and Personality*, Dorsey Press, Homewood, Illinois, 1961.

Husbands, C. and England, J., 'The hidden support for racism', *New Statesman*, vol.97, May 1979, pp.674—6.

Hylson-Smith, K., 'A Study of Immigrant Group Relations in North London', *Race*, vol.IX, no.4, April 1968, pp.467—76.

Ianni, O., 'Race and Class in Latin America', in Richmond, A. (ed), *Readings in Race and Ethnic Relations*, Pergamon, Oxford, 1972.

James, C., *Party Politics in the West Indies*, Vedic Enterprises Ltd., San Juan, Trinidad, 1962.

Jeffery, P., *Migrants and Refugees: Muslim and Christian Pakistani Families in Bristol*, Cambridge University Press, Cambridge, 1976.

John, D., *Indian Workers' Associations in Britain*, Oxford University Press, London, 1969.

John, G., 'The Churches and Race', *Race Today*, vol.2, no.10, October 1970, pp.344—46.

John, K., 'St. Vincent: A Political Kaleidoscope', in Lowenthal, D. and Comitas, L. (eds), *The Aftermath of Sovereignty*, Anchor Press, New York, 1973.

Katznelson, I., *Black Men, White Cities*, Oxford University Press/Institute of Race Relations, London, 1973.

Kerr, M., *Personality and Conflict in Jamaica*, Liverpool University Press, Liverpool, 1952.

Khan, V., 'The Pakistanis: Mirpuri Villagers at Home and in Bradford', in Watson, J. (ed), *Between Two Cultures*, Basil Blackwell, Oxford, 1977.

Khan, V. (ed), *Minority Families in Britain*, Macmillan, London, 1979.

Kiev, A., 'Psychotherapeutic Aspects of Pentecostal Sects among West Indian Immigrants to England', *British Journal of Sociology*, vol.XV, no.2, 1964, pp.129—39.

Knight, F., *The Caribbean,* Oxford University Press, New York, 1978.

Knowles, W., 'Trade Unionism in the British West Indies', *Monthly Labour Review,* vol.79, no.12, December 1956.

Kruijer, G., 'St. Martin's and St. Eustatius Negroes as Compared with those of St. Thomas', *West Indische Gids,* vol.XXXIV, 1953.

Kuper, A., *Changing Jamaica,* Routledge and Kegan Paul, London, 1976.

Lago, C. and Troyna, B., 'Black and Bitter', *Youth and Society,* no.29, June 1978, pp.17—19.

Lane, A. (ed), *The Debate over Slavery: Stanley Elkins and His Critics,* University of Illinois, Urbana, Ill., 1971.

Lawrence, D., *Black Migrants, White Natives,* Cambridge University Press, London, 1974.

Lawrence, D., 'Between cultures', *New Community,* vol.VI, nos.1 and 2, Winter 1977—8, pp.165—68.

Lazerwitz, B., 'Membership in Voluntary Associations and Frequency of Church Attendance', *Journal for the Scientific Study of Religion,* no.2, Autumn 1962.

Le Franc, E., 'The Co-operative Movement in Jamaica: an Exercise in Social Control', *Social and Economic Studies,* vol.27, no.1, March 1978, pp.21—43.

Lewis, G., 'Race Relations in Britain—A View from the Caribbean', *Race Today,* vol.1, no.3, July 1969.

Lewis, G., 'The Politics of the Caribbean', in Szulc, T. (ed), *The United States and the Caribbean,* Prentice Hall, Englewood Cliffs, New Jersey, 1971.

Little, K., *Negroes in Britain,* Kegan Paul, London, 1947.

Little, K., *West African Urbanisation,* Cambridge University Press, London, 1965.

Lomas, G., *Census 1971, The Coloured Population of Great Britain,* Runnymede Trust, London, 1973.

Louden, D., 'Conflict and Change among West Indian Parents and their Adolescents in Britain', *Educational Research,* vol.20, no.1, 1977, pp.44—53.

Lowenthal, D., 'Levels of West Indian Government', *Social and Economic Studies,* vol.II, no.4, December 1962.

Lowenthal, D., *West Indian Societies,* Oxford University Press/Institute of Race Relations, London, 1972.

Lyon, M., 'Race and Ethnicity in Pluralistic Societies', *New Community,* vol.1, no.4, Summer 1972, pp.256—62.

Lyon, M., 'Ethnicity and Gujarati Indians in Britain', *New Community,* vol.2, no.1, Winter 1972—3, pp.1—11.

Lyon, M., 'Ethnic Minority Problems—an overview of some recent research', *New Community,* vol.II, no.4, 1973, pp.329—51.

197

McDonald, F., 'The Commonwealth Caribbean', in Szulc, T. (ed), *The United States and the Caribbean*, Prentice Hall, New York, 1971.

McGlashan, C., 'The Sound System', *Sunday Times Magazine*, February 4 4, 1973.

Manderson-Jones, R., 'Minority Group Leaders', in Abbott, S. (ed), *The Prevention of Racial Discrimination in Britain*, Oxford University Press/Institute of Race Relations, London, 1971.

Manley, D., 'The Social Structure of the Liverpool Negro Community: with Special Reference to the Formation of Formal Associations', PhD Thesis, University of Liverpool, 1959.

Mannoni, O., *Prospero and Caliban: The Psychology of Colonisation*, Praeger, New York, 1964.

Mason, P., *Patterns of Dominance*, Oxford University Press/Institute of Race Relations, London, 1970.

Memmi, A., *The Colonizer and the Colonized*, Beacon Press, Boston, 1967.

Midgett, D., 'West Indian Ethnicity in Britain', in Safa, H. and Du Toit, B. (eds), *Migration and Development*, Mouton, The Hague, 1975.

Miles, R., 'Between Two Cultures? The Case of Rastafarianism', Social Science Research Council, Research Unit on Ethnic Relations Working Paper, no.10, 1978.

Miles, R. and Phizacklea, A., 'Class, Race, Ethnicity and Political Action', *Political Studies*, vol.XXV, no.4, 1977, pp.491—507.

Miles, R. and Phizacklea, A. (eds), *Racism and Political Action in Britain*, Routledge and Kegan Paul, London, 1979.

Mintz, S., 'The Caribbean as a Socio-Cultural Area', *Journal of World History*, vol.9, no.4, 1966, pp.912—37.

Moore, R., *Racism and Black Resistance in Britain*, Pluto Press, London, 1975.

Moore, R., 'Migrants and the Class Structure of Western Europe', in Scase, R. (ed), *Industrial Society: Class, Cleavage and Control*, George Allen & Unwin, London, 1977.

Mordecai, J., *The West Indies: The Federal Negotiations*, Allen & Unwin, London, 1968.

Morris, L., 'Women Without Men', *The British Journal of Sociology*, vol.XXX, no.3, September 1979, pp.322—40.

Morris, R., 'British and American Research on Voluntary Associations: a Comparison', *Sociological Inquiry*, no.5, Spring 1965.

Mullard, C., *Black Britain*, Allen & Unwin, London, 1973.

Munroe, T., *The Politics of Constitutional Decolonization: Jamaica, 1944—62*, Institute of Social and Economic Research, Jamaica, 1972.

Mussen, P. and Wsznski, A., 'Personality and Political Participation', *Human Relations*, vol.V, no.1, 1952, pp.65—83.

Nettleford, R., 'National Identity and Attitudes to Race in Jamaica', *Race,* vol.VII, no.1., July 1965, pp.59—72.

Nettleford, R., *Mirror, Mirror: Identity, Race and Protest in Jamaica,* William Collins and Sangster, Kingston, Jamaica, 1970.

Niebuhr, H., *The Social Sources of Denominationalism,* Meridian, New York, 1957.

Nowikowski, S. and Ward, R., 'Middle Class and British?—an Analysis of South Asians in Suburbia', *New Community,* vol.VII, no.1, 1978—9, pp.1—10.

Olsen, M., 'Social and Political Participation of Blacks', *American Sociological Review,* no.5, August 1970, pp.682—97.

Owens, J., 'Literature on the Rastafari: 1955—1974', *New Community,* vol.VI, nos.1 and 2, pp.150—64.

Oxaal, I., *Black Intellectuals Come to Power,* Schenkman, Cambridge, Mass., 1968.

Patterson, O., 'The Cricket Ritual', *New Society,* June 1969, pp.988—89.

Patterson, S., *Dark Strangers,* Penguin, Harmondsworth, 1965.

Peach, C., *West Indian Migration to Britain,* Oxford University Press, London, 1968.

Pearson, D., 'The Politics of Paradox: Community Relations and Migrant Response', *Social and Economic Administration,* vol.10, no.3, Autumn 1976, pp.167—81.

Pearson, D., 'Race, religiosity and political activism: some observations on West Indian participation in Britain', *British Journal of Sociology,* vol.XXIX, no.3, September 1978a, pp.340—57.

Pearson, D., 'Race, Class and Respectability: West Indian Activism in Comparative Perspective', *Sociology,* vol.12, no.3, September 1978b, pp.491—507.

Phillips, M., 'West Indian clubland', *New Society,* vol.44, June 1978, pp.585—6.

Philpott, S., 'Remittance Obligations, Social Networks and Choice among Montserratian Migrants in Britain', *Man,* vol.3, no.3, September 1968, pp.465—77.

Philpott, S., *West Indian Migration: the Montserrat Case,* Athlone Press, London, 1973.

Philpott, S., 'The Montserratians: Migration Dependency and the Maintenance of Island ties in England', in Watson, J. (ed), *Between Two Cultures,* Basil Blackwell, Oxford, 1977.

Pollard, P., 'Jamaicans and Trinidadians in North London', *New Community,* vol.1, no.5, Autumn 1972, pp.370—77.

Proctor, J., 'British West Indian Society and Government in Transition 1920—1960', *Social and Economic Studies,* vol.II, December 1962.

Pryce, K., *Endless Pressure,* Penguin, Harmondsworth, 1979.

Rex, J., *Race, Colonialism and the City*, Routledge and Kegan Paul, London, 1973.

Rex, J., 'Black militancy and class conflict', in Miles, R. and Phizacklea, A. (eds), *Racism and Political Action in Britain*, Routledge and Kegan Paul, London, 1979.

Rex, J. and Moore, R., *Race, Community and Conflict: A Study of Sparkbrook*, Oxford University Press/Institute of Race Relations, London, 1967.

Rex, J. and Tomlinson, S., *Colonial Immigrants in a British City*, Routledge and Kegan Paul, London, 1979.

Richmond, A. *et al.*, *Migration and Race Relations in an English City*, Oxford University Press/Institute of Race Relations, London, 1973.

Roberts, B., 'Protestant Groups and coping with Urban Life in Guatemala City', *American Journal of Sociology*, vol.73, 1967–8, pp.762–7.

Rodman, H., *Lower-Class Families: The Culture of Poverty in Negro Trinidad*, Oxford University Press, New York, 1971.

Rose, E., *et al.*, *Colour and Citizenship*, Oxford University Press/Institute of Race Relations, London, 1969.

Rubin, V. (ed), *Caribbean Studies: A Symposium*, University of Washington Press, Seattle, 1960.

Saunders, P., *Urban Politics*, Hutchinson, London, 1979.

Scott, D., 'West Pakistanis in Huddersfield—Aspects of Race Relations In Local Politics', *New Community*, vol.1, no.5, Autumn 1972, pp.38–44.

Searle, C., 'Grenada's Revolution: an interview with Bernard Coard', *Race and Class*, vol.XXI, no.2, Autumn 1979, pp.171–88.

Simpson, G., 'Political Cultism in West Kingston, *Social and Economic Studies*, vol.4, no.2, September 1955, pp.133–49.

Singh, P., *Local Democracy in the Commonwealth Caribbean*, Longman, Jamaica, 1972.

Singham, A., *The Hero and the Crowd in a Colonial Polity*, Yale University Press, New Haven, 1968.

Singham, A. and N., 'Cultural Domination and Political Subordination: Notes Towards a Theory of Caribbean Political System', *Comparative Studies in Society and History*, vol.15, no.3, 1973, pp.258–88.

Sivanandan, A., 'Race, Class and the State: the Black Experience in Britain', *Race and Class*, vol.XVII, no.4, 1978, pp.347–68.

Smith, C. and Freedman, A., *Voluntary Associations: Perspectives on the Literature*, Harvard University Press, Cambridge, Mass., 1972.

Smith, D., *Racial Disadvantage in Britain*, Penguin, Harmondsworth, 1977.

Smith, M., *West Indian Family Structure*, University of Washington Press, Seattle, 1962.

Smith, M. and Kruijer, G., *A Sociological Manual for Extension Workers in the Caribbean*, Department of Extra-Mural Studies, Kingston, University of West Indies, 1957.

Smith, R., 'The Family in the Caribbean', in Rubin, V. (ed), *Caribbean Studies*, University of Washington Press, Seattle, 1960.

Stone, C., *Class, Race and Political Behaviour in Urban Jamaica*, Institute of Social and Economic Research, Jamaica, 1973.

Stycos, J., Back, K. and Mills, D., *Prospects for Family Reduction*, The Conservation Foundation, New York, 1957.

Szulc, T. (ed), *The United States and the Caribbean*, Prentice–Hall, New Jersey, 1971.

Theobald, R., 'Seventh Day Adventists and the Millenium', in Hill, M. (ed), *A Sociological Yearbook of Religion in Britain*, no.7, Student Christian Movement, London, 1974.

Thomas, C., 'Meaningful Participation: The Fraud of It', in Lowenthal, D. and Comitas, L. (eds), *The Aftermath of Sovereignty*, Anchor Press, New York, 1973.

Townsend, P., *Poverty in the United Kingdom*, Penguin, Harmondsworth, 1979.

Troyna, B., 'Rastafarianism, Reggae and Racism', *National Association for Multi-racial Education*, Summer, 1978a.

Troyna, B., 'Race and Streaming: a case study', *Educational Review*, vol.30, no.1, 1978b, pp.59–65.

Wagley, C., 'Plantation-America: A Culture Sphere', in Rubin, V. (ed), *Caribbean Studies*, University of Washington Press, Seattle, 1960.

Wallman, S., 'Race relations or ethnic relations', *New Community*, vol.VI, no.3, Summer 1978, pp.306–9.

Wallman, S. (ed), *Ethnicity at Work*, Macmillan, London, 1979.

Ward, R., 'Race relations in Britain', *British Journal of Sociology*, vol.XXIX, no.4, December 1978, pp.464–79.

Watson, J. (ed), *Between Two Cultures*, Basil Blackwell, Oxford, 1977.

Weinreich, P., 'Ethnicity and Adolescent Identity Conflicts', in Khan, V. (ed), *Minority Families in Britain*, Macmillan, London, 1979.

Wells, A. and D., *Friendly Societies in the West Indies*, Her Majesty's Stationery Office, London, 1953.

Wilgus, C. (ed), *The Caribbean: Its Hemispheric Role*, University of Florida Press, Gainesville, 1967.

Wilson, B., 'An Analysis of Sect Development', *American Sociological Review*, vol.24, February 1959, pp.3–15.

Wilson, B., *Sects and Society*, Heinemann, London, 1961.

Wilson, P., *Crab Antics*, Yale University Press, New Haven, 1973.

Index

118—19, 160
and race 10, 19, 158—9, 186
and religion 123—9,
underclass 3
Coard, B. 100
Coates and Silburn 175
Cohen, S. 177
Cohen, Y. 38—9
Collins, S. 6, 163—4
Combined Caribbean Association
176—9
Commission for Racial Equality
175, 185
Community Centre, West Indian
73—7 passim, 177—9
Community Relations Commission
73, 172, 177
Community Relations Council,
Easton: 77, 173—4, 188
Conservative Party 189
Cross, C. 107
Cross, M. 19, 24, 29, 46, 53,
102, 104, 110, 124
Cultural ambivalence 121, 166,
170—1, 175
Culture shock 6, 148—9
Cumper, G. 49, 102
Cypriots 6

Daniel, W. 2
Davison, R. 1, 107
De Kadt, E. 42
Desai, R. 14
Dex, S. 155
Dominica 18, 124
migrants 44
political movements 35
religion 124
Driver, G. 155, 188

Easton 1, 43
Ethnicity 1, 178, 184
and minority status 11
and politics 10, 186

Fanon, F. 42
Fitzherbert, K. 101, 106, 116
Foner, N. 1, 2, 7, 43, 52, 107—
17 passim 155, 158—9
Formal and informal associations,
distinction 12—13
Freilich and Coser 109—10
Friendly societies 32
Frucht, R. 66, 148

Garveyism 85, 180
Glass, R. 1, 5
Gorz, A. 2, 174
Gosden, P. 32
Greene, J. 22—3, 29
Grenada 18
politics 35
Gujaratis 176
see South Asians
Guyana 18—19
black power 34
East Indians 42

Hadley, C. 42
Hall, D. 22
Hall, S. et al 177, 185—6
Harrison, I. 175
Hausknecht, M. 58
Hebdige, D. 183
Heinemann, B. 8, 72
Henry and Wilson 104—5, 122,
136
Hill, C. 126, 132—5 passim
Hindess, B. 69
Hinds, D. 153
Hiro, D. 152
Hsu, F. 122
Husbands and England 189
Hylson—Smith, K. 6

Ianni, O. 34
Indians 3, 10; see South Asians
Indian Workers' Association 187
Individualism 37—40, 152—3,